Synagogues

Meguilah: Rolls of Esther
circa 1700, wood; Parchment,
object of wership, Italy XVIIIth century,
musée d'art et d'histoire
du Judaïsme, Paris.

Paris, *View of the synagogue
in rue Buffault*
(1877, architect Stanislas Ferrand).

Synagogues

Architecture and Jewish Identity

DOMINIQUE JARRASSÉ

VILO
·
ADAM
BIRO

For
Nathanaël and Théodora

ACKNOWLEDGEMENTS
In addition to the institutions too numerous to mention which have allowed me access to their archives
and other documents over the past seventeen years, I should very much like to thank the following people
for their friendship and collaboration: Eve and Gérard Appelbaum for their expedition to Slovakia;
Sam Gruber, Director of the Jewish Heritage Council/World Monument Fund; Max Herzberg, architect;
Sharman Kadish and the Survey of the Jewish Built Heritage in the UK & Ireland;
Professor Bernard Keller for the information on Traenheim; and Mihail Moldoveanu for his links with Romania.

Summary

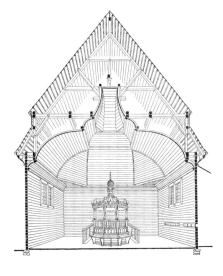

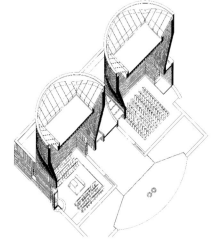

Erich Mendelsohn: Sketch-plans
for synagogues in Washington (1948)
and Baltimore (1948).

Introduction

The Synagogue and the Temple

From the outset, the bonds of art and spirituality have appeared to be inscribed in the foundations of all civilizations. Religious architecture—whether it be an Egyptian, Greek or Buddhist temple, or a cathedral or a mosque—has always been considered as the supreme form of human expression: as the synthesis of man's relationship to the world, the cosmos, and to God. The evidence of this conception is such that the synagogue, incorrectly assimilated to the Temple of Jerusalem, was included in this vision and is often considered sacred architecture. Even Erich Mendelsohn, a Jewish architect and one of the greatest artists of the 20th century, fell into the trap of this equivalence. In charge of building a synagogue, he wrote[1]: "When in 1945, shortly before the end of the last war, I was called on to build the St. Louis synagogue, I was immediately aware of the challenge involved in designing a sacred building in the spirit of our age of great changes." His functionalist approach (he maintains that the main problem of the synagogue stemmed from the flexibility of its plan) did not prevent a desire to be connected to the tradition of sacred architecture.

But the synagogue is not the Temple. The famous injunction: "They shall make me a sanctuary, that I may dwell in their midst" (Exodus 25,8), often overexploited in order to enhance its value, pertains only to the Temple. Even if the synagogue receives a spark of light and has the right to respect[2], it cannot claim to be the 'House of God'. It even appears derisory to pretend

to erect a house for God. Did not the prophet Isaiah (66,1) recount these words of God: "The heavens are my throne, the earth is my footstool. What kind of house can you build for me; what is to be my resting place?"

If the synagogue is not the Temple, it is a substitute of a totally different nature and reveals itself to be an invention of an extraordinary modernity, offering man a new place in the rite. The Temple was a sanctuary of a type common during Antiquity: a space around a hierarchically organized *cella* and served by priests. Moreover, it had a political character as the organ and symbol of national sovereignty. Its destruction could have meant the disappearance of the Hebrew state and religion, but, thanks to the synagogue, such was not the case. "The great, the true instrument of salvation for Judaism, was the synagogues, the temples (…) It was the synagogue, my brothers," asserted the Chief Rabbi of France, Zadoc Kahn[3], "that, in a way, founded, developed, and created Judaism!" The synagogue, no longer a sanctuary, became the 'house of the assembly'. The priests were replaced by an assembly of worshipers, according to a democratic process, then unknown, which placed the individual in a new role, without individualizing the cult since a quorum of ten men remained necessary. This institutional structure, flexible in its function and even more in its form, as an essential means of the community allowed the Jews to adapt to almost any historical situation and naturally served as a model for other monotheist religious spaces. It even became, during exile, the heart of all Jewish life and the place of the preservation of Jewish culture.

A synagogue should therefore contribute to make man better and not to appeal to him. Nevertheless, encouraged by the rabbis, congregations spent without counting in order to erect majestic buildings, or, when the context was hostile, to adorn them with lavish internal decoration. Who has not marveled at the goldwork of the *scuole* in Venice or the magnificently restored cupola of the Neologian temple of Szeged?

Marc Chagall, *The Synagogue* (1917), oil on canvas. Private collection.

The Mirror of an Identity and a History

Synagogue architecture only appeared and its history can only be told with the concern to create an imposing and beautiful building for the glory of God and the edification of the faithful, with this supplement of décor or of style which adds to meaning, and with the desire to enhance its cultural function in the image of the adopted societies. Over the course of its long history, it underwent numerous variations in form, but very few in function, at least not until the advent of reformism in the 19th century. This diversity of form writes the history of the Jews, of their migrations and their exiles, and also the diverse facets of an identity whose image was continuously redefined, yet remained profoundly itself. For to construct a synagogue is to construct an identity.

Following the example of the function of the synagogue which could imitate a Greek temple, an Hispano-Moorish mosque, a Gothic cathedral, a Renaissance palace or in rationalist moderns forms, Jewish identity maintained itself under a status that varied from liberty to the ghetto, and from segregation to an assimilating emancipation. It is not surprising that with such a plasticity, the synagogue was the subject, in contemporary architecture, of formal and original experiments, that its programme be revealed in the fertile support of the imagination of architects such as Frank Lloyd Wright, Louis I. Kahn or Mario Botta. But, for this reason, it remains a changing object.

Faced with the impossibility of presenting the thousands of synagogues built over the course of time and in all the countries of the five continents where Jews had arrived, this book gives priority to that which constitutes the originality of synagogue architecture: its function as the mirror of identity and a history profoundly marked by the Exile and by the community dimension. It is tempting to apply to this architecture these words of Kafka concerning Yiddish[4]: "It is composed only of foreign terms, but these are not unchanging within the language, they retain the vivacity and the haste with which they were taken. The migrations of the people cross Yiddish from end to end."

Behind the multiplicity of the historical and political experiences sustained by the Jews, and behind the variety of forms taken by the synagogue, depending upon the periods, the countries and the rites, certain constants can be discerned, as Jacob Katz notes[5]: "it seems that the relations between Jews and Gentiles were

Hammat, near Tiberias, Israel:
Synagogue pavement,
late 3rd—early 4th century. Mosaic
representing the Temple of Jerusalem.

different in each period and according to the countries concerned; but, in reality, the differences observed only constitute variants of a secular model".

On an historical level, certain crucial processes are the object of a more detailed approach. Exile that engendered the synagogue and became a key component of Jewish identity, the emancipation and its corollary, nationalization, which produced a new identity, still in question since, with the anthropology of the times, it is necessary to ask if Judaism is a religion or a race, and finally, the confrontation with modernity and the rebirth of a nation. In historicist terms, these notions are clearly translated through architecture of which the evolution determines another theme of this book: the transition from an architecture based on a language of historical styles to a functionalist approach which, far from excluding the symbolic, even goes so far as to attempt to establish a sort of modern sacredness. This perspective also explains the importance of orientalist themes, a crucial component of Jewish identity, which are covered in several chapters. Upon this rests the question of origins, the relation of otherness, even the exilic and erratic condition of contemporary man, all problems which enter into the architectural thought on synagogues.

SYMBOLIC
ARCHITECTURE

"It does not matter how a synagogue is built, nor what is its style of architecture, nor what its cost, nor how large it is, nor how large its congregation; but it does matter to what use the synagogue is put." This rabbinical homiletic leitmotiv, here taken from Rabbi Pereira-Mendes[1] who had come to inaugurate the Chizuk Amuno synagogue in Baltimore, formulates as a basic principle the submission of aesthetics to ethics. All that is needed to hold a service is a chest, a platform and a few chairs… on the condition, however, that the presence of one Scroll of the Torah and ten men transform this meeting place into a religious space. The function is attached to the Scrolls and the men and not to the furniture and the walls. All the rest is superfluous, as is shown by the pious *shtiblkh* of Eastern Europe, small rooms devoid of decoration. Admittedly, but not entirely useless, for all that is added has symbolic value.

The Tradition

THE MEANING AND FUNCTION OF THE SYNAGOGUE

As Rabbi Pereira-Mendes has suggested, it is advisable first to ask about the use rather than the image of the synagogue. What purpose does it serve? Its function is clearly expressed in the names that it has been given throughout history by the sages: *beth haknesset*, 'house of the assembly', *beth hatefila*, 'house of prayer' and *beth hamidrach*, 'house of teaching'. Yet even as a 'house of prayer', the

building itself matters little, it is the gathering of ten men, the *minyan*, that constitutes the real cultural space and not the structure. In a synagogue, the faithful pray, sing, read texts and comment upon them. They also meet in order to discuss questions concerning the community. Extremely simple, the ritual requires very few specific furnishings: a chest in which the Scrolls of the Torah are placed, the Holy Ark (*aron hakodech*), and a platform (*bimah*) from where the officiants can read and talk to the assembly. It could almost be said that all the rest has but a symbolic value. A particular prescription, nevertheless, must also be taken into account: the necessity of separating men and women. The combination of these three elements determines the basic spatial organization of the synagogue. Architects, nevertheless, have found designs of which the variations stem from the religious, even the ideological, mentalities of the congregations.

Apart from the fact that Jews were rarely the masters of their own space, these principles explain the absence of an architectural tradition: the synagogue is but a function. Its form varied according to the local architectural traditions of the adopted countries. The building, nevertheless, was laden with representational values that went beyond its primary function. Synagogues thus became an excellent reflection of the conceptions of Jewish identity and history, for, paradoxically, they were of a surprising plasticity, adopting the form of the *shtibl* in Lithuania or in the tenements of the Lower East Side in New York, of the *scuola* in Italy, of the Gothic cathedral in Bohemia, of the mosque or even the pagoda as in K'ai-Feng. But, as will be seen, to pray in a *shtibl* or a synagogue that resembles a basilica or a mosque is not without consequence. Architecture, as an instrument of assimilation, can even induce new behaviour. The Reform Jews were aware of this and attempted to modify not only the ritual but also the space itself.

Such a diversity of treatment surprised architects who were accustomed to base their work on historical models. Thus, the famous professor of architectural theory at the Ecole des Beaux-Arts in Paris, Julien Guadet, told his students[2]: "The Israelite cult, older than Christianity, and to whom riches were never lacking, could have had, it appears, given rise to an architecture with a history. But such was not the case. (…) Therefore the synagogue, heir to the Temple, is a modern programme after eighteen centuries of deliberate effacement." Guadet could not grasp the causes of such a lacuna, hence his anti-Semite suggestions, but he had understood that the programme of the synagogue required a constant actualisation which he was incapable of carrying out. He thus enjoined his students to imitate the synagogue on the Rue de la Victoire.

Although clearly defined by the Tradition, the function of the synagogue underwent an evolution throughout history that is fraught with consequences for its architectural design. The cultural function has tended to develop and to overshadow the others, at the time when the emancipated Jews were forced to reduce their Judaism into an Israelite confession. The imitation of the church reinforced this religious dimension. It was, in this context of emancipation, that the synagogue also reached its greatest monumentality, to such an extent as to rival the Temple of Solomon. The synagogue had, in effect, become a public building and the construction, from then on, became a municipal affair. It bore high, through its architecture, the new status of the Jews, but obviously only in its denominational dimension. The major change that the synagogue underwent in the 20th century was to be reinstated in an ensemble: the community centre. Modern in its spirit, particularly in American Judaism, these institutions which associate social spaces, schools and rooms for the religious service, are nevertheless a return to the Tradition.

CONSTRUCTIVE RULES

It appears surprising that a religion which so minutely regulates the least aspect of Jewish life did not enact precise laws for its religious buildings. Admittedly, the Talmud provides a few prescriptions, (resumed by Maimonides and in the *Shulhan 'Arukh*), but they are not absolutely obligatory. Some are more often than not inapplicable, such as locating the synagogue on the highest elevation in the town (*Tosefta Megillah* 4) or having it surpass the other buildings in height. The Jews felt that these were more a matter of symbolic measures to enhance the value of the building.

The orientation of the Holy Ark towards Jerusalem is a rule scrupulously respected by the Orthodox. It is based upon a reading of Daniel (6,11) who, while in exile, prayed in the direction of Jerusalem as well as upon Solomon's prayer during the inauguration of the Temple that evokes the prayer of the exiled (I Kings 8, 48). This prescription initially consisted of praying in the direction of the Holy Land. In non-oriented synagogues, the worshipers merely had to turn. The important thing was the meaning of this orientation: it defined the status of the synagogue by recalling that the only holy place in Judaism remains Jerusalem.

The separation of men and women, a rule very widely enforced, except by the liberal movements, had not been decreed, it appears, by the sages of the Talmudic period. It was justified by reference to the existence in the Temple of the Court of Women (*ezrat nachim*, a name sometimes incorrectly given to modern galleries). This court, however, was but the place up to where the women could enter with the men. The ancient texts are silent on this question. Undoubtedly women participated in the cult, then they were assigned to a special section or room. Apparently, it was during the Middle Ages that the separation became more radical with the 'women's synagogues' (*weiberschul*): rooms reserved for women sometimes located underneath those of the men (Comtat-Venaissin). This separation, nevertheless, found an architectural solution in the gallery that had already been used in Toledo in the 14th century and then made common by the synagogue of Amsterdam. Some synagogues in Antiquity had galleries, but it is not certain that they were reserved for women.

A text (*Berakhoth* 34b) stresses the need for an abundance of light in the synagogue: thus, it is desirable to have numerous large windows, twelve according to the Zohar. But here again, this light is taken in a symbolic sense. Obviously, local elements influenced the design of the bays more than the Talmudic interpretations did.

One feature appears to distinguish synagogues, the absence of images. But even this famous prohibition is very relative. It is founded on an interpretation of Exodus 20,4 where the Second Commandment decrees: "You shall not make for yourself an idol in the form of anything in heaven above or on the earth beneath or in the waters below." But it is often forgotten to recall the rest of the verse which explains this interdiction, not of the

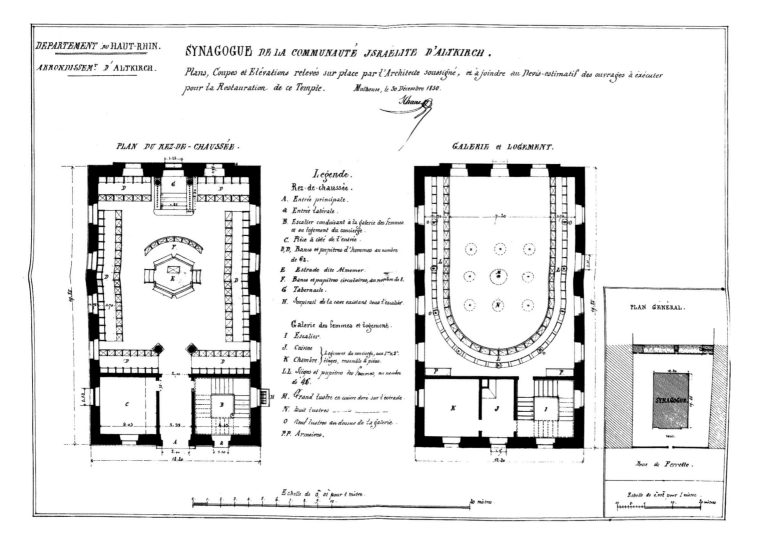

Altkirch, Alsace: *Plan for restoration of the synagogue*, by Schacre, 1850. Typical plan for a traditional synagogue with gallery and central *bimah*.

Munich, *Plan of the synagogue* (1887, architect Albert Schmidt). Engraving from the review *La Construction moderne*, 1888. Typical plan for a Reformed synagogue, with choir.

Page 12:
Venice, *Scuola Levantina*: *Bimah* attributed to Andrea Brustolon.

The Ideal Synagogue in the Nineteenth Century

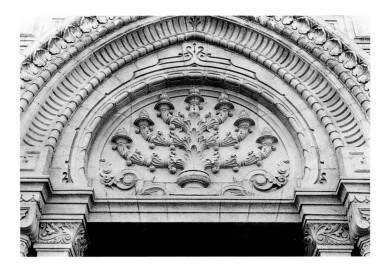

At the Ecole des Beaux-Arts in Paris, where regular competitive examinations tested architecture students' familiarity with the principal architectural types, theory professor Edmond Guillaume decided in 1886 to ask his students to design a Synagogue. Coming hot on the heels of *La France juive*, Edouard Drumont's anti-Semitic manifesto, this was the first time the Synagogue had been included in the study program. Guillaume must have undertaken extensive research for his subject outline, for the result is a kind of ideal —Orthodox Jews would call it Reformed—nineteenth century Synagogue. His students approached their task using the 'Romano-Byzantine' style then dominant in France, while sensitively opting for central plans. The outline, a blend of exact data and approximations stemming from ignorance or confusion with Christian practise, provides an accurate reflection of the spirit underlying Synagogue building at the time.

'The Synagogue is the building in which Israelites gather for their devotions. The Jewish Temple mainly comprises a large assembly hall at one end of which, in a small sanctuary, is the tabernacle containing the Scriptures. Within the choir, situated in the eastern part of the building and divided off by a railing, are the stalls of the Chief Rabbi, the members of the Consistory and the Temple's administrators; the table or altar formerly used for sacrificial rites (these have long since been abandoned); the seven-branched candelabrum; the traditional lamp; an organ to provide musical accompaniment; seats for the officiants; and various other objects forming part of the interior layout and ornamentation required by the ritual. There should also be a pulpit, so placed as to ensure that the speaker can be heard by all present.

'The seats of the Synagogue are stalls which are used only between prayers, for Jews pray standing and facing eastwards towards the tabernacle. The seating must thus be laid out with this rule in mind.

'Only men are admitted to the Synagogue, but women may participate in prayer from the gallery, which they reach by broad staircases without entering the Temple. The number of places provided is less than for the men, a reflection of the difference in the religious obligations imposed on each group.

'A large organ is necessary, together with an extensive gallery for choirs and an orchestra.

'The Synagogue to be designed here should be preceded by a courtyard—a kind of atrium—and a large vestibule with fonts for ritual ablutions. It should be accompanied by separate classrooms for each sex, a conference room with documentary storage facilities for the Consistory and a rehearsal room for the choirs. There should also be changing rooms for the officiants, lodgings for the Rabbi and the Temple staff, and toilet facilities.

'The architecture of the building should be in harmony with the fundamental simplicity of the religion it exists to serve. This religion forbids all images, but ornamentation may include Biblical quotations, the Ten Commandments, the emblems of the twelve tribes and other motifs.'

Bordeaux (1882),
detail of the central portal.

image but of the idol: "You shall not bow down to them or worship them." According to the given period in history, rabbis enforced this prescription more or less strictly. During the 4th century, as attested by the frescoes of Dura-Europos, figurative scenes were represented in synagogues, obviously not God, symbolized by a hand, but Aaron and the Prophets. The 19th century, on the other hand, was very strict in the matter and images disappeared from synagogues, except in North America. Today, the liberal synagogues, claiming affiliation to the example of Dura, have reintroduced images.

Can architecture and art—from the point of view of these principles and of the primacy allotted to the spiritual—play a role in the synagogue? Yet a rule, *hiddour mizva*, the need to add an aesthetic dimension to all duty or religious acts, justifies the recourse to art (*Houlin* 44b). It is therefore proper to honour God through beauty and

Edmond Uhry, *Plan for a synagogue* (1896). Architecture degree submission, Ecole nationale supérieure des Beaux-Arts, Paris. First used by architects from the Beaux-Arts in Paris, the Neo-Byzantine approach spread to the rest of Europe and the United States in the late nineteenth century: it emphasized the central plan and cupola, considered appropriate to the Jewish faith.

to have the concern for beauty in religious objects as well as in the buildings devoted to the cult. Moreover, the adoption of aesthetic values testifies to the perfect integration of the Jews, even to their patriotism. Chief Rabbi Zadoc Kahn congratulated the Jews of La Ferté-sous-Jouarre for having built an attractive synagogue in these terms[3]: "And in this you have followed the most ancient traditions of your religion, for they constantly commend that we seek the beautiful in the expression of faith. When it is a question of God and of the homage that we are called to render unto Him, it is our duty to use the assistance that art puts at our disposition: 'Have the concern for beauty in the fulfilment of your religious ceremonies' (*Shabbat*, 133b), such is the rule that has always dominated our private cult and even more our public cult." Thus the works of the architect and the decorator were legitimised. They were finally very free in their inventiveness and sometimes even directly responsible for the choice of styles.

THE QUESTION OF THE SACRED

Once the necessity of creating a beautiful synagogue had been accepted, there remained a difficulty, for from the point of view of the Jewish Tradition, the synagogue lacks the determining element of all religious architecture: sacredness. For this remains the attribute of the Temple of Jerusalem, and the synagogue, its substitute, does not deserve this qualification. The synagogue must not imitate the Temple, nor copy its monumentality, the ritual objects must not be reconstituted (thus the candelabra have eight branches so as not to reproduce the *menorah*), musical instruments are forbidden (as a sign of mourning since the destruction of the Temple). In short, the synagogue is not sacred. The only sanctity that it has comes from the presence in its midst of the Scrolls of the Torah. Obviously, this does not mean that it is without dignity: the synagogue must be respected, should not be sold, nor change function, unless to receive a higher function, such as *beth hamidrach*. The *Shulhan 'Arukh* specifies this fundamental relation of the synagogue to the Temple from which it receives, all the same, a 'spark' of holiness[4]: "In the Holy Temple, an atmosphere of superior life where the manifested majesty of God is renewed every day by the ritual that is celebrated there, by the piety of the pontiffs who sacrifice there and the fervour of the Israelites who offer sacrifices there, and finally, by the prayers and the canticles that rise from there to the heavens. On our synagogues, on our most modest places of prayer, there still passes a breath of this divine atmosphere. This is what according to our Sages, the prophet Ezekiel (11,16) meant by these words: 'I have scattered

them among the countries: I will be to them a little sanctuary in the countries whither they are come…'."

This absence of sacredness is one of the profound causes of the incomprehension of synagogue architecture. Architects have continually strived to rediscover the splendours of Solomon's Temple and have often extrapolated on sacred art, but totally out of keeping with the initial requirements of Judaism. It was, however, these 'errors' of interpretation that resulted in certain of the magnificent monuments presented in this book. Since the Second World War—perhaps, at times, as a compensation for the impoverishment of contemporary architectural forms—research on synagogal art has appeared with a tendency to perceive the synagogue in terms of a 'sacred space'. This is not surprising on the part of Christians who can only conceive of a synagogue in relation to a church, but it is also sometimes the work of Jews who were persuaded that art consecrates the place of worship. Similarly, in an ecumenical or cultural type of approach (such as the *Biennale de Venise* (1992) dedicated to *Architettura e spazio sacro nella modernità*) the comparison of synagogues to 'sacred spaces' falsifies and confuses the perspective. It remains difficult for most authors to acknowledge that Judaism can do without sacred spaces.

The Synagogue as a Space

For a long time the synagogue was fundamentally but an interior space, not only because living conditions frequently forced the Jews to conceal their oratories, but also because the function of a synagogue can easily dispense with the necessity of any external representation. The consequence of this concept is that only the internal organization of a synagogue concerned the rabbis and that the architects thus often found themselves at liberty to design the exterior as they pleased. Such a situation clearly reveals a conception of architecture as a mere vesture and for centuries this physical envelope changed without difficulty, passing from models based on Greek temples to those based on Christian churches. Sometimes, however, architectural forms were employed that actually took into account the internal layout and the ritual needs of the synagogue.

THE RELATION OF THE *ARON/BIMAH* AND THE PLAN

The two fundamental components which determine the internal organization of a synagogue are the Holy Ark (*aron*) and the raised platform (*bimah*). The Talmud identifies only these two elements of religious furniture.

Pfaffenhoffen, Alsace,
Parohet (1875-76). The Jewish Museum,
New York, Gift of Dr. Harry
G. Friedman in memory
of Dr Murray Last.

Mulhouse, *Present-day view
of the synagogue pulpit* (1849,
architect Schacre).

Page 19:
Berlin, *Synagogue Oranienburgerstrasse*
(1866), 1855 study for the Holy Ark,
by Eduard Knoblauch. Berlin,
Universitätbibliothek
der Technischen Universität.

The Holy Ark was, for a long time, mobile in ancient synagogues and was even occasionally carried outside according to *Taanith* 15a. Later it became attached to the eastern wall (in European and American synagogues) and gave rise to the development of niches (not always in the axis of the edifice as at Ostia) which rapidly found their definitive expression in the apse of the Roman basilica. Amongst the oldest niches attested by the archaeological record are those at Hammam Lif (3rd or 4th century). It was also acknowledged that the Ark be placed on a rather high pedestal with reference to the words of the psalmist: "In my distress I cried unto the Lord, and He heard me" (Psalm 120,1). From then on, the general plan of synagogues converged towards that of a church choir. The term itself was even used by certain Jews in the 19th century. Exemplary, but often emphatic, designs were employed in the monumental synagogues of the second half of the 19th century in Berlin, Paris and London. Here, the Ark forms an aedicule in an apse which is pierced by picture windows and sometimes even raised in the manner of a cathedral or pilgrim church choir above a crypt (as in Paris at the Rue de la Victoire or in Munich). Such a setting theatrically dramatizes the Holy Ark. Other solutions, however, were also used. In the oratories of Venice, corbelled niches, sometimes above a canal, housed the holy chest. In the wooden synagogues of Eastern Europe, multi-layered Holy Arks assuming immense proportions were simply placed next to the wall. Yet no matter what plan was adopted, the Holy Ark rapidly became the principal structural element. The general symmetry of the plan is based upon the Ark which serves as a perspective for the central nave. The Ark received the most abundant decoration by reason of its sanctity. In many modest synagogues, the only decorative element is around the Holy Ark. In monumental synagogues, however, an enhancement of this area finds expression in aedicules, the superposition of orders, and triumphal arcs which mark the entrance of the sanctuary. Such developments progress towards a more or less conscious reconstruction of the Holy of Holies of the Temple. The frequent presence of wreathed columns (in 17th century Italy and 18th century Central Europe, as at Rakovník in Bohemia in 1764) esteemed Solomonian, reinforces this symbolism. Contemporary architecture had obviously proposed original solutions: transparent and retractable Holy Arks surmounted by spires or vertical motifs were used to symbolize, in contrast to horizontal platform roofs, the spiritual soul of the composition.

The *bimah* is dependant in relation to the Holy Ark and is therefore the subject of numerous deliberations. Its position, in fact, differentiates the synagogues of various religious tendencies. The most attested tradition requires that the *bimah* be placed in the centre, for both practical and symbolic reasons. In this position, the reader or the orator is more audible to the congregation (especially in large synagogues such as that in Alexandria) and processions (*hakkafot*) can more easily take place. On the symbolic level, this configuration is both a substitution for the alter of the Temple (with prayers having replaced sacrifices) and a representation of Mount Sinai around which the Israelites gathered when Moses received the Torah. Orthodox rabbis have made the centrality of the *bimah* an imperative. Other solutions, however, have been investigated: in oratories of the Italian rite, the *bimah* is often placed against the western wall and thus forms with the *aron* an original bipolar composition, perhaps of Spanish origin. This may concur with a raising of the *bimah* and the lectern being placed on a platform as at Pesaro, Padova and in the Comtat-Venaissin (Carpentras and Cavaillon).

Centrally placed, the *bimah* is cantoned by pillars in synagogues with two naves (such as at Worms) or with four central pillars (in the so-called Polish type, but actually widespread throughout Central Europe). Most often, however, this plan gave rise to the construction of an aedicule, either a sort of chancel which was more or less elevated or (particularly in Ashkenazim areas) an octagonal platform which was usually surmounted by a baldachin or a wrought iron grill. In the 19th century, as an obvious sign of assimilation, the *bimah* was displaced towards the Holy Ark so as to form a sort of liturgical pole or choir. The reason given was that of a gain of space, but it was clearly an ecclesiastic model that was actually being imposed: the pews were transversal and the congregation assisted in the service without actively participating. Admittedly, such a plan could have existed in Antiquity, where the reader of the Torah had a lectern at the foot of the Holy Ark, but in the context of the Emancipation this new design was judged as an element of the Reform movement. Above all, it signified the abandonment of active participation in the service and was thus a separation—against nature in Judaism—between the assembly and the liturgical spaces. Occasionally, it even occurred that a chancel or steps marked this limit.

Given the importance of the *bimah* as a structural element, synagogues alternated between two major forms of organization: the basilican plan and the centralized plan. As for churches in the Byzantine world or during the Renaissance, there was often hesitation concerning the relative value of these two plans. For synagogues, however, it was not a choice between a Latin cross or a Greek cross, but of ascertaining the most appropriate model for the Jewish ritual. The basilican plan, which was based on the Greco-Roman temple and had already appeared in ancient synagogues during Antiquity, re-emerged through the imitation of church design. Furthermore, this model was also that of the Temple of Solomon, so meticulously described in the Bible. However, as it was rather difficult to accommodate a large assembly around a centralized *bimah*, numerous synagogues in the 19th century adopted a design in which the *bimah* was relocated nearer to the Holy Ark. A centralized plan best facilitates the implantation of the *bimah* in the centre, as is cited by a *responsum* of Ezechiel Landau, an 18th century rabbi in Prague, who had already advocated an octagonal plan. Numerous synagogues have thus adopted square, oval or even circular plans. This need for centrality explains the success of Neo-Byzantine designs: not only did they furnish models with centralized plans (such as Saint-Sophia) but, furthermore, demanded a domed roof which is often considered as a symbol of divine unity.

OTHER ELEMENTS OF FURNITURE

Apart from the *aron* and the *bimah*, other elements of furniture were added to the design of the synagogue, such as pulpits and organs, but these are the very symbols of the Reform that will be seen in the study of the architecture of the edifices of the 19th century. Obviously, to include a large organ and sometimes even the choir that accompanied it became a crucial question for architects, hence the frequent recourse to Christian models with galleries above the entrance or even behind the Holy Ark as in Dantzig, Strasbourg, and Essen. Since Antiquity, the practice was to honour the leaders of the community or the synagogue by installing seats or stalls that were more imposing than the other seats. In modern synagogues, veritable *cathedra* are sometimes also installed in the choir for the chief rabbis. As for the *chuppah*, the dais under which marriages are celebrated, it only entered the synagogue during the 19th century, under the constraint of public authorities and in order to consecrate slightly in the Christian manner the Jewish marriage, suspected of being but a contract. For good order but also to raise funds, the civil and religious administrations obliged the faithful to get married in the synagogue whereas traditionally the marriage had taken place in a courtyard or in the country.

Ritual objects also came to the fore, such as the perpetual lamp, *ner tamid*, frequently but wrongly compared to the fire maintained on the sacrificial altar. Introduced recently into the synagogue, undoubtedly in imitation of churches, it is most often suspended in front of or next to the Holy Ark and associates light to divine revelation (Ezekiel, 43,2) and to the Torah. This perpetual lamp assumes great importance at the inauguration of a synagogue which consists first in placing the *sefarim* in the Holy Ark and then lighting the lamp. The candelabra were used with an equivalent symbolism and in remembrance of the Temple, but in order not to reproduce the *menorah*, they usually have either eight branches or are not aligned horizontally. Not all these objects have a practical ritual function, but they add a symbolic dimension. They contribute to a certain sacralisation of the synagogue. Thus, during the 19th century, these objects multiplied. Pulpits and organs were added in the name of dignity and the behaviour of the congregation was 'disciplined' by entrusting the cult to retributed officiants. As for the ornaments of the Torah, fixed by the Tradition, they did not at that time undergo any modification, but the synagogues themselves were embellished.

Illustrating the deliberate isolation of the cultural function, annexes allotted to other traditional vocations of the synagogue were developed: meeting rooms, classrooms for the *Talmud-Torah*, marriage rooms (where the family received), sacristy (for, in certain countries, the rabbis and officiants, assimilated to priests, wore special costumes and altar boys were even instituted).

Variety of the Rites

Two factors still play an important role in the differentiation of synagogues: the local rite of the congregation and the type of associations that they have established. For the synagogue is a generic type which overlaps rather different realities and is linked not only to a history of over two thousand years full of mutations, but above all to the diverse statuses—even religious tendencies—of the communities. Confronted by modernity and the lifestyles of western societies, itself wrought upon by upsurges of mysticism and of messiahism, Judaism was transversed by divergent trends, reform movements and conservative reactions. The terminology used to denote the place of worship is in itself an indicator of these religious and social cleavages.

In fact, the opposition between the small oratory and the large synagogue has undoubtedly always existed in Judaism. Since Hellenistic times, there have been large public synagogues imitating temples and, at the same time, groups attached to a more intimate form of worship. In the 18th century, the famous opposition between Hasidism, a spiritual movement launched by the Baal Chem Tov, and the *mitnaggedim* (opponents) was archi-

tecturally materialized in buildings of a different nature. The *Hasidim* established *shtiblkh*, while the "opponents" established traditionalist synagogues and above all *yechivot*. Then both rebelled against the institutions which attempted to reconcile Judaism, the Enlightenment (*Haskalah*) and the aspirations born of the emancipation as translated by monumental synagogues. Zalman Shazar, in his *Etoiles du matin*[5], recalls his memories as a "child of the chtibel" in Steibtz. He frequented the Hasidic oratory of his father of which he says: "It was for me my real home and those who frequented it seemed to be my family"; he did not "know the large synagogue except from afar although it was nearby the Hasidic oratory" and sometimes went there to listen to a famous preacher, a renowned cantor or to settle questions concerning the community. Next door, there was still another synagogue: "Vis-à-vis the new synagogue, immense and perpetually unfinished, we retained an even greater reserve (...). It brought together those who had relatives in America or in South Africa. We, the children of the small oratories, did not enter this syna-

gogue although it was nearby except to admire the singing exercises of the new officiant at the end of the Saturday morning prayer, or to listen to the exhilarating speech of a Zionist orator". In America, these cleavages were reproduced with the *shtiblkh*, the Orthodox and the Reformed synagogues. In Western Europe as well, immigrants arriving from the East regrouped themselves into *Landmanshaften*, (associations of origin), and opened their own oratories much to the detriment of the national Jewish establishments, and of the advancement of the Reform. This had major architectural consequences, and diverse types of religious places were created.

As for the rituals, it should be added that the *minhagim* could divide the congregations according to their origins. Two major currents descended from the two poles of ancient Judaism, symbolized by the existence of two Talmuds: that of Jerusalem and that of Babylonia. The Jerusalem Talmud gave rise to the Byzantine, Italian, French and Ashkenazic rites. The latter was further subdivided into German, Polish, and other rites. The Babylonian rite spread throughout Asia and the Muslim

Paris, *Oratory*, 17 Rue des Rosiers.
Said to be the oldest oratory in Paris.

Amsterdam, *Interior view
of the Portuguese synagogue, during the
Palm branch procession at Succoth,*
engraving by B. Picart (1724).

countries, with new local variants. It is also the ancestor of the Sephardic, or Spanish, rite. Local rites also existed, such as that of the Comtat-Venaissin, which conserved traces of older rituals, blending elements of diverse origins. Mixtures are endless. The Hasidim, for example, introduced Sephardic elements borrowed from Rabbi Isaac Louria.

The hazards of the Diasporas created these very living traditions to which the congregations remained all the more attached as they were forced into exile or felt menaced with extinction. Some synagogue founders even prescribed as a formal condition the type of ritual to be followed[6]. The architectural implications of these traditions were more or less without influence on the exterior architecture of synagogues but affected the internal organization. Thus, in the 19th century, the Sephardim (who were not even Orthodox) remained faithful to the central

bimah. With the nationalization of the communities, attempts to create new *minhagim* were also made, but usually without any success. In France during the 1840s, the administration and the hierarchy tried to combine into a single group (the *minhag sarfati,* or French rite) the Jews of Sephardic rite from the Bordeaux-Bayonne region and the Jews of Ashkenazic rite from Alsace-Lorraine. In vain, the communities, although united in the same *consistoire,* continued to pray in their own synagogues. In Israel after 1948, the desire to see a united ritual established had no better success and several chief rabbis were even nominated.

The type of synagogue frequented sometimes reveals the degree of integration into the surrounding society. The terminology is eloquent: apart from the *shtibl* already mentioned, the *schoule* represents an interesting stage of the process. This Yiddish word meaning 'school'

demonstrates, as *scuola* with the Italians, the close connection between the cult and teaching. But this word is also laden with emotional connotations. It evokes the traditional synagogue indifferent to its architecture, in opposition to 'synagogue', a more neutral word, and above all, to 'temple' (the term adopted by assimilated Jews, both as a status-enhancing reference to Jerusalem and as a mark of alignment of synagogues to other religions). At the time when the famous rabbinical conferences which established the basis of Reformed Judaism took place in Germany in 1846, a columnist launched this conciliatory appeal to the leaders of the *Consistoire de Paris*[7]: "Would it not be possible, by leaving the partisans of the ancient liturgy in the *schoule* on the Rue des Blancs-Manteaux[8], and by maintaining in the *synagogue* on the Rue Notre-Dame-de-Nazareth the former *mitigated rite*, to give, by the foundation of a *temple israélite*

Safad, Israel, the *Ashkenazy and Sephardic 'Lion' Synagogues*. Both institutions were under the supervision of Rabbi Isaac Luria, known as *ha-Ari* ('the lion'). He had come to Safed, one of the 'four holy cities' of Palestinian Judaism, around 1570 and given fresh impetus to the study of the Kabbala. The two buildings illustrate the contrast between the Central and Eastern European tradition of a Holy Ark made of sculpted wood and that of the Mediterranean, with a raised *bimah* and numerous Holy Arks set into the wall.

français (French Israelite Temple), satisfaction to this large class of our fellow Jews who think that, even if religion is immutable, the cult can change and accustom itself to the ideas of each age?" He envisaged this temple, symbolically outside of the Marais district, in the Montmartre quarter. This temple "where the services would be less long, where a few of our magnificent prayers would be recited in French and those conserved in Hebrew spoken with the Oriental pronunciation, where the organ would be accompanied by a choir song composed by Halévy or Meyerbeer (...)", Ben Levi was not the only one who wished to build it. Four years later, when the reconstruction of the synagogue was under debate, Baron de Rothschild sent the project to Gottfried Semper himself, the builder of the famous synagogue of Dresden, then exiled in Paris.

This plea of Ben Levi contains another term rich in connotations: Israelite. This new term is naturally associated to the notion of the temple, since it has the same objective, to erase an overly strong sense of identity of Judaism in order to reduce it to a denomination, Israelitism, more flexible in order to be integrated into the surrounding society. The process of valorising the cultural function and the transformation of the synagogue into a public monument is strictly parallel to the mutation of the Jew into an Israelite[9]. By its location in the city, the synagogue is still the reflection of the status of the Jew in society and his identity. It is significant that the 'progressive Jews' of Cracow in order to differentiate their reform synagogue from numerous other traditionalist places of worship referred to it as the 'Tempel'. This Neo-Romanesque edifice (1860-62) is in striking contrast with the others that date from the 16th to the 17th century.

The Reform provoked violent debates and drove Judaism to organize itself. The Orthodox forged their position in face of the *Haskalah*, then of the Reform, and constructed their synagogues with a centrally placed *bimah* and without organs or choirs. The Conservatives tried hard to reconcile a religious orthodoxy slightly adapted to the times with a historical and critical vision. The Reformed congregations were split between groups that abandoned the *Shabbat* for Sunday and ordained women rabbis (qualified as Liberals) and those who were content with a few modifications of the ritual but who held nevertheless that all reference to sacrifices, to the exile, and to the return to Zion be expunged in order to be able to adopt their country of residence as their only homeland. The contours of these groups are sometimes vague and vary according to the countries involved. Moderate Orthodox tendencies became established in certain countries such as Great Britain or France, preventing Liberalism from becoming firmly established. In Hungary in 1869, following a congress in Pest, where decisions for modernization had been taken, the scission with the Orthodox hardened. After 1871, each town established or built synagogues for the different communities: Orthodox, Neologian, but also the "status quo ante", those who conserved the traditional ritual that had existed before the confrontation. These variations had their stylistic expressions. It is not surprising that the neo-Gothic synagogues of Max Fleischer were not built for the Orthodox. In Bratislava, the Orthodox obtained the demolition of a cupola on a central tower of their synagogue (1863, Ignaz Feigler) claiming that it was *hukkat hagoï*. This building was imitated in Presov by the Neologians, obviously with the cupola. As for the Neologians of Bratislava, they built a synagogue (architect Deszö Milch) with two towers crowned by domes in 1893.

Obviously, a steeple or a dome is useless in a synagogue. The stakes of these rivalries, once again, is not function but symbolic form. This search for the emblematic value of the forms is not limited to periods of assimilation during which triumphed the language of historical styles, themselves laden with a meaning of identity. It reappears in contemporary architecture and even finds expression in the emergence of a synagogal art concerned with introducing into the ritual objects, not only the forms and the modern materials, but also a sacred dimension. The sculptor Yaacov Agam, son of an orthodox rabbi, said: "My ideal synagogue would use architectural innovations to create a sacred space that would truly satisfy our needs[10]" but does not renounce symbolism, whether it be the place of the Torah in the sanctuary or the colours of the rainbow.

Paris, *Synagogue in the Rue des Tournelles*
(1876), interior elevation
near the entrance. Watercolor by
the architect Varcollier, 1878,
private collection.

II

AN ARCHITECTURE OF EXILE

Korkliai, Lithuania, *Wooden synagogue.*
In the course of its research in Lithuania
in 1993, the Centre for Jewish Art
at the Hebrew University in Jerusalem
located six of these wooden synagogues,
previously regarded as lost.
These modest structures testify to the
existence of an architectural type found
from Lithuania to the Ukraine, where
traces have also been discovered.

"En route for Quirinal, through ancient and modern Rome, the idea came to me to construct a street in Jerusalem which would be called the "The Street of the Diaspora" and where all the styles of all the ages and of all the countries of our wanderings would be represented." This vow of Theodor Herzl[1], undoubtedly inspired by the memory of the Streets of Nations presented at the Universal Expositions, was realized in a certain manner through a series of scale model synagogues, in the *Beth hatefutsot* (Museum of the Diaspora) in Tel Aviv. This notation from Herzl's journal profoundly reveals that one of the most significant traces of exile (of which it is important to remember that "to have been slaves in Egypt" is fundamental to the identity of Israel) was the ability to use the most diverse architectural spaces, not only because the essential held to the Text, to the Time and to the transmission of a tradition which is not linked to sacred forms, but because this movement between exile and the centrality of Jerusalem is the base of the specificity of the Jewish experience. Is not the plasticity of the synagogue itself—capable of adapting to any situation—the best testimony? Was not the synagogue

first born through the shock of the exile to Babylon? After the second destruction of the Temple, Judaism survived thanks to these institutions. But, as Yitzhak Baer stated in 1936, in the face of new perils, in his brief historic meditation on the *galout*, an imaginary of the exile was established in Judaism of this period[2]: "The problem of being Jewish is indissociable with the exile…" After the prophets, in the 12th century, the Spaniard Juda Halevi subliminated his nostalgia for "Zion"[3]:

"Face against the earth
Your stones I desire and my grief I hurl
To the winds of your dust…"

Henceforth, to use the words of the poet Edmond Jabès, "the homeland of the Jews is a sacred text"[4]. Exile is, thus, inherent in the Jewish existence, as much on the theological as on the historical level. When, guided by Moses in the desert, the Jewish people came into the world, was it not in the wanderings? Was not the sanctuary, the 'Tent of the meeting', already mobile? In his extraordinary aphorisms, Kafka wrote[5]: "Always ready, his house is transportable, he forever lives in his native land".

All these texts, as well as the historic events and the plastic evidence, demonstrate that exile became consubstantial with the Jewish condition, to such an extent that the Diaspora does not apply only to Jerusalem, even if the Holy City remained at the centre of religious identity and of prayers. Its effects are also felt with regards to the countries of adoption or transit, and thus created a superposition of complex exilic consciousness, reactivating the initial process, according to the operational mode of Jewish memory, that is, an assimilation of events between themselves without taking the chronology into account[6]. The expulsion from Spain in 1492 gave rise to one of the major Diasporas in Jewish history. The poets of the 15th century naturally revived the tone of the Psalms and of the prophet Jeremiah in order to deplore their departure from Spain. For was it not a new Egypt? Along with their language and the particularity of their ritual, they conserved a few interior details, but not the overall architectural solution. As for the exterior architecture of the synagogue, it adapted to new environments, and it was not until the 19th century, and the introduction of the concept of the nation-state and of historicism, that a 'style' attempted to convey a national or religious identity, more or less composed as well.

Synagogue architecture is thus, according to the American architect Stanley Tigerman[7] who applies it to all postmodern conditions, an "architecture of exile". It is an obligatory dialogue with the adopted culture, as well as with nostalgia. A place of identity *par excellence*, it adopts the expressive forms of the Jewish condition. Jews, in western countries where they are proud of their integration, have always extolled the contrast between the hovels or the ghettos which they had left and the monumental buildings that were inaugurated with pomp and ceremony. Yet this was not without a sentiment of mutilation and of nostalgia as well. Was it not before the modest Orthodox synagogues that a return to Judaism often took place, the *techouva*, more than a "temple Jew", according to the expression of Joseph Roth[8]?

The Diaspora in Antiquity

Jerusalem, *Inscription in Greek from Theodotus*, for the foundation of a synagogue, Jerusalem Museum.

Sardis, Turkey, *Synagogue*, late 4th century.

Following page:

Massada, Israel, *Ruins of the synagogue in Herod's fortress* (1st century).

Birth of the Synagogue in Babylonia and its diffusion in Ancient Israel during the times of the Second Temple

Ancient Israel, a politico-religious state, had but a single sanctuary, a single holy place: the Temple of Jerusalem. This permanent structure replaced the Tent of the Meeting (Tabernacle) which had formerly been erected on divine indications during the wandering in the wilderness after the flight from Egypt. This centralism also rested on the existence of a class of priests devoted to the cult and who did not possess any territory. The collapse of this system with the Babylonian Exile resulted in a new religious consciousness and permitted a prodigious mutation that consisted in replacing the sacrifices and rites of the Temple with study and prayer. As the prophet Hosea (19,3) said: "We wish to replace the bullocks by the promises of our lips". The Talmud (*Megillah 29a*) even retains the memory of the fact that King Joachin (Jehoiachin) took stones of the Temple to Babylon in order to use them in the construction of a synagogue. In an imaginary way, this passage emphasizes the continuity: for the synagogue was not constructed in opposition to the Temple, but as a complement. It is not surprising therefore that, with the destruction of the Temple and then the dispersion of the Jews, the synagogue, initially a complement, became a substitute. Throughout Jewish history, it played a founding role in the awareness of the existence of a community. As Charles Guignebert[1] wrote: "The regularly organized community preceded the installation of the synagogue, which became the place where this community materially became aware of itself and sought edification. It was also there that it studied. It was from there that it received its code of conduct and its discipline…". Thus, no longer priests, but rather a "people of priests" officiated, of which the masters were scribes and scholars: rabbis. From the point of view of later history, it is significant that the synagogue was very certainly born from the exilic condition[2].

A psalm (74,8), evoking the destruction of Jerusalem in 587 BC, already alludes to 'assemblies': "they burned all the shrines[3] of God in the land". Ezekiel (11,16), the prophet of the Babylonian Exile, mentions assemblies and even uses the words *miqdach meat* ('small sanctuary') that the Targum[4] interprets as an allusion to a synagogue. Such a practice, instituting prayers and readings, was in the spirit of the prophets, who were often in opposition to the kings and high priests. They condemned ritualism in the name of the faith, of the consent of the heart. After the return from the Exile, the custom of these religious reunions was undoubtedly introduced and then continued at the same time as the restoration of the Second Temple. The architecture of these early synagogues was, in all probability, in no way remarkable. These assemblies took place in communal rooms with only a chest containing the Scrolls of the Torah as furniture.

The numerous meeting places in Babylonia that are evoked in the Talmud have not left archaeological traces. Only texts and a few inscriptions supply any information concerning the synagogues of the Diaspora during Antiquity. According to the hazards of war—first between the Greeks and the Persians, then between the Romans and the Parthians—the Jewish communities developed, receiving the authorization to be administered by an exilarch, and sometimes even formed nearly independent states. Considering the important intellectual influence of Babylonian Judaism, the existence of numerous prayer and study rooms in the metropolises can be supposed, as in Nehardea (where, according to *Megillah* 29a, the synagogue is thought to have been founded by exiles taken by Nebuchadrezzar), Seleucia and Ctesiphon on the Tigris, Nisibis, and then in the academies of Soura and of Poumbedita. But little is known of their architecture. The Talmud, however, contains a few allusions. It is known (*Megillah* 26b), for example, that the *tebah* (the Holy Ark of the times) was still moveable. One day in a synagogue of Mahusa, Rabbah ordered it to be placed before the door of a room containing a corpse in order that the *cohanim* could attend the ceremony. When these regions fell under Islamic domination, numerous synagogues disappeared or were subjected to the usual restrictions.

The synagogues of Palestine, including that of Jerusalem itself, at the time of the Second Temple, are better known. Not only are they mentioned in the Talmud but also in the Christian gospels and epistles. Jesus started his public preaching in the synagogue of Nazareth (*Luke*, 4,16). He then settled in Capernaum and travelled throughout Galilee with his first disciples, and "taught in their synagogues" (*Matthew*, 4, 23; *Mark*, 1,21 and 39). Not the least fascinating aspect of the actual site of Capernaum are the outstanding ruins of a synagogue that have been preserved there. Admittedly, Jesus could not have preached in this as it dates from the 4th or 5th centuries AD, but the remains could well be on the site[5] of that known as the "Centurion" (*Luke* 7,9). The apostles as well as Paul, in their turn, began to preach in synagogues, which at that time were referred to by the Greek term of *proseuche* ('house of prayer').

Before 70, Jerusalem had 394 synagogues (according to the *Babli Ketoubot* 105a) or 480 synagogues (according to the *Yeruchalmi Megillah*, 3,1). Here again, the Acts of the Apostles (6,8) refers to "synagogues called of the Freedmen, Cyrenians, Alexandrians and the people of Cilicia and Asia". This text is all the more interesting in that it confirms that synagogues were divided according to professional groups or places of origin. Here, a major principle of this "architecture of exile" is demonstrated. Up until the 1930's, Istanbul[6] had dozens of Sephardic (*Catalan, Portugal, Aragon, Calabres, Messina*) or Byzantine (*Ahrida, Yanipoli, Edirne, Castoria, Ichtip*) synagogues named after the towns of origin. Some of these groups go back to the Byzantine period. In Italy, as of the 15th century, the oratories were also named after the country of the origin of the congregation. The Eastern European Jews who later settled in Western countries during the 19th and 20th centuries grouped themselves into *Landmannschaften* and opened separate oratories. In New York, a veritable map of Poland emerged. It appears that the principle of large centralized synagogues was an institution there. Although such buildings had existed in Alexandria, for example, is it nevertheless a model contrary to Jewish and Diasporic tradition. These large synagogues became the symbol of the Emancipation, whereas the oratory remained the privileged environment of an Orthodoxy which resisted assimilation.

The synagogue is thus a foundation in which not only the congregation, but also the leaders of the community participate. Discovered in 1913, a Greek inscription known as of "Theodotos" preserves the memory of a synagogue in Jerusalem: "Theodotos, son of Vettenos, priest and leader of the synagogue, son and grandson of leaders of synagogues, had this synagogue built in order to recite the law and to study the commandments; and the hospice, the rooms and the installation of water to accommodate foreigners. The synagogue was founded by his father with the Elders and Simonides." Besides indicating the Hellenisation of a community in Jerusalem itself, this text demonstrates the role played by the synagogue at the centre of a sort of community complex, such as are found everywhere over the centuries.

The presence of synagogues in the Herodian fortresses of Herodion and Masada are the result of conversions made by the Zealots who were entrenched there during their revolt against the Romans (66-70 AD). Nothing contradicts the possibility, however, that there were not already prayer rooms at these sites during the time of Herod. Also destroyed in 67 AD, the ruins of the only known edifice built as a synagogue and contemporary with the Second Temple have been found at Gamla (Golan). These examples demonstrate the adaptability of the function of the synagogue. Whether the prayer space was established in a pre-existing space or was specially built according to the same principle of spatial organization, the result was always the same: a room lined with seats and often supported by a colonnade.

Capharnaum, Israel, *Menorah* sculpted
on the lintel of the synagogue
(4ᵗʰ century).

Kfar Baram, Israel, *Entrance to
the synagogue* (3ʳᵈ century).

The Synagogues of Palestine: The Archaeological Evidence

Up until the Arab conquest in the 7th century, Jewish communities, and even academies, were maintained in Palestine. Archaeology has thus revealed a large number of synagogues dated from the 3rd to 7th centuries[7].

Two models should be examined in order to understand the architecture of Jewish prayer rooms, for they are not always independent and perfectly identifiable structures. The first model suggests that the synagogue emerged from domestic architecture and derived its plan and organization from the triclinium, a large dining-hall lined with benches. Such an origin agrees well with the idea that can be deduced from the initial prayer and reading assemblies. The transformations carried out in the Herodion confirm this hypothesis. The second model pertains to public civil architecture: the Roman basilica recognizable by its colonnade. The plasticity of the synagogal space allows the possibility of a dual origin to be envisaged, and even perhaps of the imitation of religious or secular buildings such as the Nabataean or Syrian meeting halls. Without it being certain that they exercised a real influence, typical plans emerge from archaeological discoveries. They oscillate between these two models with constants such as the layout of the lateral benches combined with colonnades supporting the roof.

Originally, the place of the Torah, a fundamental element for the future of synagogue design, was not fixed. The congregations used a mobile chest. The innovation consisted of resorting to a layout with an apse. This design was later combined with a precise orientation, which once again finds its principle in a text from the Exile. In Babylon, Daniel (6,11) prayed three times a day in front of his windows which were opened towards the direction of Jerusalem. Initially, it was the façades of the synagogues that appear to have been oriented towards the Holy City. Later, however, it was the niches that held the Scrolls of the Torah that were so orientated.

The evolution of the synagogue in relation to that of the church should also be considered, particularly as the influences may have been reciprocal. The plan of the synagogue in Beth Alpha strongly resembles that of a church with a narthex and side-aisles. The décor of churches, of synagogues, and even of pagan temples or of villas is also often difficult to differentiate. The chariot of Helios and the signs of the zodiac are found at Beth Alpha, but are associated with specifically Jewish motifs, such as the *menorah* and narrative scenes such as the ligature of Isaac. This demonstrates that a Jewish iconography, admittedly

based on Hellenistic models, had been established. Organizational and decorative relationships indicate that local workshops could have produced several known edifices.

In the excavated synagogues, which date mainly from the 3rd to the 6th centuries, a certain plan dominates: a rectangular room with a colonnade on two or three sides and benches resting against the walls. It appears, however, that it was at the beginning of the 6th century that the basilican plan terminating in an apse sheltering the Holy Ark and the *bimah* became dominant. Archaeologists have identified the architectural elements of the Ark and the reading platform, and in particular the chancels. This plan (a nave and two side-aisles) is also found in churches, and could have had a Roman origin. It was, nevertheless, appropriate to the ritual of the synagogue. Over the course of three centuries, annexes multiplied, and vestibules, narthex, and complementary courtyards or rooms were often added. It is not known if areas or galleries reserved for women already existed.

Rather coherent ensembles emerge from the analyses and the typology, but attempts to deduce a chronology, that many recent archaeological discoveries call into question, have proven to be uncertain. Not only are the typology and dating questionable, but the model as well. Yoram Tsafrir discusses[8] the model of the Roman basilica and rightly points out that it does not have, as do most synagogues, three-sided colonnades. He concludes that there is more "invention than copy" in the synagogues of Antiquity.

Nevertheless, certain geographic areas, such as Galilee, the Beth Shean valley and the Gaza region, have synagogues similar in their plan and décor.

Galilee, which accommodated the religious authorities of Judaism after the Bar Kochba revolt, is the richest region. Very simple synagogues occur, as at Nabratein, but there are also buildings that undoubtedly had several levels (Arbel and Meron) or façades decorated with triple portals (Capernaum and Kfar Baram) and porticos. The latter solution became extremely common. It was frequent in Galilee, but it also occurred in the south of Judea towards En-Gedi. Archaeologists have discovered around twenty synagogues with this solution as opposed to a single example with two portals. The synagogues of Galilee were excavated first (mainly by Heinrich Kohl and Carl Watzinger[9]) and, because they were often the oldest, came to represent in the eyes of archaeologists the classical example of the synagogue: a basilican plan associated with two or three interior colonnades. Later discoveries, however, have shown that other types existed, even in Galilee. Another particularity of the Galilean synagogues stems from the richness of their sculptured

Hammat, near Tiberias, Israel,
mosaic pavement representing the chariot
of Helios (late 3rd—early 4th century).

decoration. The *menorah* and other ritual objects of the Temple (Hammath), stars of David, as well as the Holy Ark itself (Capernaum and Chorazin) decorate the lintels of the façades, the capitals, or the chancels.

If the vestiges themselves are fairly abundant, several texts suggest that the number of synagogues was, in fact, much more important than the archaeological evidence indicates. Sepphoris, a prosperous city that became a major intellectual Jewish centre had as many as 18 synagogues, but only a single one has been found. Nevertheless, it presents a remarkable group of mosaics (Temple objects, biblical scenes, inscriptions).

During the 6th century, the Gaza region witnessed the construction of important synagogues. Dated to 508-509, that in Gaza is 36 metres in width and has five naves. It is decorated with a mosaic with foliated scrolls and animals, as is the nearby synagogue in Ma'on. If the basilican plan is the most frequent, it is also possible that, as in Judea, the space was arranged widthwise with the niche being placed on one of the long sides of the room. Such was the case at Khirbet Susiya where a stone *bimah* decorated with motifs such as *menorah*, palms, etc. has been reconstructed in the Museum of Israel.

The mosaic pavements, expressly authorized by the Talmud, surprise as much by their richness and quality as by their iconography. The latter attests to both an assimilation (Helios, signs of the zodiac, the seasons) and to a clear affirmation of identity (Temple objects become omnipresent symbols) and even the lineaments of narrative scenes with a high spiritual impact, such as the ligature of Isaac. The most remarkable feature of these mosaics is the reproduction of human figures which the Tradition preferred to forbid. On the artistic level, a repertoire was developed that will be found during the following centuries on manuscripts, particularly the composition representing the Holy Ark with the ritual objects or the *menorah* cantoned by lions.

Certain synagogues deserve particular mention because of the composition of the iconography of their pavements. Although, syncretic by the utilization of pagan motifs, the complexity of the compositions justifies a search for a profound religious significance. The synagogues of Beth Shean, Beth Alpha, Hammath near Tiberias, Khirbet Susiya and others present an organization in three registers which creates a progression. Near the Holy Ark, a representation of the Temple and its principal objects frequently occurs. In the centre, a zodiac and the chariot of Helios are sometimes found. At the entrance, the mosaic often has dedicatory inscriptions placed between animals (lions at Hammath), but also biblical scenes (ligature of Isaac at Beth Alpha and,

perhaps, Daniel at Khirbet Susiya). More modest synagogues simplify these representations or retain only a single element. Thus the synagogue in Hulda has a panel with a *menorah*, a *chofar*, a *loulav*, and that at Husiya the zodiac. At Japhia, it is difficult to know if a zodiac or a circle recalling the twelve tribes is represented.

Certain regions have common décors of which the origin is not Jewish. The synagogues of Gaza and of Ma'on, for example, are decorated with foliated scroll mosaics containing a complete bestiary. This type of ornamentation is also found in the churches at Shellal and at Beth Gubrin. The synagogue at Naro in Tunisia also belongs to this group. The common source is Roman. The question which arises, therefore, pertains to the value of these décors. Do these animals and objects have a symbolic function? Do the vine scrolls with bunches of hanging grapes (as in the mosaic at Gaza, donated in 508-509 AD by the wood merchants Menahem and Yeshua, as a Greek inscription shows or in that at Ma'on) have a Jewish meaning? Do they refer to the numerous evocations of the vine in the imagery of Eretz Israel or in the prophecies of Isaiah, whereas the same motifs, decorating contemporary churches, are obviously an interpretation of the vine in relation to the Eucharist? In Ma'on, however, a Judaisation occurs through the use of specific motifs (*chofar*, *loulav* and *menorah*) on the medallions formed by the foliated scrolls. Thus the same plastic language and the same common motifs demonstrate the proximity of opposing religions and cultures in 6th century Palestine, even if a concern for differentiation and for the affirmation of religious identity which led to the insertion of truly symbolic motifs is obviously detectable. An archaeological statistic clearly reveals how certain objects became dominant symbols. The *menorah* is represented in not less than 55 synagogues of the 150 that have been excavated. It has even given its name to the recently discovered 'house of the *menorot*', a 7th century synagogue in Jerusalem upon the walls of which it is painted. The other common Jewish motifs are the *chofar*, the *loulav* and the Holy Ark. They are subsequently found in Medieval manuscripts and in modern synagogues.

Numerous synagogues were damaged, not only by the conquests and reconquests of the region and by iconoclastic campaigns, but also by earthquakes. Most synagogues were abandoned by the 7th century. Some were even transformed into churches (Gerasa, 530-531 AD). Caught between the hostility of Christian Byzantium and the rise of Islam, Judaism took refuge in a few towns. Archaeology has shown that the synagogue of Tiberias, which would later be one of the four holy cities of Palestinian Judaism, was in use until the 11th century.

The Greco-Roman World: The Mediterranean Basin

It was in a Hellenistic context that the first synagogue of the Diaspora appeared. Attested by an inscription dating to the reign of King Ptolemy Euergetes (246-221 BC), a synagogue was located at Schedia near Alexandria. This text confirms a Jewish presence also known through other evidence, in particular the papyri of Elephantine, a city where a community had settled. The famous island of Delos preserves the ruins of a synagogue which could date from the 1st century BC and was used until the 2nd century AD. Undoubtedly located in a residential area, it was decorated with a marble Moses' chair of a type that was also found at Hammath and Chorazin. As is indicated by texts, several towns in Greece had very old Jewish communities, in particular Athens, Aegina, and Corinth where vestiges from the 4th to 6th centuries have been found. In Macedonia, the synagogue in Stobi, dated to the 3rd century by an inscription of the donor, is located under a church. In Plovdiv (formerly Philippopolis, founded by Philip II of Macedon), now in modern Bulgaria, the remains of a synagogue containing fragments of a mosaic decorated with a *menorah* were discovered in 1981. Even more numerous in Asia Minor, synagogues are known through several excavations: at Miletus (with some uncertainty however); at Priene, where *menorot* sculptured in bas-relief more clearly authenticate its use as a synagogue; at Apamea, remarkable for its mosaics and inscriptions dating from the end of the 4th century; and at Sardis.

The latter, one of the largest synagogues yet found, is mentioned by Josephus Flavius. This magnificent basilica was 122 metres in length. Worthy of the opulent capital of Lydia, with its colonnades, its atrium with pilasters, and its mosaics, it could hold a thousand worshipers. Such a building, associated with baths and a gymnasium, certainly resulted from an urban reorganization. Most of the synagogues known from the Diaspora were, in effect, pre-existing public or private buildings transformed into synagogues. The occupation of the town by the Persians in 616 undoubtedly brought about the destruction of this synagogue. It is not surprising to find in Asia Minor, in Tripolitania, in Ptolemaic Egypt, even in Greece and in Italy, synagogues of basilican plan, this type having become a model for all cultures.

The synagogue of Alexandria, another basilica of gigantic proportions, is attested only through texts. Described in the Talmud (*Souca* 51b), it was so large that the *bimah* was placed in the centre. It is not surprising that

Alexandria, famous for its Jewish community—which successfully completed the translation of the Septuagint—had such an edifice. "Who has not seen the double gallery, at Alexandria in Egypt, has not seen Israel in its splendour. It was built as a large basilica, having one gallery in the interior of the other. Sixty myriads of men are sometimes assembled there, as many as formerly fled from Egypt, even the double it is told. And there were, for the 71 Elders, 71 seats of gold, of which each costs not less than twenty-five myriads of gold denarii. There was, in the centre, a wooden platform, where the Hazan [cantor] stood, with flags in his hand; and, at each passage where it was necessary to intone the word: *Amen*, he signalled with his flags, and all the people proclaimed: *Amen*. The faithful never sat down, but mingled without order amongst one another. But the goldsmiths, silversmiths, coppersmiths had their places, and even the miners and the weavers. And when a stranger or a poor man entered, he immediately recognized the companions of his trade, and addressing them, he received from them assistance for himself and his family." Thus, the synagogue assembled all the faithful, but they remained, as in the smaller oratories, linked to their social and professional structures. The synagogue of Alexandria was destroyed 80 years after its construction, during the Jewish revolt against the Roman empire in 116 AD.

Around the 1st century AD, most of the towns in the Orient harboured synagogues as is shown through the peregrinations of Saint Paul. While on his way to Damascus to bring letters from the high priest to the synagogues, with the intention of eradicating evangelism (Acts of the Apostles, 9,1), he was converted. He then visited the synagogues of Thessalonica (*id.*, 17,1), Beroea (*id.*, 17,10), Athens (*id.*, 17), Corinth (*id.*, 18,4), Ephesus (*id.*, 19), etc.

The western Mediterranean basin felt the ramifications of the Diaspora, particularly in Rome where, however, its traces are rare. In Ostia, the port of Rome, on the other hand, significant ruins of a 4th century synagogue were discovered in 1961 on the site of an older structure which undoubtedly dated from the 1st century. Its basilican plan with a lateral apse and the Jewish symbols sculpted on the architrave make it a good example of the diffusion of the architecture and the décor found in the Orient. A few rare vestiges are also preserved in southern Italy, particularly at Bova Marina, near Reggio di Calabria. In North Africa, a most remarkable building was uncovered in 1884 in Naro (Hammam Lif) near Carthage. It is known above all for its mosaic, part of which is now preserved in the Brooklyn Museum: it has foliated scrolls encircling animals, but also a dedication

Doura-Europos, Syria, mural of
*The Resurrection of the Dead, the Vision
of Ezekiel.* Damascus Museum, Syria.

Doura-Europos, Syria, *Murals in the
synagogue* (244). On the niche
is shown the Temple of Jerusalem,
with to the left, the candlestick,
lulav and *ethrog* used for the feast of
Succoth, and on the right the bonds with
which Abraham bound his son Isaac.
The reference here is clearly to the Ark
of the Covenant, the Temple being on
Mt Moriah, a place of sacrifice.
The scene is dominated by the hand
of God emerging from a cloud, a motif
later found in the Beth Alpha mosaic and
in medieval manuscripts. Reconstruction
by the Diaspora Museum, Tel Aviv.

and two peacocks on a basin, a motif considered as an evocation of paradise. In France, where archaeological traces are rare, it is significant that the first mention of a synagogue, in *Historia Francorum* by Gregory of Tours, concerns the destruction of one at Clermont-Ferrand in 576 AD.

On the Edge of Empires: Dura-Europos

The synagogue of Dura-Europos, on the Euphrates near the frontier between the Roman and the Parthian empires, single-handedly writes an essential chapter in the history of synagogue architecture and decoration. Its fate, comparable to that of Pompeii, makes it an irreplaceable witness. Its discovery in 1920 called into question the basic concept concerning the origins of Christian art and iconography and opened a new field in the awareness of Jewish art. As in the case of the synagogues of Palestine, it is the pavements that have been especially preserved. It was suspected that paintings must have decorated the walls of synagogues in the 3rd and 4th centuries, but no actual vestiges had yet been found. Through extraordinary circumstances, however, three walls covered with frescoes at Dura-Europos have survived. This synagogue, completed in 244, disappeared under the backfilling materials amassed to strengthen the ramparts from an attack of the Persians in 256. It reappeared only during the excavations undertaken between 1922 and 1937 and yielded the largest ensemble of paintings inspired by the Bible[10] during Antiquity. These discoveries have subsequently incited numerous publications and key debates[11].

The synagogue of Dura, located in a residential area, was reached through a courtyard, and illustrates, once again, the use of a re-established space. An older structure, dated to the end of the 2nd century, had left a vine motif, undoubtedly symbolic, around the Holy Ark. Its western wall is the best preserved. Later, in relation to this location, representations of the Temple, of ritual objects and of the ligature of Isaac were added. A symbolism of the Covenant established between Abraham and God on Mount Moriah, where Solomon later constructed the Temple, is clearly asserted here. The programme of the second synagogue is, however, more narrative: arranged in four superimposed registers in the manner of a comic strip, the frescoes link together a series of biblical scenes of which the interpretation remains open.

Near the Holy Ark, Orpheus (obviously assimilated to David by his lyre and, beyond, to an image of the

Messiah), and Jacob's dual benediction of his children and the sons of Joseph are superposed. On the upper register, on the right, the vocation of Moses, identifiable by the burning bush, is followed by the Exodus from Egypt with the crossing of the Red Sea. On the left, Moses receives the Tables of the Law; nearby are Solomon and the Queen of Sheba. On the middle register, on the right, is Abraham (or, perhaps, Joshua or Jeremiah), then the Temple of Solomon and the capture of the Ark of the Covenant by the Philistines. On the left is Joshua (or, perhaps, Esdras or Isaiah) reading the Law, then the consecration of the Tent of the Meeting (Tabernacle) where, next to Aaron in the costume of an Iranian sovereign, are ritual objects, and finally the miraculous well of Beer (Beersheba). On the lower register, on the right, is David anointed by Samuel and Moses saved from the waters, on the left, the triumph of Mordecai associated with Ahasuerus and Esther on their throne, and finally, the resurrection of the Widow's child by Elijah.

The southern wall continues on the lower register the cycle of Elijah. The middle register offers a complementary image to the western wall, depicting the dedication of the Temple. The northern wall comprises: on the top, Jacob's Dream; in the centre, the battle of Eben ha-Ezer; and on the bottom, a very astonishing vision of Ezekiel. This fresco is the most surprising. The resurrection of the dead takes place continuously, and the prophet is depicted not less than six times, first in Iranian costume then in Greek costume. The eastern wall, less well preserved, has retained only the lower portion of two scenes which certain specialists have attempted to interpret as the struggle of David and Saul as well as the feast of Belshazzar.

The important narrative and plastic art displayed at Dura-Europos marks an original moment in the contribution of painting to the décor of synagogues, a contribution that will not be found during other periods. Here, art served the Jewish religion without restriction, but in a perspective which demonstrates that the message and its transmission prevailed over mere beauty, and that, according to an immutable principle of Judaism, aesthetics are at the service of faith. In these frescoes, even more than in the later mosaics which were more limited in their narrative development, the past (a reminder of the stage of the Covenant between God and Israel through Abraham, Jacob, Moses, and the Temple of Solomon) and the future (be it messianic or eschatologic as the vision of Ezekiel) intimately intermingle. This suggests that it is not merely a Bible in images, but a veritable convergent exegesis, in the manner of the *midrash*, to give a coherent interpretation of the covenant and the divine promises. On the whole, the textual references are identi-fied, but the major surprise, other than the high artistic quality of these frescoes that reveal Hellenistic, Roman, and Persian influences, is the constitution of an icono-graphic vocabulary of which the models are unknown. Dura-Europos, however, is certainly not at the origin of this development. This little provincial synagogue can only be the witness of a tradition already established and diffused in all of the Jewish Orient.

A final feature renders these frescoes disconcerting: the very free representation of human figures. Admittedly, God is only represented in the form of a hand, but Moses and Ezekiel are clearly represented full-faced. But why was the prohibition of representation particularly trans-gressed here? This simply confirms the historic relativity of this interdiction, which was reactivated by rabbis dur-ing certain periods, when for centuries Jewish figurative art had developed.

Influences

Archaeological discoveries have not been without influence upon the conception of modern synagogues. At the end of the 19th century, a 'historian' century *par excel-lence*, architects thought that they had found in these ves-tiges the elements for expressing a Jewish identity that specific styles had not really succeeded in conveying. It was a historicist approach, in continuity with the century, since the archaeological references served to reactivate Classicism and to subordinate its use to that which had been used in ancient Palestine. Arnold Brunner, an archi-tect of 1900, became the defender of this vision. The first American-born Jewish architect and trained at MIT, he treated synagogues in a rather eclectic fashion up until he became aware, with the discovery of 33 Galilean syna-gogues by the Palestine Exploration Fund, that there actually existed Jewish references for synagogues. He explained this in a long article in *The Brickbuilder* where he notes[12] that if "the art of Judea is the only Eastern art appropriate", unfortunately it is not suited to modern conditions and especially to the size needed for contem-porary synagogues. These archaeological vestiges, how-ever, legitimatise the use of specific motifs, such as on the colossal façade and the Holy Ark of the Shearith Israel synagogue (1897) where Brunner used coronae taken from the ruins of the synagogue of Kfar Baram. He was also inspired by the system of colonnades and amplified it. Although a specialist of monumental synagogues, he nevertheless had the opportunity to design a building close to the proportions used in Antiquity, the Harry S.

Frank Memorial Synagogue of Philadelphia (1901) which illustrated his article. In this little temple *in antis*, he used the stone and numerous archaeological motifs including a *menorah* from Kfar Baram. His taste for Classicism persisted and, in 1921, he again proposed an immense Corinthian portico for the Union Temple of Brooklyn, which was, first of all, a building containing a community centre.

Subsequent archaeological discoveries did not always have an impact. Sometimes they challenged the estab-lished principles to such an extent that it was not until the American liberal movement that they produced any effect. The murals of Dura-Europos could have legitima-tised the introduction of figurative paintings as early as the 1930s, but such was not the case, save for a few American exceptions. Nevertheless, with the creation of the new Israeli State and the evolution of Jewish con-sciousness that ensued, the influences of ancient Israel increased in American Judaism. Just as an Israeli flag accompanied an American flag in the synagogues, many synagogue designers drew their decorative inspiration from ancient art. A systematic approach was even under-taken by a congregation in New Rochelle, New York. The Beth El synagogue, inaugurated in May 1971, was designed by the architect Edgar Tafel and—at the initia-tive of a community leader, Stanley I. Batkin[13]—the building became an encyclopaedia of Jewish history. The façade, by its pilasters, is a reminder of the Temple, a *menorah* taken from an ancient synagogue being placed there. Here the symbolism is acceptable, but that the pond in the garden be the pool of Siloah demonstrates the limits of an approach that sometimes is only saved from ridicule by the quality of certain of the artists com-missioned. Each element of the furnishings is decorated. The rabbi's lectern has motifs taken from those found in 1957 at Ma'on, and the western wall obviously evokes the Wall of the Temple. The windows, by Benoît Gilsoul, reproduce the columns Jachin and Boaz, and the musical instruments of the temple. The 'pool of the Levites' recalls the mosaics of Beth Alpha, and a mural was even designed after the *Mahzor Vitry*[14]... Israeli artists were commissioned: Yaakov Agam for one of his famous stars of David[15]; Gdula Ogen, a ceramist trained at Bezalel, for the 'wall of feasts', on which ceramic panels represent the principal feasts. The sculptor Luise Kaish created a wall depicting the "eternal martyrdom" of Israel, from the Babylonian Exile to the Showa. All these artists remain symbolically abstract.

In the contemporary period, the influences of Ancient Israel are seen not in architecture, but in decoration. The artists use symbolic motifs drawn from ancient

Ben Shahn, *Ram's Horn, Menorah
and Divine Hand*, preliminary painting
for the mosaic in the synagogue
at Temple Ohel Shalom, Nashville,
Tennessee (1958). New York,
Jacob Shulman collection.

iconography: Adolph Gottlieb in his stained-glass window for the Milton Steinberg House synagogue in New York (1954, Kelly and Gruzen) or even Ben Shan reproducing the Divine hand above the faithful, as at Dura-Europos, for his mosaics for the Oheb Shalom synagogue in Nashville, Tennessee (1959). But all these elements are reinterpreted in a plastic language proper to each artist and not merely reproduced.

Nevertheless, these few examples show how an identity can be created in a contemporary synagogue which takes into account the centrality of Israel, even of the State of Israel, through the evocation of its history and its art.

The synagogues of the Diaspora in Antiquity are, in short, of great importance for a global vision of the typology concerning these buildings. As A. T. Kraabel[16] has shown, they already illustrate the very basis of this study: on the one hand, the absence of "canonical forms" which gives a large variety of architectural plans and the adoption of local methods of constructions, and, on the other hand, the tendency for the densification of space through the addition of adjoining rooms, which makes them the forerunners of community centres, a structure more fundamental for a society in exile than for Jews settled in Israel. The décor also shows how, after

the destruction of the Temple, it contributed to a certain sanctification of the synagogue, and which was to blossom at the moment of the Emancipation: the idea that Jerusalem is 'there where a Jewish community resides' is thus not a completely new notion. The synagogue was born of this tension between the feeling of *galout* and the desire of integration.

Philadelphia, Pennsylvania,
Franck Memorial Synagogue (1901,
architect Arnold W. Brunner), drawing
published in *The Brickbuilder*, 1908.

New York, *Shearith Israel* (1897, architect Arnold W. Brunner). New York's oldest Sephardic congregation commissioned a Jewish architect whose modern classicism was based on references drawn from the ancient synagogues of Galilee, recently rediscovered. Brunner stated that 'Where choosing a style for the present day is concerned, I firmly believe we must either return to the Judean originals or do as has been done in synagogue building since the dispersion of the Jews, and adopt the prevailing style in the country in question.'

The Sephardic and Oriental Diasporas

Detail of an engraving by Bernard Picart
(XVIIIth century), *Procession des palmes
chez les juifs portugais.*

Left page:
Djerba, Tunisia, *La Ghriba synagogue*,
famed for its annual pilgrimage.

Amongst the Diasporas—the veritable base of Jewish identity—that of the Sephardim is outstanding through the patrimony that it has transmitted. Moreover, it still remains alive and the term 'Sephardic' has even come to incorporate oriental Jewish communities whose ancestors had never even resided in Spain. *Sepharad* was from then on a major component of contemporary Judaism, and also perceived in contrast with the Ashkenazic world.

The dispersal of the Iberian Jews was provoked by their expulsion from Spain in 1492 when the Catholic rulers Isabella of Castile and Ferdinand of Aragon banned non-Christian religions. It was sustained throughout the three following centuries by the flight of the converted *marranos* ('pork')[1] in the face of the exactions of the Inquisition in Spain and Portugal (where some of the Spanish Jews had taken refuge in 1492). This dispersal resulted in scattering the Sephardim from America to India and in the transmission of Sephardic culture, and sometimes even their rite, to important autochthonous groups of Jews. It was in the Islamic countries that their influence was major, undoubtedly because of their knowledge acquired during the time of the Hispano-Moorish coexistence.

Although the Sephardim conserved their pure Castilian language (*ladino*) and their own culture for a long time amongst the most diverse societies, they did not—strangely enough—express their nostalgia for that which had been the "Golden Age" of cohabitation of the three religions of Spain before 1492 by the revival of a very specific architectural tradition. The synagogue had, in effect, adopted a brilliant Mudejar style, a very original Hispano-Moorish art. This style, however, was not conveyed by the Sephardim. It only reappeared during the second half of the 19th century in order to reply to an orientalist imaginary[2] that was as much non-Jewish as it was Jewish. Moreover, it was more often the Ashkenazic synagogues that were treated in this style. A few characteristics of this Sephardic identity, nevertheless, were transmitted over the centuries and their migrations.

When expulsed from Spain and Portugal, some Jews migrated to Italy, the Maghreb, and the eastern basin of

Interior of a Spanish synagogue,
Golden Haggadah, 14th century,
Ms. Or 2884, British Library, London.

Toledo, Spain, the *'Sinagoga del Transito'*
(1357).

the Mediterranean, particularly Turkey. These movements did not, however, concern only the Jews who had remained faithful to their religion and fled Spain in the wake of the edict of expulsion. The Jews who had converted in order to escape the Inquisition were also very soon induced to settle in the other countries as "New Christians". New horizons were opened for the Sephardim by those who headed towards the Atlantic ports. Portuguese Jews established a Sephardic community in the Netherlands as early as 1595. The Dutch authorities accepted them all the more as Holland was at war with Catholic Spain. The "New Christians" who settled in the southwest of France, however, had to continue to pretend to be converted until the 18th century.

Sepharad

By the 8th century, the term 'Sepharad', a place-name mentioned in the Bible meaning 'Spain', had come to indicate the entire Iberian Peninsula where Jews had long been established. Persecuted by the Visigoths, the Jewish community then flourished under the caliphate of Cordoba (until the seizure of power by the fanatical Almohads), and again under the Catholic kings that led the *reconquista*. But after 1391, anti-Jewish persecutions resumed and continued until the annihilation of 1492. Under such conditions, there remains very little architectural inheritance from this brilliant Jewish culture of Spain. Apart from a few *juderias* and *mikvaot*, only four synagogues survived, whereas originally there had been hundreds. The two most magnificent synagogues, both in Toledo, were preserved only because they were transformed into churches. Francisco Cantera Burgos identifies over 120 synagogues within the frontiers of modern Spain[3]. Nevertheless, these few edifices are a rare but major testimony of Mudejar art, an art practiced by Muslim artisans living in Christian regions, of which the jewel is the Alcazar of Seville. The surviving synagogues are all the more important because they belong to two different periods: first around 1200, then about 1350. The disappearance of these Hispano-Moorish buildings is regrettable. An elegy concerning the persecutions in Toledo in the year 1391 gives a list of seven synagogues and eight "schools" for this town[4] alone. As with many Medieval synagogues, those of Toledo were sumptuous on the interior, but their brick walls and façades did not externally differentiate them from the surrounding buildings.

The oldest of the four, which later became the church of Santa María la Blanca in Toledo, dates from around 1200[5], a period when Toledo had already been reconquered. If this building had not originally been a mosque, it strongly resembles one with its four rows of eight Moorish arches that occupy the entire space and divide it into five naves. Its Moorish décor is remarkable, covering the walls above the arches with a frieze of blind polylobed arcades and interlacings which also occurs on the capitals with crossettes and pine cones. It can be compared with contemporary mosques in Morocco, in particular with the Kouyoubia Mosque in Marrakech. The synagogue of Segovia, which became the church of Corpus Christi, presents the same plan but with three naves, and the same arcades. Unfortunately, as a result of a fire in 1899, it was too radically restored.

The other synagogue in Toledo, known as the Nuestra Señora del Tránsito (1357), is of a totally different character. The naves are replaced by a single large room which is 23 meters long by 9.5 meters wide and 12 meters in height. It is annexed to the palace of its patron, Samuel Halevi Abulafia, a minister of Pedro I who himself admired Mudejar architecture. If the arcatures are similar to those of Santa María la Blanca, the decoration itself is much more developed and is, above all, more specifically Jewish. A group of biblical citations in Hebrew are sculpted on the walls in the manner of Muslim epigraphy. These excerpts are from the Psalms and from the Prophets or allude to Bezalel, the maker of the Tent in the wilderness, and to the ritual of the Temple in Jerusalem. The stuccoes, the stalactite cornice and the framework with geometric motifs of inlaid ivory are polychrome. In the middle of the sinterlacings, organized into panels, vegetal motifs and blazons are arranged. The eastern wall is fairly well preserved. Its lower portion is occupied by a niche formed by three polylobed arches in which the Scrolls of the Torah were kept. A final architectural element of great historical importance is the presence of a gallery. For a palace, the passage between the private quarters and the religious space could obviously explain the use of a gallery. But, this is the only case known in Medieval synagogues. The presence of a citation from the canticle of Miriam during the crossing of the Red Sea seems to suggest that this gallery was reserved for women. Later, this layout became the solution *par excellence* to the question of the separation of men and women during the following centuries.

The synagogue of Cordoba, dated to 1315, more modestly presents the same elements as the Toledo synagogue. Unfortunately, only a few panels decorated with interlacings, star-shaped rosaces and inscriptions as well as a niche remain. A gallery was placed above the entrance.

As for the Jewish presence in Portugal, only a single synagogue from the 15th century in Tomar remains.

Cordoba, *View of the inside
of the synagogue* (1315).

Toledo, *'Santa Maria la Blanca'*
synagogue, (c. 1200).

Towards the Mediterranean and the Ottoman World

As a result of their migration towards North Africa and the eastern Mediterranean basin, the Sephardim came into contact with the oriental branch of Judaism and contributed to the development of a Jewish civilization which lasted until the 1950s.

Italy also attracted some of the Jews fleeing Spain. Continual movements of migration occurred according to the political changes that took place there. Stable communities, however, existed in the Papal States, in Venice and in Tuscany. In the latter, already accepted as of 1500, Jews were even invited in 1593 by the Grand Duke Ferdinand I Medici to settle in the port of Livourno. In other Italian cities and ghettos, the Sephardim founded—alongside of the *scuole tedesca, italiana, levantina*—the *scuole spagnole* (as in Venice, Ancona and Pesaro), or even retained a more precise memory of their origins, such as the *scuole Catalana* and *Castigliana* established in Rome.

It was in the Ottoman Empire, however, that Sephardic Jews sought refuge by the thousands. The sultan, Bayazid II, was greatly surprised to see King Ferdinand grow impoverished to his own advantage. Over and above expulsion, settling Jews in towns was a means of populating and energizing them, and the Turkish sovereigns did not hesitate to displace hundreds of families to do so. Istanbul, with over 1,500 Jewish families in 1477, had over 8,000 in 1535. In the port of Salonika, conquered in 1430, Jews rapidly formed over half of the population[6]. With transplantations being so common, it is easy to understand that certain names referring to the Jewish groups reveal their geographic origins. In Salonika[7], there were the *kehilot Aragon, Majorque, Catalonia, Castillia* (even called *Gerush Castilla* "the expelled of Castile"), *Portougal, Evora* (a town in Portugal) but also *Calabria* (the Jews of this Italian province were expelled in 1497), and *Sicilia*. Little is known of the material layout of these synagogues as they were often rebuilt in the 19th century. Those of Salonika for the most part were destroyed by the great fire of 1917. In any case, these religious spaces were without any exterior ostentation. The 19th century synagogues, reconstructed after the fire of 1890, are better known. With the Jewish community now in the majority, synagogues became more numerous: 68 are cited including the Beit Shaul (around 1898, Vitaliano Poselli) which can serve as the epitome of the most monumental. It presents a double-levelled façade pierced by picture windows and, over the central bay, a sort of segmental pediment[8]. A few synagogues in Istanbul, Edirne and Izmir, with equally sober façades, still bear witness to a type of planning reconciling the Byzantine and the Sephardic traditions.

In Egypt as well, the Sephardic contribution was important. Autochthonous communities obviously existed, but the enterprising Sephardim—sometimes with the support of Istanbul—played a predominant role in the culture and the direction of the communities, and even sometimes in the entourage of the pashas. No synagogues in Cairo or Alexandria are known from this period, but the reference to "the synagogues of the Portuguese" as late as the 19th century indicates the persistence of a Sephardic identity, cultural at least. Moreover, during the 17th century, Cairo had Palestinian (Ben Ezra), Babylonian and Karaites synagogues. It was in the 20th century, between the two wars, that the Egyptian communities witnessed their greatest expansion. Cairo at that time had about thirty synagogues, including the Ismailiah temple (1905) and the venerable Ben Ezra. Alexandria had more than twenty, including the Eliahu Hanabi synagogue, which had existed for a very long time, but was destroyed by order of Bonaparte. Reconstructed in 1850, it was enlarged in 1865 when two side-aisles with galleries for women were added. This synagogue, the only one still in existence today, reflects the development of this community and of its strong Europeanization. If oriental motifs appear on the interior, the building itself has, on the whole, a Renaissance appearance. A series of interesting synagogues were erected during the 19th and 20th centuries, sometimes in outlying residential districts: the Menasce temple which was founded by Baron Yacoub de Menasce (1863), as well as the Green (1900), Sasson (1910), Castro (1920), and Eliahou Hazan (1937) temples. The development of these rich and brilliant communities gave rise to a francophone Judaeo-Egyptian culture of which the poet Edmond Jabès is an excellent example. Brutally interrupted in 1956, however, a community of 80,000 souls started its migration, leaving behind them their synagogues which gradually disappeared.

The Turkish Empire became a means by which the Spanish *émigrés* could return to Palestine which the Turks had occupied in 1517. From then on, the Sephardim revitalized and even controlled the communities in Jerusalem, Hebron and Safad. Josef Qaro, the compiler of the famous *Shulhan 'Arukh* ('The Well-Laid Table') had settled in Safad, after having been born in Spain in 1488 and having lived for a while in Adrianople. These communities, however, could not have survived without the assistance sent from Amsterdam or from Livourno.

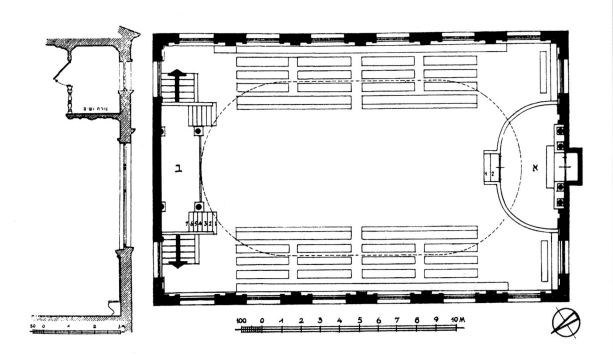

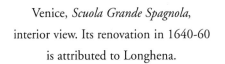

Venice, *Scuola Grande Spagnola*,
interior view. Its renovation in 1640-60
is attributed to Longhena.

Istanbul, *Galata synagogue.*

Alexandria, *Eliahu Hanavi synagogue,*
(1850 and 1865).

Solomon Alexander Hart,
*Feast of Simhat Torah in the synagogue
in Livorno, Italy*, oil on canvas.
New York, The Jewish Museum,
donated by Mr and Mrs Oscar Gruss.

Jerusalem, *Interior view of the most important of the four Sephardic synagogues, dedicated to Yohanan ben Zakai.* Known as *Kahal Kadoch Gadot,* this is also the largest of the four. *Eliahu Hanavi,* the oldest, is said to date from the 16th century. Between the two is the oratory known as *Emtsai* ('middle'). *Istambuli,* the most recent, indicates the place of origin of its founders. All were rebuilt in 1835. They survived the devastation of 1948, but were desecrated and their furnishings destroyed.

Particularly famous is the complex of four Sephardic synagogues in the Old Town of Jerusalem. They managed to survive the Jordanian occupation and demolitions in 1948, thanks to their quasi-subterranean situation, but nevertheless lost their original furniture. These buildings were located where a famous rabbi, Yohanan ben Zakkai, had taught and his name was given to the largest of these synagogues which were undoubtedly established at the end of the 16th century. A description from 1625 mentions them, but their layout is poorly known as they were reconstructed and enlarged during the 19th century[9]. The oldest is known as *Eliahu Hanavi* and the most recent is called *Istambuli*. Despite the repairs that were later undertaken, their layout and their small cupolas clearly illustrate the position of synagogues established in an Islamic context. Other Jewish communities were also present in Jerusalem, the Ashkenazim in particular. Their synagogue was established on the site of the Hurva synagogue (rebuilt in 1856-1864). The Sephardim, nevertheless, played a major intellectual and economic role.

From Istanbul and Adrianople (Edirne), the Jews of the Ottoman Empire spread into the Danubian provinces, and then moved towards Budapest and Vienna where Sephardic communities were still to be found in the 19th century. A Sephardic component played an important role in the communities of Bulgaria, Romania and Serbia. Elias Canetti, an important writer of the German language, nevertheless brought up in Judaeo-Spanish, was born in Routschouk (Bulgaria) and recalls these very lively places at the beginning of the 20th century. But many Danubian Jews came under the influence of the attraction of the West. The Stambuli and the Salonicians also emigrated towards the West, be they rich families such as the Camondo family or simple shopkeepers who settled in the La Roquette quarter of Paris where they founded oriental oratories.

Towards Amsterdam and the Atlantic Ports

Amsterdam played a primordial role in the rebirth of the Jewish communities in Western Europe. The tolerance found in the Netherlands and the economic development allowed Jewish communities of that city to build synagogues which would serve as models for communities elsewhere, and all the more so, since Amsterdam was a metropolis for the entire Atlantic zone and maintained close relations with Venice and Jerusalem[10]. Symbolic of the central role played by Amsterdam was the company that it developed "to marry orphans and poor girls of the Portuguese and Castilian Nation, living from Saint-Jean de Luz to Danzig." There were also groups of 'New Christians' more or less settled, in the south, in Bayonne and a few nearby towns (Peyrehorade, Bidache, Labastide-Clairence), Bordeaux, Nantes, and Rouen, as well as in the north, in Antwerp (where, under Spanish control, the clandestine community there was destroyed several times) and Hamburg-Altona. But it was only in the Netherlands that Jews could openly return to Judaism. There, handsome synagogues were opened as well as in the Hague (1726) and Rotterdam (1725). On the other hand, in France where rather stable groups had been constituted, they possessed only hidden oratories, of which only a few rare descriptive elements have been preserved. In Bayonne, they were confined to a few buildings of the Saint-Esprit quarter and in Bordeaux to the Rue Bouhaut and the Rue des Augustins. During the 18th century however, the 'Portuguese nation' could officially practice its religion. The fine Baroque Holy Ark of Bayonne, recalling those of Amsterdam, contrasts with the current temple built in 1837. It comes from the 18th century synagogue known as Yechiba es-Haim.

In England, after residing temporarily on several occasions, the marranos (with the consent of Cromwell who had been appealed to by the Dutch Jews) settled definitively in London in 1656 and prospered. Furthermore, the Sephardim had opened the way for the establishment of the Ashkenazic communities. Thus, despite this dispersion, the Sephardim developed their economic as well as their cultural activities. As Cecil Roth[11] remarked: "the members of the marrano Diaspora were thus truly the first modern Jews." Moreover, they also constructed the first modern synagogues, imposing, pierced by large bays, and decorated with orders. Only there was the dawn of the Enlightenment foreshadowed.

Even though they spoke Portuguese, the Jews who settled in Amsterdam adopted the vernacular architecture. The first Portuguese synagogue (1639) evokes, by its façade accentuated by pilasters and picture windows, the Mauritshuis in the Hague, built shortly before, as well as Protestant temples. The Ashkenazim, who arrived soon afterwards, opened the Grote Synagoge in 1671. Designed by the municipal architect D. Stalpaert, the materials (brick and stone), the classicising *modanatura*, and the large picture windows became a type used in a grandiose style by the Portuguese when they reconstructed their own synagogue on the plans of Elias Bouman (1671-1675). The internal layout—a major order supporting the roof and a minor order for the galleries, an imposing *bimah* near the entrance facing a large wooden Holy Ark—as well as the volume surmounted with attics

Amsterdam, *Portuguese synagogue*,
(1671-75, architect Elias Bouman).
Given the monumental
proportions of the building
—38 meters deep,
26 meters wide and some 15 meters high,

it was enormous for its time—
we can understand that it suggested
the Temple of Jerusalem.
References to the Temple can be found
in the flared pilasters of the façade,
inspired by Villalpendo's reconstruction.

London, *Bevis Mark synagogue*
(1699-1701), the Holy Ark.

Newport, Rhode Island, *Touro synagogue* (1763). The *Jeshuat Israel* congregation was founded in Newport in 1658 by Jews from Curaçao. A century later, with a view to aiding their integration into this Puritan community, the architect Peter Harrison created this remarkable compromise between the Sephardic model and the Georgian building style of the time. The synagogue was named after the Reverend Isaac Touro, minister-officiant at the time of its construction, and his sons Abraham and Judah. Wealthy businessmen, the latter made a substantial bequest to the synagogue in the form of the 'Touro Jewish Synagogue Fund'.

Curaçao, *Mikveh Israel synagogue* (1732).

Bayonne, France, *Interior view of the synagogue* (1837, architect Capdeville). The Holy Ark came from the former main oratory, known as *Yeshiva es-Haim*. The 'New Christians' did not have the right to live in the city proper, being confined to the Saint-Esprit neighbourhood on the other bank of the Adour, where the nineteenth-century synagogue still stands.

Paris, *Synagogue in the Rue Buffault* (1877, architect Stanislas Ferrand). In accordance with Sephardic tradition, the *bimah* remains in the centre.

and pierced by numerous bays were both diffused following the lanes of Dutch influence and Sephardic commerce. Examples are found in England, such as the Bevis Mark synagogue in London (1699-1701), and in the Dutch colonies. In Curaçao, for example, the *Mikve Israel* synagogue in Willemstad (1732) associated the imbrication of the two orders and classic forms of the Portuguese synagogue with the West Indian custom of spreading sand on the ground. This is also found in Kingston in Jamaica and on Saint Thomas in the Virgin Islands (*Hebrew Congregation*, 1833). From the 17th century onwards, Jewish groups settled in the West Indies. Bridgetown, in Barbados, still retains a handsome old synagogue, *Nidhe Ysrael*. It was Sephardic Jews from Curaçao, in fact, who founded the *Jeshuat Israel* congregation of Newport (Rhode Island)[12] in 1658 and built the Touro Synagogue (1763), the oldest in the United States. Here, the integration of the community into its new context was achieved by resorting to the use of Georgian references. Nevertheless, the bays and the dozen columns, as in Amsterdam or London, established a Sephardic affiliation. Moreover, the Jews of Newport had demanded assistance from the Bevis Mark congregation, which was their model. The oldest American Jewish congregation, *Shearith Israel*, established in Manhattan in 1654 (New York was then called Neuwe Amsterdam), was composed of Sephardic Jews, as was *Mikve Israel*, the congregation in Philadelphia which, after having a first synagogue (1782), built another one designed by William Strickland in an Egyptian style (1822). In South Carolina, the *Kahal Kadosh Beth Elohim* congregation of Charleston built a synagogue (1794) resembling a church. Its present synagogue, Neo-Greek, dates from 1840 (Cyrus L. Warner). Several Sephardic congregations have lasted up until today and have sometimes been revitalized by the arrival of Jews fleeing from Muslim countries.

In the Western European countries where Sephardic communities persisted, a particular element of the plan remains remarkable. Whereas many synagogues adopted, under the influence of the reform, the custom of positioning the Holy Ark and the *bimah* close together in a sort of choir, the 'Portuguese' synagogues retained the central *bimah*. In Paris, the attitude of the Sephardim shows their attachment to this *minhag*. In order to attract the 'Portuguese' to the new synagogue on the Rue de la Victoire (1865-1874)—where the *Consistoire*, with a dominant influence from Alsace-Lorraine, dreamt of fusing the different cults into a 'French rite'—the officials asked the architect Aldrophe to place the *bimah* in the centre of the building. It remained there only a few years, however, as the 'Portuguese' finally refused to associate

with the Ashkenazim. The Sephardim established their own association[13] and opened, thanks to a patron from Bordeaux named Osiris, a synagogue in 1877 on the Rue Buffault (Stanislas Ferrand) which was more respectful of their traditions: a central *bimah*, benches placed longitudinally and even orientated towards Jerusalem (an element that no Parisian synagogue respected). In fact, through another form of fidelity, the synagogue on the Rue Buffault reproduced the plan of the Bordeaux synagogue which had disappeared in a fire in 1873. Another imitation of this synagogue is found in Lausanne (1910, Charles Bonjour and Oscar Oulevey), again thanks to the patron Osiris. Thus an architectural solution can take on a significant value and inaugurate a tradition.

The Synagogues of North Africa

In North Africa, an autochthonous Judaism, integrated into the Moorish structures, had existed for centuries. The arrival of the Sephardim produced an interesting symbiosis of which the synagogues of northern Morocco are without doubt the best testimony. They also demonstrate, however, that the *megorashim* («expulsed») quickly became dominant[14], even in the older communities such as Fez (many of these had been decimated shortly beforehand, but not in the south as at Marrakech for example). Separate oratories and cemeteries were maintained for centuries. Playing a central role in the life of the *mellah*, the synagogue or the oratory sometimes belonged to the community, but in most cases to a rich or scholarly family, much to the detriment of the rabbis who regretted the dependency and the rivalry that resulted amongst the congregations. During the second half of the 18th century, however, the autochthonous custom of numerous private places of worship was revived and largely dominated religious life. The names of the synagogues attest to this evolution and show the major role played by the prominent families. Apart from the famous Danan synagogue in Fez, of which the proprietary family was autochthonous (although having also lived in Spain), many bear the names of families or masters of Sephardic origin. The forms themselves, however, are borrowed from the Moroccan context, such as the semicircular arches of the Suiri synagogue in Tangier and especially the stuccoes (stalactites, interlacings, and polylobed arcatures) which decorate the walls of the synagogues Sadoun in Fez, Rabbi Yehochua Berdugo in Meknès (1927), and Nahon in Tangier (1878). They are amongst the most sumptuous of those preserved. Classic motifs, nevertheless, were introduced under European influence as at the Nahon

212 TETUAN. - INTÉRIEUR DE LA SYNAGOGUE. L. L.

Tetuan, Morocco, *Interior view
of the synagogue*, old photograph,
Roger-Viollet.

Sanya (?), *Constantine synagogue*,
1841, oil on canvas. Musée d'art
et d'histoire du Judaïsme, Paris.
Donated by Georges Aboucaya.

synagogue in Tangier and for the Holy Ark of the Simon Attias synagogue in Essaouira (1882). Older structures are illustrated by the synagogues of the *mellah* of Fez: the Danan, which dates from the 17th century and was recently restored, and the Sabba (17th or 18th century). The former has three aligned central pillars while the latter has a central *bimah* cantoned by four pillars. Similar plans are also found in the Ashkenazic world. Historians of architecture, most of whom originated from Germany or Poland, have tended to consider this plan as typically Polish, and even speak of the "Lublin type". Admittedly, the African examples occur on a smaller scale, with a less developed stereotomy, and are often without décor, but their wide distribution in North Africa should be pointed out. It is significant that there were basic constructive methods and particularly appropriate solutions, whether they be in the Ashkenazic or in Sephardic and Oriental worlds. In Morocco, plans with two or three central pillars are encountered at Meknès-Rabbi Haïm, Marrakech-Rabbi Akan Kodech, Mogador-El Kahal, and Arazan. But even more characteristic are the plans with four pillars. Portugal has a 15th century example in Tomar and North Africa has an important but undated series (particularly among those that were studied by Jacob Pinkerfeld) in the south of Morocco (Tiznit, Assaka, Taroudant, Draa), as well as further north (Fez-Sabba synagogue, Tahala and Oujda) and even in Tunisia (Sousse and Kairouan). This question of type-plans is not without importance, for it is necessary to integrate the African synagogues into the overall vision, even if they remain poorly known on a historical level.

The Sephardim who chose to settle in Algeria mixed more easily with the autochthonous Jews in communal institutions. Only Oran (where the Sephardic immigration was later and was linked, in part, to the arrival of refugees from Tétouan during the Hispano-Moroccan war of 1859) saw the establishment of separate communities. As of 1830, France began to determine the fate of the Algerian Jews. It imposed its own model and sent rabbis trained in the *Séminaire israélite* (Israelite Seminary) to Algeria. Synagogue architecture also felt the effects of this policy.

In Tunisia, where the autochthonous element was very old and had known periods of great influence as in Kairouan around the year 1000, the Sephardic contribution was less important after 1492 than in Morocco or in Algeria. The Sephardim, transmigrating mainly from Italy, became established during the 17th century for commercial purposes. It was above all the Livournais (*Grana*) who settled and defined the social cleavages already observed in Morocco. As a minority, they did not mix

'86 ALGER - La Grande Synagogue - Place Randon

Algier, *The Great Synagogue,*
Place Randon (1865, architect
Viala du Sorbier). Here the choice
of a monumental approach highlights
the changed status of Algerian Judaism,
now organized in Consistories,
as in France. The resort to the Moorish
style points up the concern with
integration into the local context.

SYNAGOGUE DE TUNIS

FONDATION D.I. OSIRIS

Façade Principale

Tunis, *Project for the 'Osiris Foundation'*
synagogue, Victor Tondu, 1909.
The plans were presented at the 1910
Exhibition. The architect proposes
nothing less than a cathedral silhouette
for the Great Synagogue in Tunis,
but the project was ill received
by the community. The subsequent
competition was won by Victor Valensi,
son of a community leader and a student
at the Ecole des Beaux-Arts in Paris.
His highly original proposal combines
a central plan typical of the Beaux-Arts,
modernist forms and overtly
Jewish symbolism.

with the *Twansa* (Tunisians) and after 1710, separate institutions, with different chief rabbis, administered the destiny of the two communities. The Livournais, nevertheless, had to reside in the *Hara*, the Jewish quarter of Tunis, where they opened their own synagogue, *Choulhan ha-Gadol* ("the great table"). In a modern context, the role of the Livournais was primordial if only because of the fact that the books used by the Tunisian rabbis were printed in Livourno[15]. The modernization of the Jewish community of Tunis was favoured by the establishment of the French Protectorate in 1881. It is symbolized by a project launched in 1879 for a synagogue[16] which was to be constructed outside of the *Hara* (later demolished in the 1930s). An initial project, very French with its conception of a cathedral, was proposed in 1909 by Victor Tondu, an architect who worked for Osiris, the patron from Bordeaux. But, as a result of a competition opened in 1913, it was a young Jewish architect from Livourno, Victor Valensi, who received the commission. The construction of the building, however, was deferred until 1932-1937. This remarkable edifice associates tradition and modernity, the Orient and the Occident, a centralized Byzantine plan and Hebraic, even Zionist, symbolism. It is significant that the many Tunisian Jews who settled in Natanya in Israel plan to construct a replica of this synagogue for the *Centre mondial du Judaïsme tunisien* (World Centre of Tunisian Judaism). Less transposable than the Italian or Moroccan oratories, it has nevertheless become a symbol for them of an identity that they wish to preserve in Israel, even though their exile has ended.

Another important centre of Tunisian Jewish culture is on the island of Djerba, where a thousand-year-old community was established in a few villages near a place of pilgrimage, the Ghriba. This ancient synagogue sustains vivid legends concerning its origins: one recounts that the synagogue was founded by *cohanim* fleeing from Jerusalem after its destruction by Nebuchadrezzar, another relates that of a foreign girl, *el-ghriba*, whose body was found intact in the middle of the ruins of her hut after it had been struck by lightning. A synagogue erected at this site became the object of a pilgrimage which, obviously, owes much to the Muslim cult of "saints". That the origin of this edifice is very old is undeniable, but, as with all traditional synagogues in North Africa, it was regularly rebuilt and restored and therefore can not be dated. The last major works were undertaken in 1920. On an architectural level, the Ghriba is a good example of a North African synagogue: a whitewashed building in masonry with a prayer room preceded by an arcaded courtyard. The *bimah* is in the centre and the

Tunis, Synagogue in the Rue de Paris
(1932-37, architect Victor Valensi).

eastern wall is occupied by Holy Arks. The décor consists mainly of blue ceramics. Here, the courtyard was covered in order to enlarge the area of worship. So great was the notoriety of the Ghriba[17] that this type is found in many other Tunisian synagogues: as at the synagogue of Hara Kebira (one of the two Jewish quarters of Djerba), in Ben Gardanne, and in Médenine.

Other Oriental Diasporas

There are other oriental Diasporas, now termed as Sephardic, that are slowly dying out and their synagogues, with rare exceptions, are disappearing. The maximal extension of the Jews towards the East was China, where a famous community lived in K'ai-Feng. Around 1100, Jewish merchants, undoubtedly of Persian origin, who had followed the Silk Route eastwards, arrived in this town on the Yellow river and were welcomed by an emperor of the Song dynasty who held court there. A synagogue was founded in 1163. By extraordinary circumstances, the community managed to survive up until the 19th century, in spite of its distance and the destruction of its synagogue which was regularly rebuilt. An irreplaceable testimony is given by the Jesuit priests who, at the beginning of the 18th century, encountered these surprising Jews. Father Domange has left drawings of the synagogue and of the ritual (1722) which attest to a very strong assimilation, but nevertheless with an acute consciousness of a Jewish identity. This was still present when Europeans arrived at the beginning of the 20th century to study and photograph this unique community. The synagogue, however, had disappeared. In 1704, Father Gozani described the interior[18]: "There is in the middle of their synagogue a magnificent and very high pulpit, with a handsome embroidered cushion. This is the Moses' chair, on which on Saturdays and on other very solemn days, they place the Book of the Pentateuch and read from it. There is also a *Van-sui-pai*, or panel, where the name of the Emperor is written, but there are no statues or images. Their synagogue faces the West, and when they pray to God they look in that direction, and they adore Him under the names of *Tien*, of *Chamtien*, of *Cham-ti*…"

Remote descendants of those from Babylon, the extraordinary private synagogues of Uzbekistan with their stuccos and ceramics, so typical of Islamic culture, are also disappearing. The photographs by Neil Folberg[19] of the synagogues of Samarkand and of Bukhara bear witness to the last hours of these distinctive private synagogues: the houses of the Kalantarov, Tarov and Zevulanov families where the oratories sometimes date

only from the beginning of the 20th century. Through an extraordinary conjunction, these synagogues, in a certain manner, pertain to the Sephardic tradition. The Jews of Bukhara, in effect, had adopted the Spanish rite at the end of the 18th century. The Caucasus also had flourishing communities, particularly in Georgia. The Jewish Museum of New York preserves a 16th century ceramic wall from Persia, perhaps from Isfahan. Nevertheless, knowledge concerning the synagogues of these countries is very incomplete.

In Arab countries, such as Syria, Libya, and Egypt, synagogues have often disappeared. The 9th century synagogue in Aleppo, the originality of which consisted of its monumental *bimah* placed in an arcaded courtyard, was demolished in 1947. The Ben Ezra synagogue in Cairo is a basilican structure similar to the local Coptic churches. It is especially famous for its *geniza* in which, in 1896, manuscripts in their original versions, unknown *midrachim* and numerous rabbinical texts were found. Probably founded during the 9th century, reconstructed in 1039-41 after its destruction by order of Caliph al-Hakim around 1013, it was remodelled in 1892 and then again during the 1930s. The doors of the Holy Ark were bought by Solomon Schechter (the discoverer of the *geniza*) who gave them to the Jewish Theological Seminary in 1902. Consequently, a new oriental Ark more in harmony with the ancient décor, was then built in 1900. Despite of the Israelo-Arab wars, the building survived and was the object of a recent study and remarkable restoration[20] in 1992.

Jewish Communities of diverse origins have also lived in India since Antiquity and certain of them were Sephardized. The famous Jews of Cochin, who in fact first settled in Cranganore where they enjoyed large political independence, have left remarkable synagogues, including the Pardesi synagogue, constructed in 1568, and another which was later transported to the Museum of Israel. The Pardesi synagogue was partially destroyed by the Portuguese who wished, not so much to fight against the Jews, but to capture the pepper trade. In 1663, the Dutch occupied Cochin, and the synagogue was restored. The community henceforth maintained relations with the Jews of Amsterdam. During this time Sephardic Jews also settled in Cochin, and a few synagogues are found in the vicinity as at Ernakulam, Chennamangalam and Parur. The Jews of the Bombay region, who call themselves Bene-Israel and recount numerous legends about their very ancient arrival, possess more modest synagogues than those of Cochin and have become strongly Hinduized. The *Chaar ha-rahamim* synagogue was constructed in 1796 and corresponds to a

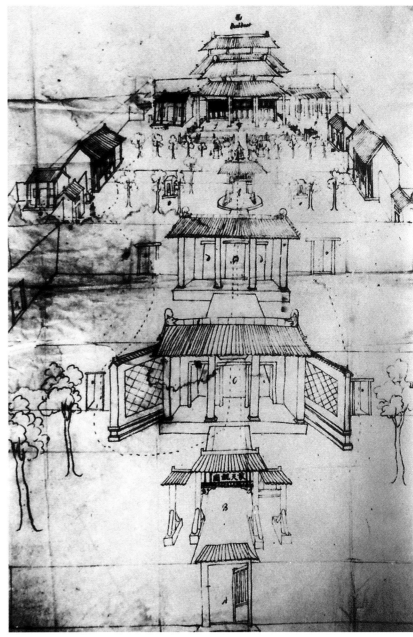

Kaifeng, China, *Synagogue.*
Drawings by Domange, 1722.
Jesuit Archives, Paris.

Cochin, India, *Pardesi synagogue*
(1568 and 17th century), exterior view.

Bukhara, Uzbekistan, *Synagogue.*

moment of revival. The others date from the 19th century. A third group of Indian Jews, originating from Iraq and the Middle East, settled in Bombay and in Calcutta as traders. As the Bagdadi (the Jews from Baghdad) did not want to mix with the Bene-Israel, the famous David Sassoon established a synagogue in Bombay in the 1830s. In Calcutta, the first synagogue, *Neve Chalom*, was established in 1831. Without having experienced the same difficulties as in the Arab countries, the Jews of India nevertheless began to migrate to Israel and the Western countries during the 1950s.

Aleppo, Syria, *The Great Synagogue*
(9th century), destroyed in 1947.
Old photograph, Museum of the
Diaspora, Tel Aviv.

Cochin, India, *Pardesi synagogue*,
interior view.

Cairo, Ben Ezra synagogue
(11th century and 1892),
detail of the Holy Ark.

Brooklyn, New York, *Kol Israel*
(1987, architect Robert Stern).

Influences

For the Sephardim, the process of maintaining a cultural identity passes more rarely through architectural influences than it does in the Ashkenazic world. It is significant that the Spanish Jews, who conserved Judaeo-Spanish (Ladino) as their language, did not transplant their Mudejar art. Even if they retained a certain form of nostalgia, at least those who left Spain directly, the marranos who settled in Holland clearly opted to adopt Dutch architecture. It is in the Ashkenazic synagogues of the 19th century that references to the Alhambra are found, with as an alibi the existence of the synagogues of Toledo. But it was, above all, in the imagination of the non-Jewish architects that this fascination for Spain germinated, which was seen as a Golden Age. The preoccupation of stressing the Sephardic origin of certain communities was also widespread in Ashkenazic circles as well. It is not rare then that orientalist motifs were used to emphasize it as in the Spanelska synagogue in Prague (1867-1868) or the Türkischer Tempel (1885-1887). The latter, constructed in Vienna by the architect Hugo von Wiedenfeld, has a chantourné portal and polylobed Moorish arches to recall the Ottoman origin of this community which was founded in 1736. This choice influenced the new synagogue of Sofia (1905-1910) where the Viennese architect Grünanger combined Neo-Byzantine, laden with a national dimension in the capital of the new kingdom of Bulgaria, and orientalist motifs. Even in Western Europe, this process also occurred. In Manchester, where there were already three Ashkenazic synagogues, the Sephardic synagogue, on Cheetham Hill Road, was designed by Edward Salomons (1874) so as to be recognized by its Romanesque and Oriental forms. The congregation, however, did not come directly from Spain but from Turkey, Egypt, Romania and Italy.

In the contemporary period, the United States (with a social system that favours identity groups and that has an obvious predilection for references is the ideal architectural context for demonstrating that the Sephardic congregations still claim their origins[21], all the more so in that their members have sometimes only recently arrived from Turkey, Morocco, the Middle East or even Israel. Consequently, significant motifs in the décor can be encountered. Built in 1963, the Spheroid Temple in Cedarhurst (Long Island) is a very modern structure with a large parabolic roof under which Bertram Bassuk installed a synagogue and a weekday oratory. The latter, although the community is essentially of Turkish and Greek origin, has an arcade imitating that of Santa Maria la Blanca. Moreover, the brick façade of the synagogue that Robert Stern (1987) built in Brooklyn for the *Kol Israel*, a Jewish congregation from the Middle East, might well refer to the exterior of the well-known synagogues of Toledo. Sometimes, it is the furnishings, the Holy Ark, the *bimah,* or the benches, that recall the traditional layout of the country of origin.

The Sephardic emigration, the transport of a few synagogues to Israel and the project of constructing a replica of the synagogue of Tunis in Natanya, reveals the second tragedy which, next to the Showa, characterized the history of the Jews in the 20th century: a new Sephardic and oriental Diaspora. Jews from Muslim countries had to seek refuge in Western countries, where they revitalized the declining and decimated communities, as well as in the recently founded State of Israel. Communities which had been established for over a thousand—even two thousand—years, in Egypt or Iraq had to set off again on a new exile, but this time to Zion.

Prague, *Synagogue Spanelska* (1867-68,
architect Vojtech Ignac Ullmann).
Prague's Altschul synagogue
had been used by Iberian Jewish refugees
after their expulsion; when it was
demolished and replaced by
a new synagogue on Dusni Street,
care was taken to recall
its origin via its name and the use
of the Moorish style.

The Ashkenazic Diaspora

Jacob Epstein, *The Spirit of the Ghetto*,
1902, illustrations for the book
by Hutchins Hapgood.

Left page:
New York, *Eldridge Street Synagogue*
(1886, architects Herter Brothers).
Detail of the doorway.

Tzostianetz, Ukraine, View of the *shtetl*,
photograph taken in 1888.
Musée d'art et d'histoire
du Judaïsme, Paris.

Issachar Ryback, *The old synagogue
in Vilnius,* Lithuania, lithograph in *Shtetl,*
published in 1923. Musée d'art
et d'histoire du Judaïsme, Paris.

From Ashkenaz to Yiddishland

In the Bible, Ashkenaz was the grandson of Japheth, son of Noah. His name came to indicate the Germanic world. Rashi of Troyes (1040-1105), the great Medieval scholar, when he mentions Germany—where he studied—used this very word. Ashkenazic culture was formed between the northeast of France and the Rhine Valley, but was then displaced under the effect of expulsions and incessant migrations, so much so that the contours of this Diaspora, as that of the Sephardim, remain vague. The Jews who settled in Central and Eastern Europe in the 16th century were of diverse origins even if the Jewish worlds were never compartmentalized. The displacements of the centres of gravity, nevertheless, were noticeable during the course of the second millennium. Western European Judaism—which had been flourishing in Spain, France and the Rhine Valley from the 11th to 15th centuries—was decimated by the Crusade. Countries such as France found themselves without Jews. A migration towards the East began. It was in Poland that the majority of European Jews sought refuge: a certain degree of autonomy was even granted to them by the Council of Four Lands, an organization that existed from the 16th to the 18th centuries, during the time of the radiance of Poland (from 1569 until the division). In the 18th cen-

tury, there were more than 150,000 Jews in Lithuania, 130,000 in Galicia, 75,000 in Poland. The impact of this migration was primordial for the constitution of contemporary Judaism since it gave birth to one of the most original Jewish cultures, the *yiddischkeit,* and led to the construction of thousands of synagogues. Communities defining themselves as Ashkenazic are found from Northern Italy, Alsace, and the Netherlands to Russia. But this Diaspora was to be decimated during the 20th century. If it did not disappear altogether, it is because in the 18th century a new wave of migrations, this time from east to west, had begun and knew a phenomenal magnitude around 1880-1900, Ashkenazic Judaism profoundly marked the New World, but also South Africa and Australia. At this time, there lived on the borders of the Russian, Austro-Hungarian and German empires about six million Jews of which two and a half million were to emigrate towards the West, and in particular to the United States, a country which had in 1937 more than four and a half million Jews, 95% of whom came from Eastern Europe.

The living conditions of the Jewish communities in Central and Eastern Europe were such that synagogues experienced on an architectural level a new development, even an originality that presupposes a certain autonomy. Two types, marked by the use of either masonry or of wood, emerged between the 16th and 19th centuries, depending on whether the communities were settled in a town and its outskirts, or in a village. The latter gave its name to a reality specific of small towns where the population could be mainly Jewish and engender a particular culture and sociability, the *shtetl*.

"The small town is located in the middle of a flat land that borders no mountain, no forest, no river. It gives onto the plain. It begins with small huts and ends with them. Houses take over from the huts. Then the streets begin. One goes from south to north, the other from east to west. The market is at the intersection. The station is at the end of the north-south road (…). The town has two churches, a synagogue and about forty small houses of prayer[1]…."

Besides this description borrowed from Joseph Roth[2], the *shtetl* is also well-known through the paintings of Chagall, as well as through sociological studies such as *Olam*[3] or *La Flamme du shabbath*[4]. All are tinged with nostalgia and of a surprising sublimation, as the *shtetl*, for having sustained an original form of Jewish life, was also often a miserable and frightening place. Zborowski and Herzog gave "the" synagogue a nearly abstract description, as a mere type, while totally ignoring the splendors or the original structures that had sometimes been used: "The large synagogue, the *shul* properly called, is of a more careful construction than the other places of worship in the shtetl, even if it lacks the magnificence that can be expected of a church. Its exterior aspect submits to the architectural style of the region. The interior is in no way remarkable. Long benches are placed facing east. Their backs serve as a support for the readers of the following row. In the centre, stands a platform surrounded by a balustrade, the *bimah*, with the table where the reading scrolls may be spread. The *bimah* also serves for the sermon, for important announcements concerning the community, for appeals for funds for the poor of the *shtetl* and for exposing individual grievances . The only decorative element is the Ark of the Torah, a sculpted wooden chest, placed to the east of the middle of the *mizrakh*. A curtain of velvet or satin, covered with embroideries, is hung in front of its sculpted doors."

On the architectural level, however, it should be noted that synagogues—especially wooden synagogues—present certain remarkable features which, with the initiation of ethnological investigations at the end of the 19th century in a context of the awakening of national identity and of the exaltation of the popular roots of Jewish art, were the object of numerous studies. Russian painters such as Issachar Ryback and El Lissitzky, who belonged to the most avant-garde movements (expressionism and constructivism) made records of the paintings of the synagogues of the valley of the Dnieper in 1916. They were marveled by the culture of these artists. In Poland, a group of scholars, architects and historians, including Szysko-Bohusz, Zygmunt Gloger, Mathias Bersohn, Majer Balaban, and Szymon Zajczyk, collected documents and published these buildings which have nearly all disappeared. The stone synagogues, on the other hand, built mostly during the 16th and 17th centuries fared better and a few remain. Characterized by their construction materials, two types emerged of which the usage was determined by the local environment: urban or rural.

Stone Synagogues

Towns usually had stone synagogues, which were concentrated in the imposed Jewish districts. The best known examples are in Prague and Kazimierz. In Prague where, along with the famous Gothic Altneuschul synagogue (14th century), the community, organized into a veritable Jewish town with its own town hall, had the Haute, the Maisel, and the Klaus synagogues amongst others. Kazimierz, a district adjoining Cracow, teemed with synagogues and oratories. The oldest, undoubtedly inspired by that of Prague, as a result of the presence of numerous Jewish emigrants from Prague, is called the 'old', 'Stara'. It presents a plan that can serve as a type-model for masonry synagogues of this era. Sometimes, it is a courtyard, the *schulhof*, that regroups all the community buildings including, obviously, the synagogue and the prayer space. Such is the case at Vilnius, one of the capitals of Judaism described as the 'Jerusalem of Lithuania'.

In these masonry synagogues, dating from the end of the Middle Ages or from the Renaissance, three types of plans are identifiable that correspond to major solutions for the organization of the interior space. The most basic is a single square or rectangular nave, which is applicable only to modest structures such as the synagogues of Bamberg (13th century, now destroyed), Rouffach in Alsace (1288-93), and Sopron, in Hungary, which, in use during the Middle Ages were abandoned around the 1520s. This type of plan is obviously not an Ashkenazic specificity and is also found in southern countries, as for example in the 13th century synagogue recently discovered in the handsome complex of Montpellier, best known for its *mikve*.

The second type of plan stems from the model of the chapter house, that is to say, a layout with two naves covered by groined vaults resting on two or three aligned central pillars. The oldest model is found in the Romanesque synagogue of Worms (1174-75, with the addition in 1212-13 of a '*weiberschul*', a room for women). Its twin pillars are decorated with capitals of which the abacus bears inscriptions recalling the construction of Solomon's Temple (I Kings, 7, 40-41). This plan, also found in Christian buildings, caused an organizational difficulty for the Jews. The *bimah,* in order to be in the center, was caught between two pillars. The same problem was apparent in the other important model, Gothic this time, that is the Altneuschul of Prague and which is found in the Stara of Cracow in the 15th century. The 13th century synagogue of Ratisbonne had three central pillars. Destroyed in 1519, it is known through an engraving of Altdorfer. Rachel Wischnitzer[5] notes that this plan can be adapted to Renaissance aesthetics and survived in Poland up until the 18th century. She mentions the synagogues of Chelm and of Vilnius (*Kloyz*).

The third model was very subtle and its solution of spatial organization actually took into account the function of the synagogue. A central bimah was surrounded by four pillars that supported barrel vaults of which the springers rested on the pilasters of the lateral walls. This system, which covers a large square volume, was widely diffused in all of Central and Eastern Europe between the 16th and 19th centuries. According to Rachel Wischnitzer, it first appeared in 1567 at the Maharsal synagogue[6] in Lublin. Alfred Grotte reports[7] that of Lvov (outside of the town) in 1632. It is certainly the most widespread type and is found in Poland at Przemysl (1592-95), Pinsk (1640), Tykocin (1642), in Lithuania at Slonim (1642) and Nowogrodek (1648), in Galicia at Rzeszów (two synagogues) and Lancut where the pillars still have their decoration, at Maciejow in Volhynia (1763 or 1781). This plan is often of the famous fortified synagogues, that is, synagogues having high defensive walls, towers, imposing attics, such as Lutzk in Volhynia—of which the construction was authorized in 1626 by specifying its defensive role— Pinsk or Zolkiew (1692). It is remarkable that the plan with four centralized pillars became diffused in Bohemia, at Mikulov (formerly Nikolsburg,1550, remodeled in 1723) and in Hungary (Mad and Bonyhad in Hungary, 1795) where it still was found in 1822 at Apostag. Symbol of the Ashkenazic emigration, it is employed in a surprising manner in Israel, at Safad (Ari synagogue), in connection with a characteristic sculptured wooden Holy Ark.

Worms, Germany, *Synagogue* (1174-75), old interior view.

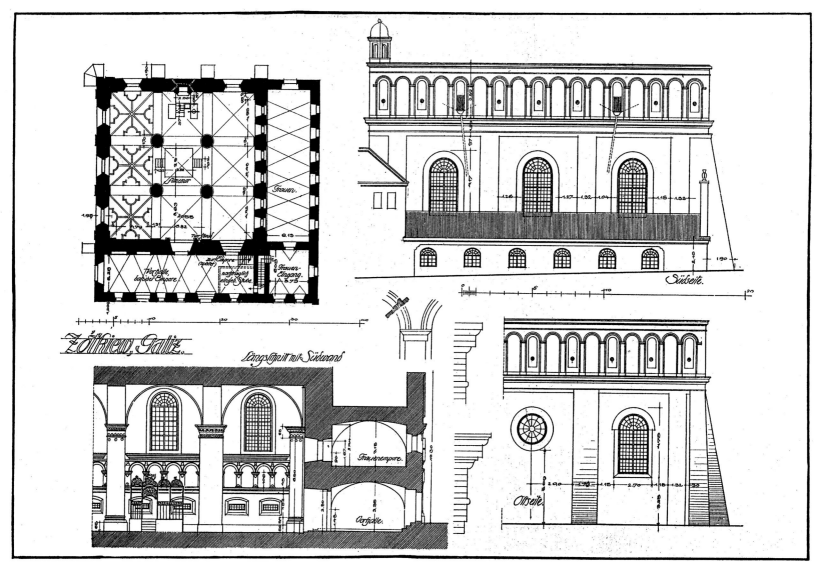

Zolkiew, Ukraine, *Synagogue* (1692),
Elevations by Alfred Grotte, 1911-14.

Lancut, Poland, *Synagogue*
(17th century), interior view.
The paintings date from the 18th century.

Luboml, Ukraine, *Synagogue*,
drawing by Georges Loukomski.

However, the purely Ashkenazic dimension of these types of plans, emphasized by historians of German or Polish origin who were unaware of the African and Oriental synagogues, should be qualified. Type-plans with central pillars aligned or arranged in a square, as has been seen, are also common in North Africa.

In the Central European countries, at the beginning of the 16th century, the Renaissance developed under Italian influence and favoured the use of synagogues with square or rectangular plans without pillars encumbering the space. On this principle were constructed the synagogue of Remo in Cracow, that of Taz in Lvov, designed by an Italian architect, Paolo Romano, in 1582, and that of Szydlów (1699). This influence is also seen in the Classicizing décor—Holy Arks decorated with orders and triangular pediments—or Baroque—*bimot* with wreathed columns. The Stara synagogue in Cracow was remodeled around 1570 by Matteo Gucci. The large arcaded attics that surmount it, date from this time (where certain authors have attempted to see a firebreak). Very widespread, it is found at Lutzk, Tarnopol, Zolkiew, Brody, Luboml…

This type of synagogue in masonry, with Renaissance or Baroque décor, persisted until the 18th century and spread throughout all of Central Europe. Today, Poland has, even after numerous destructions during the last war, a group that reveals the wealth of synagogue architecture of these centuries: Pinczów (beginning of the 17th century), Zamosc (1620), Lesko (beginning of the 18th century), Przysucha (end of the 18th century). Although built according to Italianizing constructive methods, multi-levered Holy Arks are also found, as at Orla (beginning of the 17th century) or Siemiatycze (1795). At Jassy, on the frontier of Romania and Moldavia, the oldest surviving Romanian synagogue was constructed in 1670-1671 on the initiative of Rabbi Nathan Hanover. It has, in a domed structure, a Holy Ark of a type widespread from Poland to Moldavia, two-storied and a coronation of lions and an eagle, a composition that is found in the synagogues of Romanian Moldavia from the beginning of the 19th century, Botosani (1834) or Falticeni (1838).

In Bohemia, and in Prague in particular, Renaissance and Baroque developed with splendor, even in the ghetto.

Bohemia also has an interesting series of small masonry synagogues which are similar to those of Poland, in Chodová Planá (Kuttelplan, 1759), Lázné Kynzvart (Königswart, 1764), Nové Sedliste (Neuzedlisch, 1786). The synagogues of eastern Germany, characterized however by richer external forms and larger bays, can also be attached to this type: for example in Souabe, Ichenhausen

(1781), Altenstadt-Illereichen (1802), Krumbach (1819). This model remained in use for a few decades in synagogues of small towns. Nevertheless, an important stage of this confrontation between the Polish models and their adaptations in western monarchies, is marked by the synagogue of Berlin, designed by Michael Kemmeter in 1712-14 Heidereuter street. It was correctly recognized as a symbol of the Prussian tolerance of the times, as King Frederick William I was present at its inauguration. Its large bays are inspired by Dutch models but its Holy Ark however, is typical of Central Europe and would not be amiss in a Polish wooden synagogue. This synagogue opened a new era.

Wooden Synagogues

The most surprising type of synagogues that ever developed in the Ashkenazic world was that made of wood[8]. Wooden constructions were a local tradition and many possible origins of these synagogues have been suggested, including Polish churches and lordly manor houses. Certain forms even imitate stone architecture. Yet this would be a simplistic vision, for the use that the Jews made of it,—for at this time carpenters, joiners and decorators could be Jewish—is profoundly original. Numerous studies undertaken since the 19th century concerning these structures (which are no longer preserved) with a few minor exceptions, except through photographs, show that the diffusion of the wooden synagogues originated in Podilia then spread to the rest at the Ukraine, to Poland, Lithuania, Belarus and even beyond, to the West as far as Bavaria and to the East to Russia and Siberia. It also appears that with time the spaces became more complex. Initially, these synagogues were but simple rectangular prayer rooms covered by a wood and shingle roof. This type is found as of the end of the 17th century in Podilia and Galicia (Janów Trembowelsky, Smotrich, Michalpol). Later, annexes were added comprising towers, galleries and several stories. The most famous rise to great heights through an interplay of superimposed roofs that has sometimes led historians to evoke pagodas. It is in the interior that these buildings differ by their harmonious systems of roofing. The layout with four central pillars between which was placed the *bimah*, can be found here, but, whereas they supported only a rather low ceiling at Nowogród and Sidra (district of Bialystok), they reach extraordinary heights and combined different levels of galleries and vaults: for example at Olkienniki and Valkininkai (Lithuania), Sniadowo (northeast of Poland), Suchowola and Wolpa (Belarus); balustrades, pendant keys and wooden friezes decorate these roofs. The region corresponding to southern Lithuania, western Belarus and the district of Bialystok has the most complex synagogues. The *bimot* and the Holy Arks there are also remarkable masterpieces.

Another form of evolution consisted in multiplying the annexes and the volumes around the large central hall, first as additions, according to a principle already seen in masonry synagogues. In the Atneuschul of Prague, certain galleries could have been added later in order to accommodate the women, the stairs that give access to them were often placed on the exterior (Pilica, Warka). Additional rooms were added on three sides, sometimes there were vestibules surmounted by external galleries as at Yarishev, Kamenka Bugskaya and Jablonów in the Ukraine. The constructions of the 18th and 19th centuries often have peristyles, as in Poland at Lutomiersk (designed by Gillel Benjamin of Lask, 1763-65), or Kórnik (1767), Mogielnica (19th century). Specialists also distinguish a type of edifice with two lateral towers on the façade. It was widespread in the same region as the buildings noted above, in Belarus (Grodno, Narovlya, Wolpa, Suchowola) and around Bialystok (Zabludów), but also in Poland (Nasielsk). Attesting to their late character, the Polish synagogues of Gombin (18th century) and Sierpc (19th century) have towers crowned with bulbs similar to those of the stone synagogues.

As of the 17th century, synagogues—which then offered but a simple interior vessel covered by barrel-vaulting—received a painted decoration of which only a few examples remain. The most famous ensembles are even signed: the paintings of Mogilov (1710, Belarus) by Haïm Segal, and those of Chodorów (1714, Ukraine) by Israel Lisnicki. The former were recorded in 1916 by El Lissitzky and Ryback who were sent on an ethnographic mission. Lissitzky left a text that is all the more important in that all theses paintings have now disappeared. He relates[9] how, in his search for the popular sources of Jewish art, he went to Mogilov and was amazed. A rich bestiary, both local and exotic, realistic and symbolic, with the zodiac occurring next to the major symbols of Judaism, *menorah* and the Tables of the Law, landscapes including scenes of Jerusalem or divine evocations, Biblical inscriptions, are all intermingled in a system of foliated scrolls and of medallions covering the ensemble, such are the characteristics of these paintings that reveal an art both popular and scholarly, where intermingle scenes from daily life, religious references, copies of motifs from books or engravings. Most of these elements are found in the two famous synagogues of Mogilov and

of Chodorów. The zodiac is also found in Targowica, the fantastic animals in Grójec (end of 18th century-beginning of 19th century), and the landscapes in Warka (1811-17). The favorite colors of these artists appear to be red, ochre and brown. The motifs are drawn in black. In Jablonów, the decoration is based on texts arranged as on the manuscripts. The artists moved from one town to another and their traces are found in several synagogues. Thus, Yehuda Leib decorated the synagogues of Przedbórz, Szydlow, Pinczow and Dzialoszyce; Haim Segal, those of Mogilov, Kopys and Dolginov. The tradition of these travelling painters was attested in the 18th century by the works of an artist from Brody who was active in Bavaria, Eliezer Sussman. Panels painted by him between 1733 and 1740 are preserved in Bechhofen, Horb, Unterlimburg and Kirchheim. More modestly, but belonging to the same decorative movement, the paintings rediscovered in 1990 in an Alsacian village, Traenheim[10], attest to how artists and models circulated. This oratory (1723), hidden in a loft, has inscriptions and a few motifs which are also found in Prague.

Just as remarkable as the paintings, the sculptures draw from the same popular sources and from books. This art is applied especially to the Holy Arks where the interlacings of the foliated scrolls were infinite, even on the colonnettes. A complete bestiary weaves its way through the interlacings. The layout of the décor of these Holy Arks has been correctly compared to the *tass* (pectoral) adorning the Torah. The same Baroque taste for arabesques, foliated scrolls and profiled motifs is manifest. A coronation, composed of the two lions of Juda and often an eagle, completes the composition. Certain were proceeded by a stairway framed by an introductory arch, a layout that obviously suggests the *mirhab*: Zelva in Belarus (18th century). The most handsome and elevated, dating from the 18th century, are found in Janów Sokólski, Sidra (district of Bialystok), Grodno, Wolpa (Belarus), Olkienniki, Valkininkai and Saukenai (Lithuania), always in the same zone. There again, the artists became renowned, such as the sculptor of the Holy Ark in Uzlany (end of the 18th century), Bayer Ben Israel. The other current type of Holy Ark was then widespread throughout Europe: a chest framed by Classic orders.

These sculpted multi-leveled Holy Arks are not particular to wooden synagogues. They also decorate stone synagogues as is seen at Plonsk (Poland), Zolkiew (Ukraine), Orla and Siemiatycze (district of Bialystok).

A further element allowed the cabinetmakers to use their imagination, the *bimot*: they are often of original conception, some are surmounted by voluted baldachins,

Wolpa, Lithuania, *Synagogue*

(18th century).

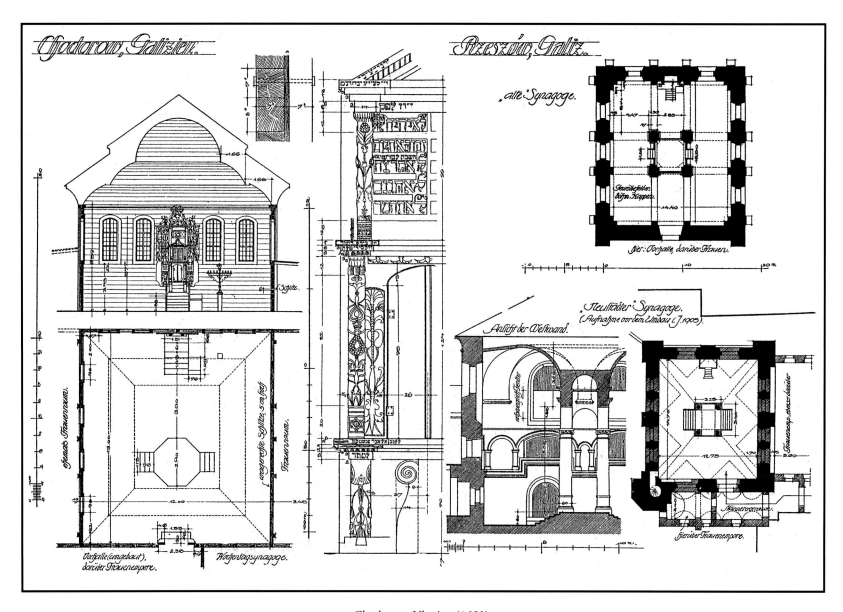

Chodorow, Ukraine (1652)
and Rzeszów, Poland (17th century),
Synagogues, elevations by Alfred Grotte
(1911-14).

Jewish carpenters, postcard.
Collection Gérard Silvain.

Suchowola, Biélorussie,
View of the Holy Ark (18th century).

Synagogues paintings

El Lissitzky first came into contact with the synagogue paintings of the Dniestr valley as a member of ethnographic expeditions searching for the popular roots of Jewish art. The text that follows recounts the feeling of awe he experienced in the synagogue at Mogilov. The drawings made by his group led to the re-creation of the paintings in the synagogue at Chodoróv, now on display in the Museum of the Diaspora in Tel Aviv.

This was truly something special, like those surprises in store for me when I first visited a Roman basilica, a Gothic chapel, Baroque churches in Germany, France and Italy; or like a crib, bedecked with a fine veil embroidered with flies and butterflies, in which the infant suddenly awakes in surroundings sprayed with sunlight; such, perhaps, is how it looks inside the synagogue.

The walls—made of oak logs—rang when struck. Above them, the ceiling looks like a tent of wooden planks. All the rivets are exposed—no deception, no fantasy. The work is by a cartwright from top to bottom, but the entire shape was organized by the painter with just a few basic colors, so saturated that an entire vast world lives here, blossoms forth and fills up this none-too-large cube.

The interior of the synagogue is embellished, from the backboards of the benches to the entire length of the walls and up to the very top of the 'tent'. The synagogue, quadrangular on the ground floor, rises to an octagonal tent ceiling, exactly like a skullcap. Three-cornered boards mask the passage from four corners to eight corners. The ceiling panels are organized with a striking sense of composition. This is something entirely contrary to the laws of primitivism; rather, this is the fruit of a great culture. Where does it come from? The master of this work, Segal, says in his inscriptions, with the most noble inspiration: '...for a long time I have been travelling about the living world...'

(...)

The focus of the whole building is the ceiling. On the western side, above the entrance, are gigantic lions with peacocks below. The lions hold two shields with inscriptions, the lower one being the master's memorial to himself. On the three-cornered northern and southern planks of the tent, like a frieze, are placed side by side carnivores and their prey, underwater and on the earth. In the sky above, stars burst forth in flowers. In the water, a fish is being seized by a bird. On the earth, a fox carries a bird in his mouth. A bear climbs a tree looking for honey. Birds carry snakes in their beaks. The fleeing and running figures are really people. Through their quadruped or feathered guises, they stare with human eyes. This is a remarkable characteristic of Jewish folk art. Isn't that a rabbinical face on the lion's head in the zodiac painting in the Mohilev synagogue?

Above the frieze, a voluminous, fully developed line ornament bursts forth, capturing the entire ceiling within its ring. Further up, there is a row of stamps of a somewhat oriental design—perhaps from a Mauritanian assemblage—composed of a complicated entwining of rope, a motif which brings to mind Leonardo da Vinci's drawing for the stamp of his academy. And I remember I saw in Milan, in the Castello, a room whose ceiling is also attributed to Leonardo, which made use of comparable rope ornamentation.

Above them, arranged in a row, stand the twelve zodiac signs in roundels all linked to one another. The zodiac pictures are very unusual, and some of the drawings are remarkably laconic and vigorous. The archer in the zodiac, for example, is depicted with one hand holding the bow, the other hand drawing on the string. The latter is the 'strong' hand, the 'punishing hand' of the Bible. In the very center of the 'skullcap' surmounting everything is a three-headed eagle, a fusion of the Polish and Russian eagles.

On the eastern side, above the Holy Ark, there are lions again, but here they hold the Tablets of the Law, and dangling from them a large, sacrificial fowl seizes the Holy Ark. On the sides are two panoramas. On the left, or the north wall, is an imaginary representation of Worms, a seemingly cursed town in the clutches of a dragon, and with a Tree of Life. On the other side, the northwestern side, are Jerusalem and the Tree of Knowledge.

On the three-cornered board that covers the passage from the wall to the ceiling on the northwestern side, is the legendary wild ox. On the northeastern side is a wild goat; on the third plank, in the southeast, is the Leviathan; and on the fourth plank, to the southwest, is an elephant with a saddle on his back.

On the walls, there are boards with inscriptions, holy objects from King Solomon's Temple, additional ornaments, and all kinds of living creatures.

The painter's wealth of forms seems inexhaustible. One can see how it all poured out as from a horn of plenty, how the hand of the virtuoso

neither tires nor resists the rapid flow of thoughts. On the back of the Holy Ark, I discovered the first brush sketch, the 'outline' of the entire picture, which serves as the basis for further elaboration in color. This particular 'outline' was cast on the wall by a master of remarkable discipline whose brush is completely subordinated to his will.

The coloration of the painting is amber-pearl with brick-red rays. It is not to be grasped; it lives and moves because of its own specific luster. On all four walls there are windows on the uppermost reaches. The sunlight flows around and around at each hour on each wall with a different light effect, especially on the sloping parts of the ceiling. This provides the

whole work with a continuous play of light. The painting, with all its transparency, is very thick; from the heaviest pigments—ochre, lead-white, cinnabar and green, to the lightest color tones—blue and violet.

Where does this stream come from? How did this cloud burst and precipitate such a salubrious downpour?'

El Lissitzky, article published in Yiddish in Rimon/Milgroim, no. 3, Berlin, 1923. Translated as 'Memoirs Concerning the Mohilew Synagogue' in Ruth Apter (ed.), *Tradition and Revolution. The Jewish Renaissance in Russian Avant-Garde Art 1912-1928*, The Israel Museum, Jerusalem, 1987, pp. 233-34.

Chodorów, Ukraine,
Ceiling of the synagogue, painted by
Israel Lisnicki in 1714.
Re-creation at the Museum
of the Diaspora, Tel Aviv.

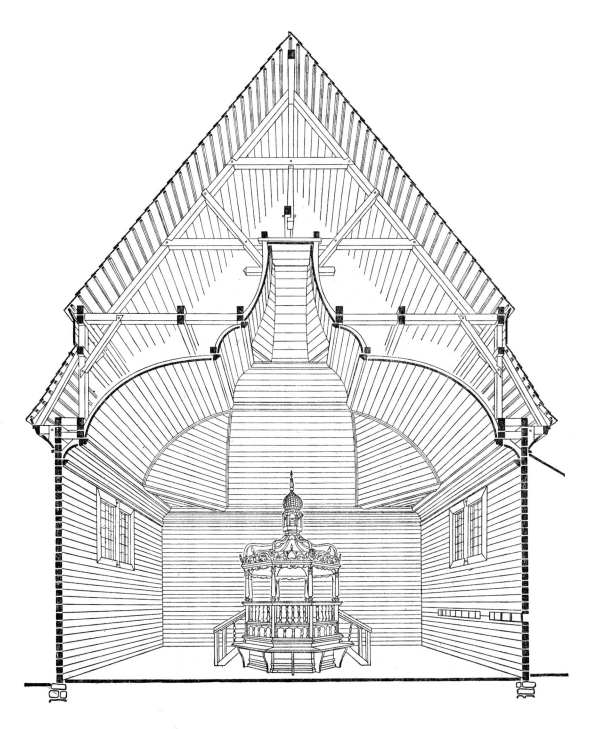

Gvozdec, Ukraine, *Interior
of the synagogue* (XVIIth century),
old photography.

Gwozdziec, Ukraine,
Section of the synagogue,
after M. and K. Piechotka.

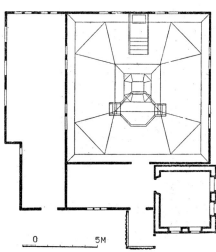

0   5M

Vilnius, Lithuania, *Choral Synagogue*
(1890, architect Grozenberg).
The only surviving example of its kind.
Present-day view of the interior.

Venice, *Scuola Grande Tedesca*
(1528-29), interior view.

others forming veritable aediculea with an octagonal covering and twin stairways (Grodno, Sniadowo, Sopockinie, Zabludów). The baldachin can assume enormous proportions such as at Jubarkas (1870, Lithuania) or be covered with exuberant Baroque motifs (Olkienniki, Przedbórz). Sometimes an aesthetic link is established through a play of curves between the baldachins of the *bimot* and the arches of the buttressed vaults (Gwozdziec).

In the 19th century, wooden synagogues are found throughout Russia, from Parnu on the Baltic Sea to Kouba, (near Baku) on the Caspian Sea, in Krasnoïarsk, Kansk and Irkutsk in Siberia, but these structures, often imposing, were constructed at the end of the 19th century according to very different principles than the Polish or Ukrainian synagogues: they seek the monumentality and the classic ornaments of the masonry buildings that they imitate.

From Exile to Exile

In search of new lands where they could live more freely, the Ashkenazic Jews permanently experienced waves of migrations, mostly from east to west. But also towards the south. Northern Italy was thus profoundly marked by an Ashkenazic presence. Yet sometimes communities were established during Medieval migrations, for traces of Ashkenazic ritual before the expulsion from France have been found in the communities of Asti, Fossano and Moncalvo. The layout of Ashkenazic synagogues in Italy clearly differs from oratories of the Italian or of the Spanish rites. In the Piedmont and the Duchy of Montferrat, the octagonal *bimot* are in the center and often have a traditional baldachin: there are magnificent examples dating from the 18th century at Carmagnola, Casale Monferrato, Chieri (now in Turin), Cherasco, refined examples of Baroque with wreathed colonnettes, decorated panels, volutes… and more modest ones at Moncalvo and Saluzzo. The Ashkenazic layout is also encountered in Venetia. It is significant that the Scuola Grande Tedesca of Venice, established in 1628, and the synagogue of Conegliano Veneto originally had central *bimot*, but these were later moved into niches according to the Italian model during the 19th century.

Such Baroque *bimot* are found in Germany, demonstrating connections that were established between the Ashkenazic communities. In Ansbach, the synagogue designed by the architect Leopold Retti in 1744-45 presents a Holy Ark and an octagonal *bimah* with wreathed colonnettes, as is the case in Leutershausen (1755) nearby.

Jan Ten Compe (1713-1761),
View of Amsterdam showing
the Ashkenazy synagogues and,
on the left, the Portuguese synagogue.
Oil on canvas. Private collection.

London, *The Great Synagogue*
(1790, architect James Spiller),
lithograph by T. Rowlandson, c. 1819.

Toronto, *Holy Blossom Synagogue* (1897),
old view of this Orthodox synagogue,
now being used as a church.

Such furnishings even reached Israel where Ashkenazic synagogues were established in Jerusalem and in Safad according to the same principles. During his voyage in 1931, Chagall was not disorientated when he painted the interior of the synagogue of Safad, because it contains a typical Holy Ark. On the other hand, during other emigrations, these forms tended to disappear, as in Holland.

When the Netherlands became a tolerant refuge for the Jews fleeing Spain, Ashkenazic Jews also obtained the authorization to reside there and to construct synagogues. They concentrated on the same plot of land and formed a representative ensemble. The first, designed in 1670-71 by Daniël Stalpaert, the municipal architect, was the Grote Synagoge. It followed the type-plan of Dutch temples, with its portal surrounded by orders and its large picture windows. The Holy Ark is a common type with a pediment. Other religious spaces were added over the next hundred years: Obbene Sjoel (1685-86), Nieuwe Sjoel (1750-52), Drit Sjoel (1777-78). Today, this ensemble is occupied by the Jewish Museum of Amsterdam, but some elements of the ritual furniture are preserved. In London, the Ashkenazim also had benefited from the right to rehabilitation negotiated by the Sephardim. Their first synagogue was at St Helen's, Bishopsgate (1690), where they soon became the majority and, in 1722, built the Great Synagogue on Duke's Place ; in 1726, the Hambro' (demolished in 1892) ; and a third synagogue on Leadenhall Street at Bricklayers' Hall. In plan, they differ little from the design of Sephardic synagogues. The most remarkable construction is the neo-Classic Great Synagogue rebuilt by James Spiller in 1790. As famous as its architect, it quickly became a major curiosity in London. Unfortunately, it was bombed in 1941. The Ashkenazic immigrants then swarmed to England and constructed numerous synagogues during the 19th century: a quarter of London, the East End, took the aspects of a ghetto, even a *shtetl*, so much so that the poor Jews from Eastern Europe poured in and brought the number of Jews in England to 300,000 in 1914.

The Ashkenazic Diaspora also developed in the British colonies: Canada, Australia, and South Africa. Canada already had a small Jewish community as of the 18th century, but it was in the 20th century that tens of thousands of Jews from Central and Eastern Europe arrived and formed Yiddish speaking congregations. In 1914, there were more than a hundred synagogues. They were concentrated in Toronto and Montreal, but Jews also participated in the conquest of the West. These pioneers sometimes built wooden synagogues. These structures had nothing to do with those of Lithuania or of Galicia, but

Port Elizabeth, South Africa,
Old Synagogue.

Havana, Cuba, the *Patronato Synagogue*
(1956).

were based on the famous Mid-West 'balloon-frame' framework and differed little from a simple farmhouse. Nevertheless, a few[11] synagogues, such as Winnipeg (1893) or Melville in Saskatchewan (1932), offered a few traits borrowed from Eastern Europe.

In large cities, Toronto and Montreal, the construction of synagogues intensified as of the 1890s, following the aesthetics close to those of the models of the United States. In Montreal, Shaar Hashomayim, erected in 1886, mixed Gothic and Oriental turrets, then in 1922 a neo-Byzantine synagogue (Melvin Miller). Holy Blossom, an Orthodox congregation, constructed in Toronto an enormous synagogue with two towers and a cupola (1897). In Ottawa, Adath Jeshurun dates from 1904 (J.W.H. Watts). But it was the 1930s that witnessed the greatest development of congregations, with a predilection for immense brick constructions with semicircular portals decorated with sculptures, for example in Toronto, Anshei Kiev (1926, B. Schwartz), Anshei Minsk (1930, Kaplan and Sprachman), Holy Blossom (1938, Chapman and Oxley). This type also persisted after the Second World War, in Montreal with Shaare Zion (1947, Eliasoph and Greenspoon).

In Australia, the 1840's saw the creation of communities in Sydney, Melbourne, Adélaide, Hobart. At the end of the 19th century, communities were established in distant centres such as Perth and Brisbane. Until the Second World War, they were nearly exclusively Ashkenazic immigrants who founded these communities. It was not until 1962 that a Sephardic synagogue opened in Melbourne. The architecture of Australian synagogues followed the fashions of European historicism and did not conserve the memory of *Yiddishland*. The neo-Egyptian style, on the other hand, initially knew a surprising success, then Orientalism became more affirmed (Perth, 1897): in Sydney (1878), the Gothic dominates, but the arches are polylobed.

Emigrants were also attracted to towns that were born by the discovery of gold or diamonds. In New Zealand, apart from Auckland which had a community as of 1840 and a synagogue (1885), Dunedin constructed a neo-Greek synagogue in 1882 (Louis Boldini) during the gold rush. In South Africa, a community was organized in Kimberley, the diamond town, as early as 1871 and the first monumental synagogue dates from 1876. Pretoria constructed an Orientalizing synagogue in 1898.

In Latin America as well, the Ashkenazim played a key role, even if the Sephardim obviously were settled there first. In Cuba, the oldest synagogue of Havana, the Chevet Achim Temple, dates from 1914, but it is only an ensemble of rooms on several stories. In Mexico City, the

Buenos Aires, *Synagogue of the Congregación Israelita de la República Argentina.*

Modern Ghettos

During the 20th century, the notion of the ghetto para-doxically saw a revival. For it ended by referring to, in Western countries where the rights of the Jews were indis-putable, the districts where the Jews who emigrated from Eastern Europe settled in priority. The sociologist Louis Wirth, using the example of Chicago, gave a very famous analysis of this notion[12]; concerning the modern ghetto, he states: "it illustrates, in a picturesque fashion the means by which a cultural group expressed its ancient heritage even when it was transplanted to different habi-tats, the permanent filtering and renewal of its members and forces, thanks to which the community maintained its integrity and its continuity." And he pointed out that as, in the former ghetto, the center of life remained the synagogue, the place of socialization, of the control and of settling internal affairs, even familial.

In the 1930s, Egon Erwin Kisch, a well-known reporter from Prague, visited all the modern ghettoes and gave them a literary form in his *Histoires des sept ghettos*. He speaks of Amsterdam, Prague and the *Pletzl* in the Marais district of Paris… Whitechapel had already served as the setting for the novels and short stories of Israel Zangwill[13]. This tradition is found in Budapest in the *Histoires du Huitième District* of Giorgio and Nicola Pressburger of which a chapter describes the "immense and mysterious temple" installed in a former warehouse[14], "where, the men that I saw everyday quarreled, dealing and exhausted at work, appeared to be metamorphosed into meditative specters, striped in black prayer scarves."

New York, with the Lower East Side, Harlem, and Brooklyn, is the very image of the modern ghetto. That is to say, no longer an imposed and enclosed quarter as in the 16th century, but a district that attracted waves of new emigrants. As of 1902, Hutchins Hapgood had clearly described this "spirit of the ghetto"[15] that Jacob Epstein, himself born in the Lower East Side, illustrated. A map of Poland could be drawn, or the residential zones of the Russians according to the implantation of the var-ious Jewish congregations in New York. Not satisfied by innumerable *shtiblkh*, they sometimes constructed mon-umental synagogues to which they gave the names of their congregations[16], often Anshe ('people') followed by the name of the town of origin. In the Lower East Side, the oldest, Norfolk Street, is that of Anshe Chesed (1849, Alexandre Saeltzer), with a Gothic appearance, gathering together Germans and Poles. On Willett Street, the Bialystoker synagogue (1905), a former church was equipped with a wooden Holy Ark and even an eagle. On Attorney Street was built the Erste

Justo Sierra synagogue is a very colorful Gothic variation. But it is obviously Argentina which is the most marked by Jewish immigration from Eastern Europe. The present community is still 85% Ashkenazic. Between 1840 and 1945, Argentina received 225,000 Jews, some of whom participated in the famous agricultural experiments of the Jewish Colonization Association of Baron Maurice de Hirsch. These Jewish farmers and gauchos obviously established synagogues in their villages, along with schools and other institutions. Attempts of the same type were also undertaken in Brazil, in the state of Rio Grande do Sul. However, it was the 1920s that saw the organiza-tion of more structured communities and thus the con-struction of more ambitious synagogues. The Jews flocked to the larger town: in Brazil, Rio de Janeiro and Sao Paulo had synagogues (Isr. Roder) as of 1929, and in Argentina, Buenos Aires, Rosario and Córdoba. The architectural forms, adopted as of the 19th century, tend to persist and the European or North American solutions persisted: thus the synagogue of the Congregación Israelita de la República Argentina, in Buenos Aires, on Libertad street, oscillated between neo–Romanesque which was common in Western Europe and Palaeochris-tian allusions similar to those of Emanu-El in New York.

Above and opposite page:

Jacob Epstein, *The Spirit of the Ghetto*,

1902, three illustrations for the book

by Hutchins Hapgood.

Galitzianer Chevra Synagogue (1884), on Forsyth Street the Mishkan Israel Suwalki Synagogue (1901), on Pike Street the synagogue of the Sons of Israel Kalwarie (1903), and on Rivington Street that of the Erste Warshawer Congregation. Many used the term 'Anshe': on Madison Street Etz Chaim Anshe Wolozin (1890's), on 7th Street that of Anshe Ungarin, then Anshe Abatien, Anshe Baranove, and Anshe Mezeritch. Moreover, these congregations moved, fused and returned to their synagogues. The geography of the ghetto was thus shifting. Finally, as a result of the social evolution of its members, the congregations left the ghetto. Today, more than a few synagogues now shelter an Hispanic church or even a Buddhist temple, as is the case of Agudas Anshei Mamod Ubeis Vead Lachachomim (1940).

In Brooklyn, a large number of synagogues were built, but undoubtedly even more *yeshivot* and Hasidic oratories. *L'Elu* by Chaim Potok (1967) familiarized his public with the *shtiblkh* of Williamsburg. The one that the father of the narrator frequented was a former grocery shop and that of the rabbi an apartment. In Brooklyn, certain congregations, nevertheless, had more space than in Manhattan and built monumental synagogues such as Beth El (1920, Shampan and Shampan).

It is impossible to choose an architectural predominance in this eclectic ensemble of synagogues, that had more Classic and Medieval elements than Orientalist ones. Some motifs, such as the woodwork and towers with bulbs, evoke Eastern Europe.

The East End in London also witnessed an influx of Jews from the east, 150,000 between 1881 and 1914, who established oratories and a few synagogues. The following chapters will evoke the East London Synagogue of Stepney Green, and the Anglicization undertaken with the support of the United Synagogue as early as 1876. German immigrants created Machzikei Hadath and transformed a former church in Brick Lane into a synagogue, Spitalfields Great (1898). During this time several *hevrot* with evoking names such as Vilnius, Wlodowa, Dzikover or Plotzner were established and a Federation of Minor Synagogues (1887) was even established. An orthodox group, Adath, organized the North London Beth Hamidrash (1886), but their places of worship essentially remained oratories. Israel Zangwill, the Zionist novelist, described several.

Similarly in Paris, after the 1860s, the immigrants settled in the Marais district, then in the arrondissements (districts) of eastern Paris and even beyond in a few suburban towns. There as well, oratories proliferated and it was necessary to await Guimard's building on the Rue Pavée (1914) in order that the Russo-Polish communities

New York, Lower East Side,
*The faithful leaving a synagogue
on Rivington Street in 1911.*
Current state of two synagogues
on East Sixth Street. A veritable ghetto,
this migrant neighborhood contained
dozens of synagogues whose names
re-create the geography of Central
and Eastern Europe. Population shifts
mean that most of the synagogues
are now abandoned or have been
transformed into Hispanic churches.

Venice, *Scuola Grande Tedesca* (1528).

were equipped with a real synagogue[17]. The *Consistoire* of Paris, on the other hand, in order to control the immigrant groups as much as it could, sometimes even offered them synagogues. In the 18th arrondissement, in 1907 a synagogue in a former theatre on the Rue Sainte-Isaure was established by its architect Lucien Hesse. It was reconstructed according to a modernist solution by Germain Debré in 1939. This same architect, with Lucien Hesse, had already constructed for the Jewish immigrants of the 20th arrondissement the "Temple of Belleville" (1930) with financing by Baron Edmond de Rothschild.

The synagogues of these 'ghettos' played a primordial role in the consciousness of a Jewish identity. The different Jewish establishments obviously established procedures of nationalization and, as in France, even used civil laws in order to try to close private oratories. But, submerged by the influx of immigrants, they had to come to terms and let them remain. There was a confrontation between monumental synagogues in which the recent generation felt uncomfortable and the *sthiblkh*, sometimes a bit repugnant, but warm and authentically Jewish.

But, for others, the 'ghetto' was not far off. The nostalgia of childhood and a few identity crises led them back to the synagogue. The hero of *A Walker in the City* (1951) by Alfred Kazin, undertook a return to the sources which was triggered off by the prayer of the survivors of Bergen-Belsen. He returned to Brownsville and, at the subway exit, went to the synagogue. This ascent into time, as Rachel Ertel[18] suggests, is a return to the *shtetl*. In the famous pre-Zionist novel, *Daniel Deronda* (1876), George Eliot marked the return to Judaism of the Anglicized protagonist by his visit of synagogues, initially in Frankfurt, in the *schule* and not the large synagogue, and then in the East End of London. In quest of his identity, he roamed through the small shops and in the small synagogues of Whitechapel. The same approach takes the young Israelite of *L'Enfant prophète* (1926) of Edmond Fleg to the 'ghetto' of Paris: he fled "the large empty synagogue" animated only for marriages and on Friday evenings in the Marais, undoubtedly the synagogue on the Rue Pavée[19]:

"I returned to the Ghetto, but alone. It was Friday evening. It was raining, it was dark in the strange street."

Who will take me to this house, too tall, with its windows too narrow and too brightly lit?

It is their synagogue, I believe. Yes, their synagogue. (...)

They enter to pray, I did not dare enter. They are together; they feel that they are together. And I, I stay alone, under the rain like a poor man. Why?"

In the construction or reconstruction of identity, the orthodox synagogue, above all the precarious oratory became the alternative to a model of assimilated Judaism, even monumentalized. As the Galicean Jews for the Viennese or the 'Polaks' for the English or French Jews, these synagogues were 'the ghetto' and revived exilic consciousness that monumental synagogues, to be seen in a following chapter, sought to smother.

Influences

Already in the 1900s, more than one American congregation had, strangely enough, recognized that in the 'zone of residence' that the members had fled, was not a lost paradise as expressed through the architecture, as reflected through the memory of the *shtetl*. Oscar Israelowitz even qualifies this tendency of the "*shtetl* revival.[20] Obviously, wooden frame architecture has American sources, but the examples that are given are convincing considering the bulbed towers, the sculpted Holy Arks. All were established around 1900: the Temple of Israel (1900) and the First Independent Hebrew Congregation (1905) in Queens, Ohav Sholom, on Thatford Avenue, and Temple Beth El, on 12th Avenue, both built in Brooklyn in 1906, Montefiore Congregation (1906, Daumer and Co.) in the Bronx. This movement is found in other cities and states, but sometimes obviously combined with the means of construction used by the pioneers. Thus, can the synagogues of Port Gibson in Mississippi (1891, Barlett and Budeineger) and of Corsicana, Texas (1900) be compared with the models of the *shtetl*? Their onion domes support this interpretation, but the shingles that covered the tower in Port Gibson could also pertain to the typically American *shingle style*. In Canada, numerous traces of Eastern Europe are also found in the synagogues constructed around 1900, not only in Toronto and Montreal, the two Jewish centres of the country, but also in Ottawa. Thus in 1904, the former Adath Jeshurun combined bulbed-onions and brick (John W.H. Watts) and has a wooden Holy Ark with two turrets.

On the other hand, after the Second World War and the Showa, the *shtetl revival* saw a new phase: the communities chose, independently of their origin to honor the memory of *Yiddishland*, for the architecture, as often the literature, can be anamneses. For Ashkenazic Jews settled in the West, the sentiment of exile was already very strong: "to leave Poland, is to be exiled from exile itself" wrote Henri Raczymov in *Contes d'exil et d'oubli*[21]. With the Showa, the wrench was doubled. The "lost world" of

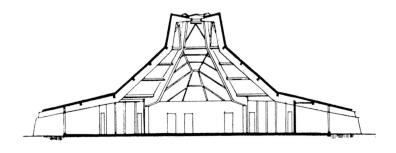

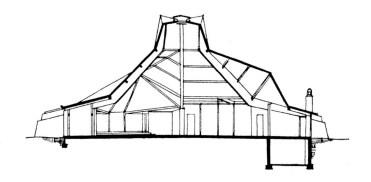

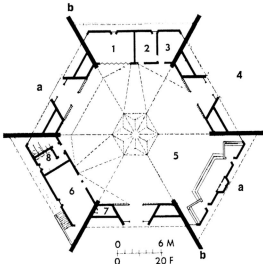

South Norwalk, Connecticut,
Temple Shalom (1964, architects
Oppenheimer, Brady and Lehrecke).
Illustration taken from
Progressive Architecture.

Brooklyn, New York, *Ohav Shalom
Synagogue*, 1906. Old photograph.
The United States and Canada became
focal points of migration by Eastern
European Jews, who brought with them
their architectural customs,
wooden buildings, taste for façades
with towers and onion domes, and so on.
A kind of '*shtetl* revival' took place
which marked an entire generation,
from the large synagogues in Manhattan
and Brooklyn to the little oratories
of the pioneers.

AN ARCHITECTURE OF EXILE

the *shtetl* is subliminated: to the largely imaginary recon-situtions such as *Olam* there corresponds architectural influences, both as a reply to the tentative of extermina-tion and to a reaffirmation of identity. This tendency once again represented in the present *Yiddishland* that is the United States, a form of memorial.

Oppenheimer, the architect who constructed the Shalom Temple of South Norwalk in Connecticut (1964), clearly states[22]: "I wish to make this building tan-gible proof that Polish synagogues have not been com-pletely destroyed, but that their spirit in some way con-tinues. The form of the synagogue roof recalls the tent form that made up the earliest synagogues and restates their continuity". With a centered hexagonal plan (based on a six-pointed star), this synagogue presents, in effect, a high shingle roof surmounted by a sort of six-pointed lantern. In the interior, the beams and planks are exposed. Wooden roofs and ceilings are also used for Beth Jacob in the suburbs of St. Paul, Minnesota (Jeremy Mayberg), in Raleigh, North Carolina (1978, Kehrt Shatken Sharon). In the latter, the value of the past is also reinforced by the reuse of a wooden Holy Ark from 1867 (from Detroit) around which is conceived the worship space. In Lakewood, New Jersey, the Sons of Israel con-gregation constructed a synagogue (1963, Davis, Brody and Wisniewski) recalling Poland by its roofing. The Gates of the Grove Synagogue (1989, Norman Jaffe), in East Hampton, New York has more ambitious allusions: for the profile of such a roof here is not only a reminder of Polish synagogues, but also a Cabalistic motif, the reproduction of the letter *yod*, of which the numeric value (10) also determines the symbolism of the windows and the prayer alcoves. Light, which the *Zohar* praised, is equally very meticulously used in this synagogue where it penetrates through the interstices between the roofs and plays on the clarity of the Alaskan cedar that covers the interior. The exterior is covered with shingles, and the ensemble is built in the natural setting of a site where trees have been respected. There, an American aspiration already illustrated by Frank Lloyd Wright is seen. Louis I. Kahn, one of the greatest American archi-tects of the 20th century, who could not complete his best projects for synagogues, nevertheless left a plan for a small wood frame synagogue in Chappaqua, New York (1966-1972). This approach is not surprising for an architect born on an island in Estonia, Saaremaa, and who had this personal vision of assembly spaces, delivered in one of his poetic expressions[23]: "this is what space means to be: a place to meet under a tree".

It appears that it is the wooden synagogues, all now destroyed, but not only by the Nazis—that have struck the imagination of architects by their originality, revivify-ing a form of historicism which was still to bloom with the post-modern tendencies of present American architecture.

East Hampton, New York,
Gates of the Grove Synagogue (1989,
architect Norman Jaffe).

III

AN ARCHITECTURE OF IDENTITY

Exile, fundamental to Jewish identity, is inscribed in synagogue architecture. It gives it a variety of character, and imposes a plasticity yet not without expressive capacities, for Jewish identity is also built through history, through the confrontation with the societies who had shaped the status of Judaism, whether it be that of exclusion or that of assimilation. With the transition from the ghetto to citizenship, the Emancipation and its corollaries, nationalization and assimilation, the Jews were confronted with a new phase of their history and of their identity. Henceforth, the Jewish condition was not thought of only in terms of religion and of exile, but also in terms of history. The historicist process, which shocked European societies at the end of the 18th century by committing them to the road of nationalities and of nationalistic excess, also profoundly affected the Jewish condition. Along with the concepts of language, of race, and of territory, architecture became a major force, as the "writing of the people[1]" and as the spearhead of nationalism and identity: for each nation a style that exalts its origins and its own particularities, and for each religion a style that is appropriate to its history and its spirituality. What will the Jews be in the face of these unitary constructions, for whom the dispersal had bestowed a mixture of languages and fragments of discontinuous history, had also prevented the development of a specific art and thus synagogues had drawn from all styles?

With this mixture of styles, a new dimension of the synagogue appeared: an identity that was expressed for and by others. By opening onto the street, the synagogue suddenly had to convey Jewishness, not towards the congregation for whom this message is totally unnecessary, but towards the exterior, for the other citizens, who for the most part were ignorant of the realities of Judaism and thought of it as conforming to their own model. The departure from the ghetto, as the *mellah* and the *hara*, thus found its expression in architecture, monumentality and an anchoring in national history. These constructions of identity, however, followed the "progress" of the anthropological sciences and architects soon felt obliged to convey Jewishness by resorting to an architecture that drew it legitimacy either in the memory of the Temple of Jerusalem which archaeologists took pleasure in reinventing, or in an Orientalism which was borrowed from Muslim cultures. Architects, more often non-Jewish, thus contributed towards making Semites out of the Jews by imposing on them synagogues which looked like mosques or Alhambras. A very powerful imaginary developed, relayed even by a Jewish nationalism which developed during the second half of the 19th century, Zionism. Even the architects, often Jewish, refused it and endeavoured, on the contrary, to convey the integration of the Jews through the use of national styles such as neo-Romanesque and even neo-Gothic.

The 19th century was that which saw the greatest number of synagogues built in Europe. It was thus the century of the recognition finally acquired by Judaism, at the price of its denominalisation however. But it was also the century that, with the new status of the Jews, there developed a modern form of antijudaism: anti-Semitism. All these aspirations, all these imaginairies, all the friction of admission into modernity and standardization are reflected in this architecture.

From the Ghetto
to Emancipation

Map of the Street of the Jews, Frankfurt,
engraving by Matthäus Merian (1628).
The ghetto is the narrow curved street
closed off at each end.

Left page:
Krakow-Kazimierz, *Stara Synagogue.*
Originally medieval, the building
was subjected to a Renaissance
renovation by architect Matteo Gucci
in 1557.

Preceding page:
Vienna, *Seitensstettengasse Synagogue*
(1826, architect Josef Kornhäusel).
This synagogue had no street frontage.

Frankfurt a/M

Joseph II. 1765.1790.

Leopold II. 1790.1792.

Die neue Synagoge

der israelit. Gemeinde

eingeweiht am 23. März 1860.

Segregation, desired by all, logically followed from the nature of Jewish, Christian, and Muslim religions and societies, since each one of these faiths contains an indisputable truth. This basic schema, constant beyond the local and historic circumstances, governed social relations from Antiquity until the 18th century which saw the emergence of rationalistic values and of a relativism which, by introducing the notion of tolerance (although still ambiguous), allowed a redefinition, not so much of identity but of social status. The Middle Ages developed a mode of excluding Jews that tended to harden in the following period and persisted, in most countries, until the 18th century. The exit from the ghetto or the *Judengasse* was slow but proved to be a major change. Since the destruction of the Temple, it was the real rupture: the sentiment of *galout* was called into question. Jews could from now on—as citizens—loosen their ties with their community structure, from the *kehila*, a framework from which it had been very nearly impossible previously—barring conversion—to have left. Implementation of exclusion through physical enclosure - in particular quarters or streets—had not, however, prevented the construction of synagogues which in certain places reveal a prosperity and a degree of culture then rarely attained. The Renaissance and the Baroque blossomed in the ghetto, and became forms of integration and stages in the process of acceptance that led to the Emancipation.

Previously an outsider, the Jew was now submitted to non-Jewish jurisdiction, in the name of the famous principle of *Dina de-malkhouta dina* (the law of the state is the law). Yet he also remained Jewish just the same for a greater part of his daily activities and, above all, for intra-community relations, following an equilibrium that the ghetto had managed to preserve throughout its history. As a citizen, the extension of non-Jewish jurisdiction to all domains entailed the denominalization of his identity and even allowed him, if the case arose, to entirely elude from the rest of Jewish jurisdiction, now confined to the sphere of religion. During Antiquity and in the Middle Ages, a messianic hope had upheld the communities. The Messiah would one day overthrow the ephemeral kingdoms of nations and restore the sovereignty of Israel. This basic principle of *galout,* dimmed by the Emancipation and the messianic hopes, was transferred to the Napoleonic

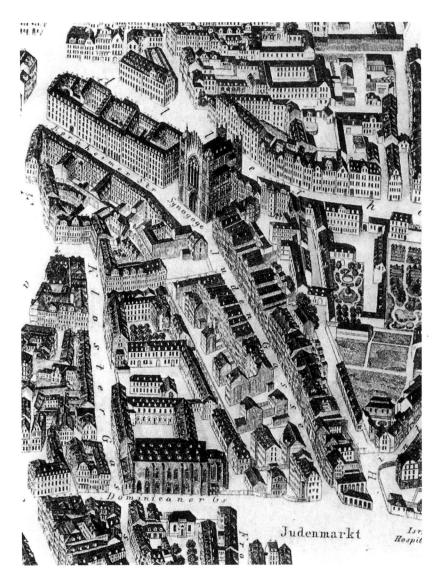

Map of Frankfurt c. 1860.
The ghetto no longer exists,
but the street is exactly the same and
the new synagogue has just been added.

Inauguration of the Frankfurt synagogue,
23 March 1860, lithograph.
Frankfurt, Jüdisches Museum.

Code and to more or less utopic political systems. Patriotism seized the emancipated Jews and drove them either to reject or to spiritualize the concept of the return of the exiled to Zion.

Preceding the Emancipation, experiences such as Marranism, already evoked in the Sephardic world, as well as modern humanism and rationalism—which tend to reduce religion to nature—prepared a new conception of Judaism. Models were elaborated—from Rabbi Yehouda Loew to Spinoza and Moses Mendelsohn, already capable of envisioning the process of the separation of Church and State—that prepared the conditions for a mutation of Jewish identity. Yet these doctrines developed in a context of the weakening of community structures[1], linked to socio–economic difficulties, to disputes challenging rabbinical authority, and to an increasing temptation to become integrated into Christian societies which had become more tolerant under the influence of the Enlightenment.

The *Haskalah* (Jewish Enlightenment) based itself on this recognition of the human quality common to men of different religions and on an education freed from the hegemony of the Talmud. At the same time as Lessing, Herder undertook a redefinition of man and culture that he historicized: rationalism and humanist universalism, which underlie the emancipating vision, were quickly swept aside by Romanticism. The way was then open to the process of nationalization, a crucial factor in order to grasp the aesthetic choices of the architects of the 19th century.

The Hidden Splendors of the Ghetto

During the Middle Ages—as symbolized by the blindfolded Defeated Synagogue on the doors of cathedrals or the legal status of *dhimmi* in Muslim societies—Judaism, having lost its status of election, was humiliated by restrictive measures, particularly concerning the places of worship. Not only were synagogues frequently destroyed or transformed into churches or mosques, following upsurges of religious zealousness in the dominant society, but even when tolerated, they were subjected to rigorous supervision. In Muslim, as well as in Christian countries, the old synagogues were accepted but the construction of new ones was forbidden. Their height was limited in Cairo[2] just as it was in Rome: they could not be taller than the smallest mosque or church. It is thought that many synagogues have floors sunken below the street level in order to have a higher and more imposing interior space. Even in 1743, Bishop d'Inguimbert of

Carpentras demanded that the reconstruction project of the synagogue, located upstairs in a crowded *carrière*, be lowered in height so as not to exceed that of the cathedral of the Saint-Siffrein.

However, it must be understood that this segregation process was legitimized by both communities. During the Middle Ages, the rabbis reinforced the Jewish abhorrence of the idolatry cult of the Christians. The Hasid[3] states that the sand and lime which remains after the construction of a church can not be used to build a synagogue. Admittedly, this rigorist trend was undoubtedly in the minority, but the period undeniably saw the reinforcement of *houkkat ha-goï*. The end of the Middle Ages and the Renaissance witnessed the establishment of the ghetto. It was but one of the traditional forms of segregation (and of integration), a form sometimes even appreciated by the Jews themselves since it provided them with their own space as well as with protection. Jews had, in fact, always grouped together in certain streets or quarters for convenience as well as for security. The city elders had sometimes even forced them to do so, creating a *Judengasse* or even a *Judenstadt* in the Germanic countries, a *Juderia* in Spain, or a *Mellah* in Morocco. This segregation, however, was not always strict and Christians still lived in these areas. The ghetto, on the other hand, surrounded by walls with gates watched by guards, reinforced this separation. For this reason, the ghetto could have contributed to the reinforcement of Jewish identity by the part of autonomy that it implied. In Prague, there was even a *Judenstadt* which was administered by a municipal council that sat in a town hall, complete with banners and symbols (including the *Magen David*).

The word 'ghetto', now a generic term, is of Italian origin. It was in Venice in 1516 that Italian and German Jews were moved to a specific quarter, the *Ghetto nuovo* (new foundry). In the Papal States, where segregation was longstanding, the ghetto was instituted in 1555 by a papal bull of Paul IV *Cum nimis absurdum*. The ghetto of Rome did not definitively disappear[4] until the unification of Italy in 1870. In other places, the establishment of ghettoes consisted of closing off a street already allocated to the Jews. In Avignon, a papal possession, a ghetto was established in 1458. In Carpentras, a *carrière* (the local term for a ghetto) was requested by the town in 1460 and its enclosure was obtained in 1486.

The *Judengasse* of Frankfurt, decreed in 1462, was maintained up until the 19th century. It is famous for its configuration and for having been the birth place of Mayer Amschel Rothschild. As evidence of the diffusion of the term, this quarter was already referred to by the word ghetto[5] as from the middle of the 17th century. The

Jacob ben Asher, *At Prayer in the synagogue*, a miniature from the *Arba'a Turim* ('The Four Orders'), Mantua, 1435. Vatican, Apostolic Library.

ghetto and its synagogue burned in 1711, fire being one of the principal scourges of these crowded quarters with their overpopulated and overly high buildings. The synagogue was reconstructed with sobriety. The exterior presents no distinctive character and the interior is groin-vaulted in a rather archaic mode of construction. The contrast with the Heidereutergasse (1712-14, Michael Kemmeter) synagogue, built at the same time by the Jews of Berlin, is significant. The culture of the ghetto influenced this building, but it should be noted that the attachment to these places remained very strong. The end of the ghetto did not always mean, however, the abandonment of the Jewish quarters. The new synagogue, of neo–Gothic inspiration, inaugurated on the 23rd March 1860, was still located on the *Judengasse*, whereas the right to reside in the rest of the town had been acquired in 1824.

It is interesting to note that the ghetto, having become the symbol of exclusion, and the other modes of settling Jewish communities in towns, represent an important phase in the evolution of Jewish consciousness. The walls did not prevent intellectual exchanges and even a rather brilliant cultural life.

Venice, *Exterior view of the Scuola Grande Spagnola.* In the ghetto the synagogues inside apartment blocks were often characterized by successions of curved windows indicating the interior worship areas. Buildings in the ghetto were taller than elsewhere in the city: here the *Scuola Grande Spagnola,* which included a gallery, occupies the entire top floor of the building, its corner situation also allowing for lighting via the windows on each side of the Ark.

Ferrara, Italy, *Scuola Spagnola,* Via Mazzini (17th century).

The Italian Ghettos

Between the 16th and 18th centuries, Italy systematically organized its ghettos. The only exception was in Livorno where the Duke of Tuscany authorized the establishment of Jewish merchants in order to develop the port. For this reason, it was almost always oratories located upstairs that were built, and all the extravagance of the Baroque was concentrated in the interior. These layouts are obviously inspired by the *scuola* of the Christian brotherhoods. Moreover, each rite (Italian, German, Spanish, Levantine…) planned to install its own oratory, and these rivalries were often translated by ostentatious decoration. But also by traditions such as an extravagantly decorated central *bimah*, usually octagonal and with a baldachin, placed under a lantern in a *scuola tedesca* whereas the Italian plan consisted of a bipolar layout with the *bimah* being affixed to the western wall facing the Holy Ark. The bays of these oratories were often arched and five in number in order to evoke the Pentateuch. Although located on the upper levels, certain of them had galleries for women: crowded and closed by canopies, these galleries, sometimes circular, appear to be inspired by the theatres of the times. This was not, obviously, surprising as the architects and the artisans working for churches or patriarchs were summoned to the ghettos. A tradition even suggests that Baldassare Longhena, the author of the Santa Maria della Salute, remodeled the *Scuola Grande Spagnola* of Venice around 1640-1660. The decorative taste was the same on each side of the wall, and if the wreathed columns—so frequent in Baroque designs—are considered to be derived from the Temple of Solomon, it was certainly under the influence of the altar canopy of Saint Peter's in Rome, designed by Bernini, that they became common.

Venice, attracting Jews from all horizons, created three ghettos: the *nuovo* (1516), the *vecchio*, granted to the Levantines in 1541, and the le *nuovissimo* (1633). The oratories multiplied. In 1528, the Scuola Grande Tedesca (remodeled in 1732-33), the Scuola Canton (1531), also Ashkenazic, the Scuola Levantina (between 1538 and 1561), the Scuola Italiana (1571), the Scuola Grande Spagnola (before 1584 and remodeled around 1640), the Scuola Luzzatto, and the Scuola Meschullamin. The most remarkable element of these oratories is the Holy Ark: decorated with orders and with pediment, it is gilded. Particularly lavish, that of the Scuola Grande Spagnola, with its double fronton, has been compared to the altar of the Vendramin chapel in San Pietro del Castello de Longhena. It was imitated in the ghetto at the Scuola Levantina. The *bimot* were also covered by baldachins copied from Bernini. Venetia had other communities

possessing richly decorated oratories, Conegliano in which the ghetto dates to 1635 and the synagogue from 1701-19, and Vittorio Veneto which has a synagogue related to that of Conegliano. Padua offers the Tempio Grande of German rite (1525), the Spanish synagogue (1617) on the fifth story of a building, and a synagogue of the Italian rite (1548).

The Piedmont also had numerous communities established in ghettos. These were initially installed in Turin in 1679, then in all the other towns[6] as of 1723. As for the synagogues, sometimes older, they all followed the German rite and had a central *bimah*, most often octagonal and surmounted by a baldachin. Their decoration is surprisingly rich in contrast to the external walls. A profusion of sculpted motifs, gilded stuccos, balustrades, and wreathed columns, and lamps characterize the synagogues of Casale Monferrato (1595 and enlarged in the 18th century), Cuneo, Mondovì, and Asti. The same richness is encountered in the ghettos of the Papal States, in Ancona where the *scuole* of the 16th century of Italian and Levantine rites are found, and in Pesaro, a town bestowed with Italian and Spanish oratories. In Rome, where the ghetto was established in 1555 near the Tiber, very restrictive measures obliged Jews to concentrate their oratories in a single building. Three followed the Italian rite (the Scuole del Tempio, Nuova, and Siciliana), and two followed the Spanish rite (the Scuole Catalana and Castigliana). Their decoration was equally more restrained than elsewhere, as if the proximity of the Pope prevented the deployment of the splendors of Venice or of northern Italy. The building itself disappeared during urban renewal in 1893, but the furniture of the Castigliana, for example, was reused in the actual Tempio Spagnolo.

Ferrara, an important Jewish centre had had, under the dukes of Este, printing houses and a large number of synagogues. Its annexation by the Pope in 1598 provoked its decline. Only three synagogues were authorized, one for each rite, and in 1626 the ghetto was decreed. It is fascinating to see that the nuances of identity related to these rites were still perceptible in the 20th century. The novelist Giorgio Bassani has described[7] his awareness of being an 'Italian' Jew: his family had a bench "at the Italian synagogue, up there on the second floor, instead of having it on the first, at the German synagogue, so different with its severe congregation, almost Lutheran, with their bourgeois soft felt hats". He also felt different from the congregation "a little odd" at the Levantine synagogue, "located on the third floor of an old house on the Via Vittoria", which, in opposition to the Italian rite adopted "quasi-Catholic popular and theatrical forms",

Cavaillon, France, *Present-day view of the synagogue* (1772). Here tradition sets the officiant in the gallery.

Carpentras, France, *Present-day view of the wall of the Holy Ark*, with an 'Elias chair' in the niche. The chair is part of a regional tradition which has it that the prophet Elias, taken up to heaven in a chariot of fire, often returns to oversee certain ceremonies. A wineglass is set out for him during the Passover *seder*, a place is reserved for him at circumcisions and a miniature chair is installed in the synagogue: a handsome example, perched on a cloud, is to be found in Cavaillon.

the religion "remained essentially a cult to be practiced by a few in semi-clandestine oratories where it was advisable to go at night and sleek by small groups through the darkest and most disreputable streets of the ghetto".

A large number of other Italian towns had a ghetto and oratories in their midst, Verona, Mantua, Reggio Emilia, Modena, Bologna, Florence, Siena, etc., but also towns under Italian occupation such as Dubrovnik where a synagogue, established in the 15th century and remodeled in 1652, still survives.

Avignon and the Comtat-Venaissin[8], papal possessions, were enclaved in France. If the Comtadin rite was original, the synagogues of the *carrières* were absolutely Italian in design. During the Middle Ages, communities had existed in several townships such as Valréas, Pernes (where a ghetto was even established in 1504), but after 1624, only the *carrières* of Avignon, Carpentras, Cavaillon

and L'Isle-sur-Sorgue were tolerated. Prosperity brought the reconstruction of four synagogues during the 18th century of which two still survive: one in Carpentras (1743-1776) and the other in Cavaillon (1771-74; contractors Antoine and Pierre Armelin, sculptor Jean-Joseph Charmot, and the iron craftsman François Isoard). The synagogue of Avignon (1766-67) was destroyed by a fire in 1845. All of them attest to an Italian influence. They are located upstairs, have bipolar plans associated with a surelevation of the lectern of the officiant on a platform, (as at the Scuola Spagnola of Pesaro or the Italiana of Ancona) and Holy Arks decorated with festoons, volutes and other rococo motifs.

Prague, exterior view of the *Altneuschul*
(14th century). The Jewish town hall
with its famous bell-tower is also visible.

The Judenstädte of Central Europe

From the 15th to the 18th century, the Ashkenazic Diaspora found refuge in Poland and prospered. There were not ghettos in the strict sense, but rather imposed quarters. The most significant was undoubtedly in Cracow where the Jews had first lived in the town, but were later expulsed after a fire in 1494. They then settled in Kazimierz, a village which was afterwards integrated into the city. This Jewish town had a market, baths, printing houses and synagogues. It had an autonomous administration which acquired a large religious and cultural influence. As of the middle of the 16th century, the Renaissance was seen through the construction of several synagogues. As previously mentioned, the plan of the Old Synagogue had two naves with central pillars, and a vaulting that dates from the first synagogue still built in the Medieval spirit. After a fire in 1557, it was remodeled by the Italian architect Matteo Gucci who gave it Renaissance decoration. At the same time, Israel Isserles rebuilt a private oratory, the Remo synagogue (named for his son, Moses Isserles) in the aesthetic fashion of the time as is perceptible in the Holy Ark. The Haute Synagogue also dates from the 1550s. Several private synagogues were established during the 17th century: the Kuppah synagogue (1600 ?), the Popper synagogue (1620) named after a rich merchant, and the Isaac synagogue (1638) named after Isaac Jakubovicz, the financier of King Wladyslaw IV: barrel vaulted, they present an essentially Renaissance *modanatura*. The following decades, troubled by wars, were less favorable for buildings and the community declined.

In Bohemia and Moravia, provinces under Austrian control, the Jewish streets were often composed of ghettos, even in small towns such as Mikulov (Nikolsburg, beginning of the 15th century), Boskovice (15th century) and Trebíc, undoubtedly established in the 16th century and one of the best preserved in Europe. In Bratislava, the ghetto, imposed after several expulsions during the 16th century, was outside of the town. In Budapest, while the traces of several Gothic synagogues were found in Buda, the Jews were expelled around 1710 and had to settle on the fief of a more tolerant lord in Obuda. It thus appears that the Jewish settlement was not limited to a particular quarter but depended on the decisions of the local lords. For a long time, Pest was forbidden to the Jews.

The most famous ghetto is the Jewish town of Prague which even had its own cemetery. From the 13th century, the Jews of Prague benefited from royal protection as direct subjects of the king and could even constitute an autonomous administration. This, however, did not prevent exactions, or even massacres as in 1389, a year that saw the destruction of the Altschul. The Jewish town, situated on the right bank of the Vltava, near the central market, grew over the centuries, even if it was enclosed by walls. Its full development was attained at the time when Rudolph II of Habsburg, mounted on the throne of Bohemia in 1576 and restored its privileges to the Jewish city. The Renaissance then developed in the ghetto, particularly under the impetus of Mordechai Maisel (1528-1601), financier of Rudolph II who also assumed the management of the Jewish town. To him is owed the famous Jewish town hall (1565-68, Pancratius Roder; reconstructed in 1763-65, Josef Schlesinger), situated just next to the Altneuschul synagogue. The town hall was symbolically decorated with a tower and a clock with Hebrew characters of which the hands turned counterclockwise, from right to left. Maisel constructed the house of the *Hevra kadicha*, enlarged the cemetery and paved the Jewish town. He also appears to be at the origin of the construction of the Haute Synagogue (1568), initially accessible from the town hall and remarkable for its vaults with decorated ribs (the Holy Ark, installed after a fire, dates from 1691). Finally, he built his own synagogue, known as Maisel, (1591-92, Juda Coref de Herz and Josef Wahl) which, according to witnesses was of great splendor. But, damaged by fires in 1689 and 1754, it was reconstructed in a neo-Gothic style (1893-1905, Alfred Grotte). At that time there lived in Prague the Maharal, Rabbi Yehouda Loew ben Bezalel, the author of "*The Well of the Exile*" (1599), and to whom is also attributed the creation of the golem. The prosperity of the ghetto of Prague, which continued during the 17th century despite the hostility of the people of Prague who considered the increase of the Jewish population to be excessive, found expression in the construction of a series of Baroque synagogues: the Klaus Synagogue (1694) which replaced several small *Schules* (*klausen*, cellules) which had burned in 1689, the Zigeuner, founded in 1613, but reconstructed, after a fire in 1710, and the synagogue of the Grande Cour, founded in 1626 by Jacob Bashevi of Treuenburg (the first Jew ennobled in the Habsburg Empire) and rebuilt in 1708. They have barrel vaults richly decorated in stucco, finely worked grills for *bimot*, Holy Arks embellished with orders, pyramidians, frontons, etc. Unfortunately, both the Zigeuner and the Grande Cour Synagogues were demolished during the rehabilitation of the ghetto in 1906. The ghetto also had its private synagogues.

Towards Emancipation: Haskalah and Renunciation of the Exile

The ghetto and the Jewish street were symbolic of the social status of the Jews in the 16th and 17th centuries. With the Enlightenment, there began a period of transition that saw synagogues open, even sometimes with a handsome façade, yet they still remained either located in the old Jewish quarter of the town or hidden and unseen from the street. A few countries, however, went further in their tolerance. After the Union of Utrecht (1579) which proclaimed religious liberty, this new vision was manifested in the Netherlands through imposing synagogues, pieced by large bays. In Amsterdam, where two migratory movements (the Sephardic and the Ashkenazic) converged, the construction of a 'Portuguese' synagogue in a local style was authorized in 1639. This structure architecturally evokes the Mauritshuis, and its galleries appear to be borrowed from Protestant temples. Germany of the Aufklärung also saw buildings constructed that symbolized the tolerance that Lessing advocated, particularly in *Nathan le Sage* (1779). The king of Prussia helped with the construction of the Berlin synagogue and was present at its inauguration in 1714. The building, externally resembling a Protestant temple, follows a model that was used for about a century in the states of certain enlightened princes: Halberstadt (1699-1712), Ansbach (1746, Leopold Rietti), Westheim (around 1750), Ichenhausen (1781) and Krumbach-Hürben (1819). The duke of Anhalt-Dessau even asked his architect, Friedrich Wilhelm von Erdmannsdorf, who was in charge of the buildings in the Wörlitz park, to construct a synagogue there (1789-90). He designed a picturesque circular tempietto (resembling the temple of Vesta but without any external Jewish character) for this park that already had several Roman temples, a Pantheon, and a Gothic house. There was even a pagoda not far away, in the Oranienbaum park. In fact, such a building illustrates the persistence of the exceptional status of the court Jews, rather than a real evolution of mentalities.

Germany, thanks to the philosopher Moses Mendelsohn, was then, nevertheless, the centre of a debate, typical of the Enlightenment, concerning the place of Jews and the consequences of new concepts of humanity: that the Jew was a man, even a citizen. One of the most famous pamphlets, on this question, was " *Uber die bügerliche Verbesserung der Juden (on alleviating the civil disabilities of the Jews)*" by Christian Wilhelm Dohm which appeared in Berlin in 1781 and was translated into French in 1782. Admittedly the *Reasons for Naturalizing the Jews* by John

Berlin, the *Heidereutergasse* Synagogue
(1714, architect Michael Kemmeter).
18th century engraving showing
the synagogue during the celebration
of *Purim*. Private collection.

Prague, interior view of the *Altneuschul*.
This 'Old New Synagogue' is the oldest
still in use in Europe and is famous
for its Gothic architecture, its location
in the historic Jewish quarter
and its wealth of legendary associations.
Its style shows a distinct Christian
influence, while the fifth rib
in its groined vaults is often
interpreted as a means of avoiding
the form of a cross.

Lunéville, France, *Synagogue*
(1784, architect Augustin Piroux).
This fine Baroque façade was hidden
by a house until the First World War.

Wörlitz, Germany, *Synagogue*
(1789-90, architect Friedrich Wilhelm
von Erdmannsdorff).

Toland (1714) had preceded this work, but the context of the 1870s was crucial in the process of the Emancipation, whereas Toland's treatise had had but a punctual impact. From then on, the educational means in particular of a 'regeneration' of the Jews was in place. It should be noted, however, that the naturalization of the Jews held to their strangeness: Dohm himself, so understanding, qualified them as "unfortunate fugitives from Asia"[9], a vision which quickly reemerged. Herder, who highlighted the irreducible sense of national identity, considered the Jews as "paradisiacal plants"[10] and wished to impose upon them the adoption of "European laws".

In the Austro-Hungarian Empire, Dohm's ideas influenced Joseph II. In 1782, the emperor proclaimed an edict of tolerance that instituted an educational system based on the assimilation of the Jews. Henceforth (at least theoretically), all trades were opened to them, but of whom it was demanded that the teaching of the Talmud be counteracted by secular studies. Obviously, civil equality was not envisioned, but the defamatory laws were abolished. As for synagogues, their status varied little. In Vienna itself, the first large synagogue opened in 1826, but—although designed by the court architect Josef Kornhäusel—it remained hidden behind other buildings and had but a single portal on the street.

France—although less concerned than Austro-Hungary which was then inhabited by 260,000 Jews and had recently (1772) acquired Galicia—resumed the debate. Malesherbes, minister of Louis XVI, prepared, on the heels of his work in favour of Protestants, a reform that resulted in 1784 with the abolition of the infamous tolls. But during the same year, the construction in Lorraine of two monumental synagogues at Nancy and at Lunéville was authorized by the king. The latter, finished in 1785, built according to the plans of Charles Augustin Piroux, presents a Baroque façade decorated with garlands, royal symbols, and an inscription in Hebrew thanking the king. However, symbolizing the first stage of the process of emancipation, it was only authorized on the condition that it be built behind a house which hid it. Its inauguration was an event: the Abbé Grégoire, *curé* of a nearby village, who would be the champion of Jewish emancipation during the coming Revolution, pronounced a sermon in Lunéville on this occasion. As for the synagogue of Nancy, by the same architect, finished in 1788, it was erected on the edge of the town and without a façade.

The Revolution of 1789 as the champion of a universalistic vision of the rights of man and of the citizen (already inscribed in the Constitution of the United States of America in 1787) hastened the process by which the rights of the 'Portuguese' Jews as citizens were

Jean Lubin Vauzelle Angerville,
*Interior of the Bordeaux Synagogue,
with the Architect Corcelles,* between 1812
and 1840. Paris, Musée d'art
et d'histoire du Judaïsme.

Bordeaux, *Synagogue in the Rue Causserouge* (1812), lithograph by Willy. Bordeaux, municipal archives. As self-appointed King Hiram to the local Jewish community, the Christian architect Arnaud Corcelles dreamed of re-creating the Temple. His façade includes a series of symbols borrowed from the Bible, the columns of the Temple, a candelabrum, twelve palms representing the tribes and the Tables of the Law in majesty. The openings derive from Aaron's miter as interpreted for that of Chief Rabbi Sintzheim, president of the Sanhedrin organized by Napoleon in 1806.

acknowledged on the 28 January 1790, and by according emancipation to all Jews the 27 September 1791. The opening of synagogues was from then on free (except under the Terror), but the communities—rather disorganized during this period of transition—only managed to maintain or install oratories. For there was a counterpart to emancipation, as was explicit in the notorious remark of the Count of Clermont-Tonnerre[11]: the disappearance of the 'Jewish Nation'. It was thus necessary to renounce the exile and to enter into a nation that was still very Christian and to denominationalize Judaism. It is to the honour of France that this admission was not, as it was for a long time in Germany, the price of conversion. French revolutionary logic, argued in the same speech by Clermont-Tonnerre, established that religious liberty, as was inscribed in Article 10 of the Declaration. In Germany, many were ready to convert in order to attain emancipation. This phenomena wreaked havoc amongst the well-to-do and even amongst Mendelsohn's own children. David Friedländer carried this argumentation to its extreme limit. He understood that the last rampart must be assaulted[12]: "The most powerful advantage that Jews can turn to good account is to eliminate more and more in their hearts the nostalgia of the Messiah and of Jerusalem, following the example of reason that rejects this hope as chimerical". By the 1860's, this was done in the prayer books that were expurgated of allusions to the restoration of the Temple and the return to Zion.

Neo-classicism: the Style of the Emancipation

Concerning synagogue architecture, the consequences of the renunciation of Zion were primordial, for emancipation was materialized by a search for monumentality. It forced the synagogue, and consequently the entire Jewish community, to redefine its place in the city and to mark its presence by a denominative façade. Parallel to the nationalization of the Jews, the synagogue went from a private status to that of a public building. The construction of a synagogue, even if it still remained incumbent upon the Jews themselves for a long time, became an official operation occasioning the collaboration of administrative officials: ministries, municipalities and various architectural services. In 1808, Napoleon equipped French Judaism with a very rigid administrative system, the *Consistoires* (Consistories). He even had inscribed in the decree that created these institutions (which played a major role in the denominationalization of Judaism and the nationalization of Jews) the requirement of assembling

Portrait of Rabbi Sintzheim,
anonymous, oil on canvas,
early 19th century.

the congregations in a single synagogue[13]. Large buildings must thus be built. The *Consistoire* of Bordeaux, established in 1808, immediately adopted the decree[14]: it undertook as of 1809 to replace the various oratories by a "temple". This term itself, which then appeared, concentrated all the values invested in the new synagogues: Emancipation, obviously, but also the acknowledgement of the acquired dignity which should be conveyed by a new comportment, and finally, the officilisation of the status of the Mosaical or Israelite denomination. These adjectives attempted to obliterate, parallel to the promotion provided by the notion of 'temple', the negative connotations of 'Jew'. This regeneration required the abandoning of numerous traditions judged obsolete, incompatible with the status of citizen, the synagogue became the instrument and the mirror of this mutation. In Bordeaux, the new ideas were immediately proclaimed. Chief Rabbi Andrade announced at the inauguration of the "temple des Israélites" (Israelite Temple): "If the tomb that contains the ashes of the pious men and sages of Israel were to be reopened, if life was returned, they could contemplate the splendor of a rare solemnity, unique perhaps in the brilliance of Juda, we would hear them exclaim in rapture: Is it a new Jerusalem that emerges with us from the shades of the tomb? What beneficial star, Lord, on the scattered remains of your people? (…) This temple, elevated under the auspices of the greatest of Monarchs, boldly proclaims the benefaction of the Eternal. No, Israelites, you will no more be reduced to take refuge on Mount Modin, nor to make the subterranean an asylum for the practice your religious laws: Napoleon, protector of all religions, had us hear these words of life: *And you too, Jacob, build your altars!*"[15] The leitmotivs of the rabbinical homiletics were in place: on one hand, the affirmation that Jerusalem is there where a community is established, and on the other hand, the evolution (sometimes quasi-messianic) that represents the transfer of the oratories and of the *Schule* from the Jewish streets to an honorable street or square of the town. Henceforth, all inaugurations saw these themes developed. In 1861, Rabbi Maier gave his blessings on his "very dear Stuttgart, our Jerusalem". Rabbi Isaac Levy in Porrentuy, in Switzerland, said[16]: "every time that one of our old Synagogues disappears in order to make room for a larger and more beautiful one, it is the dark image of the past that fades in order that we can perceive the radiant face of modern civilization."

To renounce exile, in the sense of the *galout*, was underlying in all these speeches. In 1872, Chief Rabbi Zadoc Kahn, towering from his pulpit, was explicit[17]: "The Temple, it is true, will be rebuilt a second time on Mount Moriah. But already Judaism has recognized that its destiny is not tied to the existence of this sacred monument. Jerusalem is no longer only in Jerusalem. Jerusalem is everywhere where a community of the faithful live, everywhere where a sanctuary is built to adore the Almighty and study the Law."

The passage from the hidden oratories and the *Schule*, with a private or semi-private character, to the synagogue, a public place of worship, is the very symbol of emancipation. The question which thus arises concerns the type of architecture for an "Israelite temple". The Emancipation process began at a time when architecture was dominated by a return to Antiquity. References to Greek temples were even seen as valid for churches. Neo–Classicism offered a greater universalistic plastic language more in harmony with the ideals that had governed these aesthetic changes, which moreover the Revolution had exploited. Judaism, a religion now recognized by the State, also found in neo-Classicism a style of integration. Although, architects were more or less incapable of conceiving a synagogue outside of the model of a church or of the Temple for which the Classical forms were welcomed. Thus, the basilican plan triumphed in this period and externally the neutrality of the pediment appeared to convene to a denomination which was discreetly emerging from the dark.

For two decades, discretion was the rule and all decoration remained interior. The large Ashkenazic synagogue in London (1790, James Spiller) used the design of Bevis Marks, and was without an entrance on the street or any distinctive sign. This was also the case in Paris, even thirty years after the Emancipation. The first synagogue in Paris (1822, Sandrié de Jouy), with a handsome basilican plan and Doric columns, had no external decoration. The situation is identical in Karlsruhe (1798-1806) where the synagogue, designed by the chief municipal architect, Friedrich Weinbrenner, is nevertheless on a courtyard, and in Munich (1826), where the colonnade of red marble constructed by Jean-Baptiste Métivier has no external counterpart. In Germany, where civic rights were granted to Jews progressively according to the states, neo–Classicism was conjugated with a certain discretion. The architects, nevertheless, employed a few neo-Egyptian touches, expressing an attempt to develop a specific character.

Neo-Classicism also became widespread in the synagogues of Central Europe with the same connotations: imposing porticos of the synagogues designed by András Landherr in Obuda (1820-21) and in Abony (1825) show that tolerance was more visible in Hungary than in Vienna. Similar porches are also found in Hungary at

Karlsruhe, Germany, *View of the
courtyard and inner façade of the synagogue*
(1798, architect Friedrich Weinbrenner),
watercolor by Abraham Stähelin, 1816.
Basle, Kunstmuseum.

Baja (1845-46), in Slovakia at Liptovski Mikulá_ (1846), in Poland at Kepno (Kempen,1814-15, Fryderyk and Karol Scheffler), Wroclaw (Breslau, Storch Synagogue by Karl Langhans, 1827-28) and Wielun.

In the Unites States, where neo-Classicism was closely associated with republican and federal ideology, a few synagogues of congregations formed during the 1840s were built in this style, as at Charleston (1841, C. L. Warner), and Baltimore, Lloyd Street (1845, R. C. Long).

Neo-Classicism thus corresponds with the transition of the ghetto to acknowledgement. By its prestige, it transformed the synagogue into a public monument. Admittedly, it was often necessary to wait a generation in order that the exteriors had a more ostentatious character. Between 1830 to 1840, depending upon the country, the process was concluded, but at this time an architectural debate was launched that challenged neo-Classicist hegemony in the name of nationalism, a theme to which Jewish communities were very sensitive, for patriotism therein stood out. Architecture was once again called upon in order to translate the motto, of the Consistoire central des Israélites de France (Central Consistory of the Israelites of France), was not less valid anywhere else: Religion and Nation.

Obuda, Hungary, *Façade of the synagogue* (1820-21, architect András Landherr).

Baltimore, Maryland, *Lloyd Street synagogue* (1845, architect R. C. Long).

Architectural Styles and National Affiliation

Paris, *Installation of the Chief Rabbi of Paris at the synagogue in the Rue Notre Dame de Nazareth: the Prayer for the Emperor.* Engraving from the *Monde Illustré* of 13 January 1869.

Left page:
Paris, *Synagogue in the Rue de la Victoire* (1874, architect Alfred Aldrophe).

Israel Zangwill, 'Anglicization', *Ghetto Comedies* (1907)

'The Great Synagogue itself took on a modern, thoroughly English note of gaiety, as of a dining room; freshly gilded, stripped of its quiet intimacy, with electric light replacing the antique candelabra and casting a dazzling whiteness over this winter's afternoon.

The pulpit—yes, the pulpit—was draped with the Union Jack, and looking towards the loggia of the *Parnass* and the *Gabbai*, she saw it occupied by gold-belted officers. Somebody whispered that the tall one over there, his chest studded with medals, was a Christian nobleman, a Knight of the Order of the Bath, 'a great honor for the Synagogue'…

What! Were Christians coming to Jewish ceremonies then, the way she herself had attended a Christian service? Yes, it was true, you could see a white cross on an officer's sleeve. And before the eyes of all these outsiders the cantor began intoning on the steps of the Ark, and lighting the great seven-branched Hanukah candlestick. In truth, the world was changing before her very eyes.

And when, in turn, the Chief Rabbi advanced towards the Ark, she saw that he was wearing a strange red and white robe (in her ignorance she imagined it too to be a military uniform); and, stranger still, a helmeted soldier followed him and drew back the curtain concealing the richly ornamented Books of the Law. Then, amidst all this pomp, burst forth a sound that filled her with a feeling of exquisite sweetness. An organ! an organ in a synagogue! This truly was Anglicization!

…There followed a sermon whose doubly appropriate text had been chosen from the Book of Maccabees: "One Jew in every ten," declared the preacher, "flew to the defense of the Queen's territories against the bold invader. Their beloved country had no more devoted citizens than the children of Israel living under its flag.

Joyfully, but without surprise, they read in the Jewish press the names of more than seven hundred of their own who had spontaneously volunteered to serve Queen and country. Many others, left unmentioned, had also set off, and proportionately they provided more soldiers—from the colonel down to the humble bugler—than their numbers would have led one to expect. Thus were the Englishman, and the Jew whose Holy Writ he has adopted, united in spirit and in ideals; let us not then be astonished if Europe's Anglophobes are also anti-Semites."

Then the preacher, the entire assembly standing before him and the Union Jack unfurled, recited aloud the names of all those Jews who had died for England on the distant *veldt*. Heads were bent as the names echoed in the silence of the synagogue.'

The fundamental shift from Jewish to Israelite identity coincided with an aesthetic revolution. Firmly rooted in the philosophy of the Enlightenment, Neoclassicism still had advocates for whom its architectural language remained the only fitting one, its principles seen as having been shaped by the ancients in the context of a relationship with nature that guaranteed its universality. The arrival of historicism—'the greatest revolution ever to take place in Western thought', in the opinion of Friedrich Meinecke—thoroughly modified the bases of an architecture no longer set in nature but in history. Even Classical art was now no more than the art of the Greeks, the product of one culture among many. This historical relativism, which Isaiah Berlin[1] prefers to call pluralism, combined with the notion of a national spirit—Herder's *Volksgeist*—to generate a quest for origins in which each culture, each nation drew on its history for the appropriate aesthetic principles. Thus we find Goethe contemplating Strasbourg Cathedral and exclaiming passionately over 'German architecture'[2]! In terms, then, of the process involving language, culture, the arts and national identity, the situation of the Jews was a difficult one in that they no longer constituted a nation as such; despite its lofty ancientness, their specific history, except when secularised and consigned to a distant past, remained an obstacle to incorporation into the history of the various countries they lived in. And yet their presence since time immemorial in those countries continued to be extolled.

The second aesthetic consequence of this mutation was an architectural theory based no longer on general principles or programs, but on the use of historical styles that took on specific national connotations and were intended to serve various secular and religious ends.

Brussels, *Prayer for Léopold II,*
King of Belgium in the Brussels Synagogue
(1889), oil on canvas
by Jacques Emile Edouard Brandon.
Brussels, Musée juif de Belgique.

The synagogue as an instrument of national affiliation

On the morning of the inauguration of the little Alsatian synagogue in Lauterbourg (Albert Haas) on 1 October 1845, Rabbi Isaac Libermann, trained at the rabbinical school in Metz, went first to the old synagogue for the leave-taking prayers and delivered a sermon in German. The procession bearing the *sefarim* then moved on to the new synagogue, where the rabbi mounted the pulpit and gave a sermon in French. The abandoning of Yiddish for sermons was already required by the Napoleonic Code: like the Talmud, the sense of exile and such practises as the selling of *mizvot*, now considered unworthy, its disappearance was to be part of the forging of the new Israelite. Nonetheless Kafka was to point out to his assimilated fellow-Jews more than sixty years later, 'You know more Yiddish than you think…' With language, architecture is one of the most effective instruments and symbols of integration, of the process of national affiliation. This latter takes place at two levels: firstly via the adoption of new modes of behaviour, adaptation of ritual and the intrusion of symbolic elements of an architectural nature, be it recourse to the basilica plan, inclusion of a bell-tower or the use of a pulpit; and secondly via the choice of a historical style giving concrete expression to integration into the adoptive nation and an authentically patriotic dimension.

Emancipation brought the modern Jew face to face with a crucial and totally new issue: identity was no longer a simple matter of dialogue with the host culture, the demand now being for integration founded not on respect for individual differences, but on eventual assimilation. The price to pay, then, was a degree of dejudaization. It was true that the exigencies varied between a centralist, assimilationist country like France and one built on immigration like the United States, where there was a greater respect for the identity of groups of differing origins. Yet if Gallicization took place, so did Americanization. Leon A. Jick[3] stresses, for example, that in the United States of the 1840s, in parallel with rabbinical use of English for sermons, the building of a synagogue was an act of patriotism and 'a symbol of belonging in the new society. Jewish immigrants were thereby announcing their conviction that they had become American Jews'. Moreover their use of the word 'temple' implied rejection of the traditional belief in a messianic restoration of the Temple of Jerusalem.

Obviously such a process could only have taken place in the nineteenth century, when states were defining themselves as nations and searching for a linguistic, cultural and even racial coherence on which to base their national identity. The Jews then had to abandon their traditional 'ethnic' identity in favour of Israelitism, that is to say of simple religious difference, and become, for example, French, English, Hungarian or German Israelites. Each community was affected by this shift in time with political change in the European countries, where Jewish emancipation often coincided in time with a rising assertion of national identity. Assimilation became more pronounced, even in such multi-national states as the Austro-Hungarian Empire; for while the population might include Austrians, Hungarians, Czechs, Galicians and Ruthenians, Jewishness did not constitute a nationality. Assimilating to the point of oneness with the nation, the Jews became ardent patriots, rejecting the extraterritorial alliances foreshadowed by such groupings as the Universal Israelite Alliance—founded by integrated Jews in 1860 to aid their less fortunate coreligionists—and later openly affirmed by a Zionism that was itself a nationalist reaction to anti-Semitism. In the French context, for example, exists no finer declaration of love for the nation than the farewell speech made by Chief Rabbi Isaac Levy at the Colmar synagogue on 6 July 1872, following the German annexation of Alsace. Justifiably famous too is the article 'Germanity and Jewishness'[4] (1915) by philosopher Hermann Cohen, in which the author strips Jewish messianism of its national dimension to equate it with Kant's ideal humanism. He then goes on to demonstrate the 'intimate harmony linking Jewishness and Germanity', ultimately reaching the conclusion that the world's Jews 'are bound by a duty of piety to Germany, for it is the mother country of their soul'! By contrast the Zionist novelist Israel Zangwill[5] mocks Western Jews become 'passionate Hungarians, thoroughbred Italians, flag-waving Americans, loyal Frenchmen, imperial Germans, enthusiastic Dutchmen…'

National affiliation is also apparent in the Christianisation of the synagogue. The monumentalism and sacralization of the place of worship, the dignity of ceremonial procedures now entrusted to officiants were pretexts for the introduction of pulpit and organ; in addition there was the creation of a sort of choir by amalgamation of the *bimah* and the Holy Ark and the wearing of ceremonial

robes by rabbis officialdom tended to see as Jewish priests—with, by extension, Chief Rabbis as bishops and Consistories synagogues as cathedrals. All these factors made the synagogue a 'Jewish church' that ought not to appear less dignified than its Catholic and Protestant sisters; as a testimony to assimilation pushed to its absolute limits, church and synagogue are seen as one and the same.

The presence of a pulpit, sometimes imposed by the Consistories on traditional communities by means of ministerial subsidies, is one of the symbols of national affiliation. Appearing in the Bordeaux synagogue in 1812, by 1822 the pulpit had made its way to Paris and elsewhere.

In a short story aptly titled 'Anglicisation', Zangwill describes the patriotic feeling that drives a young English Jew to enlist for the Boer War, then to seek marriage with a Christian woman who ultimately rejects him. Through the eyes of the protagonist's mother he recounts the pompous memorial ceremonies at the church and the synagogue, where she discovers the organ and the pulpit draped with the British flag. Judy Glasman[6] has shown how the United Synagogue—which, like the Paris Consistory, had its own architect, Nathan Solomon Joseph—generated a conception of the typical synagogue including such evident factors for anglicisation as the use of the basilica plan with galleries and moving of the *bimah* towards the Holy Ark while giving it monumental proportions designed to inflate the dignity of the rabbi. Paul Lindsay adopts this analysis, offering[7] as 'the most extreme example of the "anglicised" arrangement' the Hammersmith Synagogue (1896, Delissa Joseph). Just as the Paris Consistory aimed attempts at Gallicization at the Jewish immigrants of the city's eastern districts, Anglicisation was extended to the Jews of London's East End. The *shtiblekh* here were rooms in buildings also containing shops and workshops, and the notables did their best to 'anglicise' local Eastern European Jews by pressing them to build more monumental synagogues, a process Judy Glasman describes as 'architectural colonization'. The East London Synagogue in Stepney Green was one of the first to be built in this vein. Established in 1887 with its own architect, Lewis Solomon, the Federation of Minor Synagogues adopted the idea and rejoiced, in its 1896 report, at the spread of the model synagogue.

However there was open resistance to the new interior model from Orthodox groups. In Paris in 1911 nine groups of immigrant Eastern European Jews banded together to form the *Agoudath hakehiloth de Paris* and planned to build a synagogue that would keep them independent of the Consistory. Other Russo-Polish groups would have liked the Consistory to grant them

Chief Rabbi Zadoc Kahn,
photograph by Nadar. Paris, BnF.

Paris, *Installation of the Chief Rabbi*
of Paris at the synagogue
in the Rue Notre Dame de Nazareth:
the Prayer for the Emperor.
Engraving from the *Monde Illustré*
of 13 January 1869.

147

Dresden, *Interior of the synagogue*
(1840, architect Gottfried Semper),
old photograph. The Moorish interior
is in marked contrast
with the Neo-Romanesque exterior.

use of the synagogue in the Rue des Tournelles, which local Alsatian Jews were using less and less. This would have meant increased Gallicization, as a report addressed to the Consistory[8] points out: 'Among our immigrant brethren are many who, more used to France and sensing the danger of a separatist movement among the immigrants, sincerely wish to see a continuing spirit of fraternity between French and immigrant Jews while readying the latter for complete assimilation into the great family of French Judaism.' However the Rue des Tournelles synagogue was to remain 'French', although this did not mean the *Agoudath hakehiloth* was completely opposed to modernity and integration: in its prospectus the president, J. Landau makes it clear that 'We no longer need to take refuge in temporary, private premises where our children refuse to accompany us. We shall have a large synagogue with all modern conveniences.' Nor did he need to specify that the *bimah* would be in the centre and that there would be no organ or pulpit. The architect called on being none other than Hector Guimard, there was an evident desire to reconcile the religious tradition and architectural modernity. In choosing Guimard, it should be noted, these Orthodox Jews were also cutting free from the Christian ecclesiastical model: throughout the nineteenth century the other major sign of national affiliation had been the adoption of current church styles, in particular medieval references offering—especially in the Gothic context— the dual advantage of spiritual significance and a point of anchorage within the national history. It is hardly surprising then, that so many nineteenth-century synagogues opt for the same styles. And yet national affiliation could also take other forms.

Neo-Romanesque: variation on a religious and national style

Once it had been demonstrated that the Greek temple possessed no inherent superiority and that as a pagan structure it was perhaps inappropriate and no more than a foreign body on the national soil, use of the Romanesque and Gothic styles celebrated by Goethe, by Chateaubriand's *Génie du Christianisme* and by the Romantics, began to spread, notably in response to demand from the Church. Committed to integration, the synagogue felt obliged to follow and several Jewish architects produced theoretical justifications for this recourse to the medieval.

Germany was especially marked by the Neo-Romanesque *rundbogenstil,* the work of Munich architects and

Paris, *Project for a synagogue,*
elevation (1850) by Gottfried Semper.
Semper Archive, E.T.H. Zürich.

Coupe longitudinale.

Metz, France, *Project for a synagogue,*
section and elevation
(1844) by Nicolas Derobe. Metz,
Archives départementales de la Moselle.

Metz, France, *Exterior view*
of the synagogue (1850, N. Derobe).

836 Homburg. Die Synagoge. L. L.

Homburg, *Synagogue* (1866).
Old photograph. Example of a common
Neo-Romanesque style,
with two towers flanking the façade.

of Heinrich Hübsch, the style's theoretician. In 1834 in Kassel, where the Jews had succeeded in preserving civil rights accorded under Napoleon, the architectural competition for a new synagogue saw victory go to the Neo-Romanesque camp led by state architect August Schuchardt and his assistant Albrecht Rosengarten, a member of the local Jewish community. Their building retained many Classical features, but the two-tower gabled façade, which was to become a model, the round arches, the rose windows and the Holy Ark all showed Neo-Romanesque tendencies. Opened in 1839, this synagogue is the keynote for Harold Hammer-Schenk's chapter on 'style as demonstration of German nationality'[9]. In an article[10] the young Rosengarten justified the choice of Romanesque as being less typically Christian than Gothic, but at the same time deeply rooted in German history. Later, in his *Dictionary of Architectural Styles* (1857)[11] he sharply criticized Oriental trends in synagogues, continuing to champion the Neo-Romanesque. In this spirit he built a number of synagogues in Hamburg: Alte and Neue Klaus (1853), the 'Portuguese' (1855) and Kohlhöfen (1857). The Kassel model made its way to Mannheim (1855, Lendorff), Francfort-Isr. Religion Gesellschaft (1853) and as far afield as Moravia, where it was used in Pohorelice (1855, Muschel), Brno (1855, Schwendenwein) and Jihlava (1863), Linz in Austria (1877) and Gliwice in Silesia (1861, Lubowski and Troplowitz).

The other major contribution to the establishment of the Neo-Romanesque as the emancipation style in Germany is the Dresden Synagogue (1840) designed by Gottfried Semper, a key figure in nineteenth-century German architecture. Entrusted with the project by a community recently granted civil rights still falling short of full emancipation, he created a square building given a Romanesque touch by its octagonal central tower—reminiscent of San Lorenzo in Milan, certain German churches and, according to Semper, the tent in the desert—and its use of Lombard bands. The exterior indicates a firm desire for integration into German culture, but the interior ornamentation, by contrast, is in a Moorish vein, featuring stucco work copied from the Alhambra in Granada. This interior-exterior duality, which was to reappear in Tübingen in 1882, probably reflects the conciliatory attitude advocated during the Enlightenment by Moses Mendelsohn, who advised the Jews to 'be German on the outside and Jewish on the inside'. Living in exile in Paris after the 1848 revolution, Semper was commissioned by Baron James de Rothschild to design a replacement for the synagogue in the Rue Notre-Dame de Nazareth (1850) and submitted

Hanover, *Exterior view of the synagogue*
(1864-70, architect Edwin Oppler).
Old photograph.

a proposal taking the Dresden approach further, making the towers and the entry more monumental while abandoning the Moorish references. Paris would thus have been endowed with a building whose square plan and Neo-Romanesque aesthetics were distinctly at variance with the French tradition; however the Paris community opted instead for a basilican edifice with a more orientalist feel[12].

The Neo-Romanesque enjoyed widespread success in Central Europe, where the Kassel model, for example, was often further enriched—in addition to numerous series of blind arcades—with two side towers. The type of tower developed in the 1860s was to reach its culmination in the 1890s with the Grand Synagogue at Plzen (1892, Max Fleischer and E. Klotz), the second-largest in Europe and restored by the Czech Republic in 1995-97. Here the towers take on the proportions of those in Budapest. Most of the variants on this theme are to be found in Poland, notably in Bytom (1869, Freuding), Bydgoszcz (1884) and Racziborz (1889), but other examples exist in Trnava in Slovakia and in Debrecen in Hungary (1896), where the Viennese architect Jacob Gartner opted for the two-tower approach he was to use again in Vienna's Kluckygasse and Siebenbrunnergasse Synagogues, dating from 1900 and 1908 respectively. This style was also well received in Western Europe, several examples being built in the German-annexed Alsace-Lorraine, at Dieuze (1907) and Soultz-sous-Forêts (1897); the latter was copied from, or based on the same model as the synagogue at Saint-Louis (1907, Alexandre Louvat).

Alsace shows a pronounced Romanesque influence: the 1845 design by architect Albert Haas for Lauterbourg gave France its first Neo-Romanesque synagogue, a little ahead of Metz, left with no choice in the matter. The trend continued with the synagogues in Thann (1862, Victor Heilmann), Bergheim (1863, Auguste Hartmann), Westhoffen (1868) and those built by the architect Roedrich at Hatten (1870) and Wissembourg (1872). However it was with the German annexation that this style came to dominate: notable examples are the synagogues designed by the Alsatian Albert Brion at Obernai (1876), Barr (1878) and Rosheim (1882), those to be found in villages like Bambronn (1895) and that of Strasbourg. In the case of the Strasbourg Synagogue the plan by Karlsruhe architect Ludwig Levy—a specialist who alternated between Neo-Romanesque and Neo-Moorish—seems to symbolize the desire to Germanize not only the Jews but Alsace itself. Inaugurated in 1898, the synagogue is a faithful imitation of such Rhine Valley cathedrals as Worms and Speyer and as such sets Strasbourg firmly in the context of German history. Synagogues drawing on the Neo-Romanesque so dear to the heart of Kaiser Wilhelm II—square plan, octagonal tower over the crossing, staircase turrets and large rose windows—were also built by Joseph Kleesattel in Düsseldorf (1904) and Mülheim (1907) and by the firm of Cremer and Wolffenstein in Königsberg (1896) and Dessau (1909). The latter designers, however, opted for domes rather than towers, following a model originating with Edwin Oppler.

A Jewish architect from Silesia, Oppler had spent three years working with Viollet-le-Duc and by 1863 had developed a Neo-Romanesque style whose variants he tested in competitions. For his winning entry in the competition for the Hanover Synagogue, completed in 1870, he chose a national architectural form, a 'Germanic Romanesque style of the twelfth century'. In applying it, however, he did not hesitate to use a Latin cross design with a high dome at the crossing and blind arcades and rose windows as decoration. As Carol Krinsky[13] has astutely pointed out, the overall approach is highly reminiscent of that of Victor Baltard's church of St Augustine (1860-74), the connection being a possibility in that Oppler visited Paris in 1859 or 1860. In explaining his choice of a 'German style', Oppler was highly critical of the Moorish approach, for him unrelated to Judaism. Reminding his readers that synagogues have always been built in the national style, he writes[14] that, 'The German Jew should also build in a German spirit and a German style.' He used the same arrangement for the synagogue in Wroclaw (1865-72), in his projects for the competitions for Nuremberg (1868), Munich (1872) and Karlsbad (1874), in which the domes take on gigantic proportions, and for the synagogue at Swidnica (1877). The winner of the Munich competition was another Neo-Romanesque proposal (1877), that of Albert Schmidt[15], whose initial drawings, like those of other competitors were worthy of royal pavilions or Arabian Nights palaces. The Neo-Romanesque as an extension of the approach proposed by Semper seemed thus an appropriately sober manner of celebrating emancipation.

It would seem that Oppler's work also bore fruit in Berlin during the 1890s, with Cremer and Wolffenstein again making appearances with Lindenstrasse (1891) and Lützowstrasse (1896). In their quest for a new monumentality, Germany's last historicist synagogues were above all experiments in combining Neo-Romanesque, Byzantine and modern building possibilities, examples being the Fasanenstrasse Synagogue in Berlin (1912, Ehrenfried Hessel), the Friedberger Anlage Synagogue in

Wroclaw, Poland, *Section of the synagogue,*
drawing by the architect E. Oppler,
c. 1870. Stadtarchiv, Hanover.

Strasbourg, France, *Exterior view*
of the synagogue
(1898, architect Ludwig Levy).

Dijon, France, *Present-day view*
of the synagogue
(1879, architect Alfred Sirodot).

Frankfurt (1904-07, P. Jürgensen and J. Bachmann) and others in Poznan, at the time still called Posen (1907, Cremer and Wolffenstein) and Bamberg (1910, J. Kronfuss). The most original however, with its circular worship area set into a wedge-shaped piece of land, is the synagogue in Essen (1913, Bernard Korner): here Neo-Romanesque and rustication are used in a most distinctive way reminiscent of the work of Richardson.

Other ventures in Neo-Romanesque variation took place in Hungary, subsequent to the synagogue built by Ludwig Förster at Miskolc (1861-63): that of Tata (1861, Ignác Wechselsman) and continuing up until the 1880s (Mezöcsát). The 1860s also saw the spread of façades with semicircular gables in Vác (1864, Abis Cacciari) and Pecs (1864, Gerster and Frey), the model surviving until 1911, when it was used in Constanta, Romania. Neo-Romanesque was also common in Poland, from Lodz (the synagogue on Wólczanska Street) to Warsaw (1902, Zalman Nozyk).

Chicago, *Present-day view of the Anshe Maariv Synagogue* (1891, Adler and Sullivan). This highly original building harmoniously combines such Eastern European references as the roof and the immense, wood-lined nave with Sullivan's characteristic use of the Neo-Romanesque. His personal style is also visible in the ironwork decoration.

Brussels, *Interior view, detail of the Holy Ark* (1878, architect Désiré DeKeyser). Having a Consistory similar to those in France, Brussels built a synagogue imitating the Romano-Byzantine monumentality of those in Paris and Lyon. The choir and galleries are decorated with a group of symbolic stained glass windows. A Temple in miniature, the Holy Ark is reminiscent of that in Lyon, described in the architectural press in 1865.

In France synagogue architecture was to make the 'Romano-Byzantine' its favourite style for several decades; but with the exception of the synagogue in Dijon, which has the authentic silhouette of a Romano-Byzantine church—complete with crossing!—the buildings in question are essentially Romanesque. Such was the choice of Alfred Aldrophe, architect to the Israelite Consistory of Paris, who built the synagogue in the Rue de la Victoire (1865-74) after the Consistory's rejection of his initial proposal as too ecclesiastical in tone. His façade was to influence that of the Portuguese synagogue in the Rue Buffault (1877, Stanislas Ferrand). Under the patronage of Cécile Furtado-Heine, Adrolphe was to provide Versailles with a Romanesque synagogue in 1886). The Byzantine touch is more evident in the synagogue built by Abraham Hirsch in Lyon, behind the Consistory building (1864), at a time when a journalist from the *Univers Israélite* was denouncing the church model in an article on the Aldrophe project[16]: 'It is strange that Israelite architects—as has also been the case in Lyon—should have a predilection for applying Christian forms to synagogues.'

It seems that in France, where the Neo-Gothic was met with misgivings, it fell to the Romano-Byzantine to symbolize in its Romanesque aspect the religious func-

tion and in its Byzantine aspect a discreet indication of Oriental origins. Like the institution itself, this 'consistorial' model was exported to Brussels (1878, Désiré DeKeyser) and there too a commission found the style too Christian, its preference for an Oriental source generating the counter-argument that the Romanesque was in fact of Syrian origin… At any rate, this attempt at assimilation was ill-received.

In the United State the Neo-Romanesque merged into the prevailing eclecticism. In partnership with Otto Blesch, a German-Jewish architect from Prague, Leopold Eidlitz introduced it to New York in 1847 with a synagogue for the Shaaray Tefila congregation on Wooster Street. The model is perhaps the Allerheiligenhofkirche (1826-1837) in Munich, built by Klenze after a visit to Sicily, and this may explain why some Americans have seen Eidlitz and Bletsch's synagogue as 'Byzantine'. However, in the hands of such imaginative architects as Frank Furness and Henry Richardson medieval styles also provided scope for truly original interpretation: a Romanesque ground plan is perceptible in the Rodeph Shalom Synagogue Furness built in Philadelphia with his associates Frazer and Hewitt, but the dominant impression created by the asymmetry of a façade flanked with a tower and the use of Oriental motifs for the windows and the interior is one of wilful picturesqueness. Louis Sullivan, who spent some time in Furness' studio, created a personal style out of a Richardson-derived Neo-Romanesque approach featuring massive round arches and the rustic effect of rough-cut stone. Sullivan went on to build the Anshe Maariv Synagogue in Chicago in association with Dankmar Adler, a member of the congregation there; the originality of the building lies in its superposition of two different volumes, the use of rustication, the large wooden nave and the foliate decoration typical of the Sullivan approach.

Gothic: a response to anti-Semitism?

It hardly needs to be said that the other principal influence in religious architecture from the 1840s onwards was the Gothic. Initially Christianity, seeing in it the supreme incarnation of its spiritual ideal, had taken it over and made it primarily religious; as the national style par excellence, the Gothic took on such marked ideological proportions that several countries claimed to have sired it. It seemed in most cases ill-adapted to the Jewish form of worship; even pro-integration Jewish architects of the time like Albrecht Rosengarten were opposed to it and it was essayed on only a few occasions, notably in countries such as the United States and Holland where it carried less of a historical and ideological charge. Synagogues embellished with Neo-Gothic motifs—ribbing and pinnacles, for instance—were opened in Cincinnati (1848) and San Francisco (1866, William Patton). One of the period's most interesting buildings was created in New York in 1850 for the Anshe Chesed congregation of German Jews by Alexandre Saeltzer, himself of German origin. Its main features are its two towers and its decorative gables and pinnacles, in which the press saw a reference to Cologne Cathedral that would never have been permitted Jews in Germany itself. Several other Gothic buildings were constructed, among them the Temple Brith Sholem in Kentucky, but it also happened that congregations bought former churches in the same style.

What followed was an eclecticism similar to that which in England resulted in most Victorian synagogues' drawing on the Romanesque or the Gothic, albeit in orientalized forms marked by additions or idiosyncratic motifs; the synagogue in Sydney, Australia is an example of this trend. In the United States the Mikve Israel Synagogue in Savannah, Georgia (1878, Henry G. Harrison) was handled in a late English Gothic style, while Rabbi Wise's Temple in Cincinnati (1866, James K. Wilson)

was a Gothic structure enriched with two minarets and Moorish decoration. The same stylistic mix can be found in New York at the Emanu-El Synagogue (1868, Leopold Eidlitz and Henry Fernbach) and in Portland at Beth Israel (1887).

In Holland eighteenth and nineteenth-century synagogues often combined Neoclassical features with Gothic elements—especially tierce-point windows—or at least with the relatively austere, brick-based Gothic that had developed in Northern Europe. Examples of this style, especially from the period 1820-1840, are countless[17]—they include Gouda (1827), Haasksbergen (1828), Tiel (1837-40) and Weesp (1840)—but can also be found throughout the century, Schiedam (1859) and Culemborg (1868) being interesting illustrations. The Neoclassical synagogue at Kampen (1847) is dominated by a Holy Ark in the Flamboyant Neo-Gothic style.

In the midst of all this eclecticism the Gothic tended to lose its significance, especially in a Protestant country where national identity looked back less to the Middle Ages than to the Renaissance. In Central Europe, by contrast, the tardy but stunning success of Neo-Gothic was doubtless due to its value as a symbol of national integration, but also, more surprisingly, to its spiritual aspect.

A proponent of integration, Rabbi Max Grunwald, then in Hamburg prior to moving to Vienna, published in 1901 a memorandum entitled 'How are Synagogues Built?'[18] After a review of the various styles adopted down the ages, he concludes with a condemnation of orientalism: 'To the extent that they set out to emphasize the «Oriental side» of Judaism, they were unconsciously aiding such enemies of the Jews as Lagarde.' In his view the most suitable style is the Gothic, as the architectonic expression of prayer. 'Only one style,' he writes, 'represents in concrete and moving fashion the human aspiration towards God and, at the same time, absolute confidence in the granting of prayer; the style of which Heine said, 'We feel here the elevation of the spirit…with these colossal pillars the spirit soars towards Heaven', and of which it is also said, 'These walls, these pillars are made for eternity'. 'The Gothic style.' The rabbi then goes on to remind his readers that the Gothic is not a Church monopoly… He justifies his choice by a consideration of the character of the Gothic which, like Judaism, is both Western and Oriental. Yet over and above its spiritual implications, it would seem that for Rabbi Grunwald the Gothic is also a means of responding to the virulent anti-Semitism of the time. In this he shares the point of view of the Viennese Jewish architect Max Fleischer; the two may have met when the rabbi moved to Vienna in 1903, but by then Fleischer had already been building Gothic synagogues for twenty years.

Fleischer was a veritable synagogue specialist, building some ten in all. His plan for the Schmalzhofgasse synagogue in Vienna in 1883-84 was relatively sober, but with the Müllnergasse and Neudeggergasse projects (1889 and 1900-03 respectively) the façade acquires two spires, while the interior and the Holy Ark are given richly Gothic moldings. All these features are to be found on an even more generous scale in Bohemia in the Reform Synagogue in Ceské Budejovice (1888): here, the building not being squeezed in between two others, the entire Gothic structure can spread its wings, especially the flying buttresses and the side aisles beneath them. The façade, it goes without saying, has its two spires. Ernst Hiller has demonstrated[19] how the overall approach could have been inspired by the church of Brigittenau in Vienna, built by Friedrich von Schmidt, one of Fleischer's masters. The undisguised likeness to a church was openly defended by the architect on several occasions. Presenting his first synagogue in Vienna in 1884[20], Fleischer readily acknowledged the Christian reference, outraged that architects ignorant of Judaism should have imposed the Oriental style and basing his stand on the example of Oppler who, he asserted, built in the Gothic style. For Fleischer there was no questioning Gothic's rightness for the times—times, he implied, stamped with the anti-Semitism of a Karl Lueger.

In the late nineteenth century Bohemia, where the Prague Altneuschul was the living symbol of Jewry's proud link with the Middle Ages, was the setting for a use of Neo-Gothic that would seem to have had the same implications as in the Austro-Hungarian capital. Fleischer built in Bohemia too, sometimes in a Neo-Renaissance style. In 1837 the Prague Altschul had been given a Neo-Gothic renovation, a standard practice also to be found at the same period in such German cities as Fürth (1831) and Regensburg (1841), where synagogues had existed since medieval times. However Neo-Gothic rebuilding really only took on substantial proportions in Bohemia, even a synagogue like that in Trebíc, dating from the seventeenth century, being rebuilt in this way. The Meisel synagogue, mentioned above, was similarly remodelled between 1893 and 1905 by the erudite architect Alfred Grotte[21], who bedecked with pinnacles a building dating from the late sixteenth century.

At least as much as the justifications put forward for the use of Gothic, the reservations expressed show that the style question was not simply one of a formal correspondence between a set of goals and a building type.

Ceské Budejovice, Czech Republic,
Synagogue (1888, architect
Max Fleischer).

Prague, *Façade of the Maisel synagogue*
(1893-1905, architect Alfred Grotte).

Nor, despite the arguments so frequently advanced in favour of Gothic, was it one of economics. The primary consideration was that of the symbolic value, the historic dimension attaching to different styles; for the actual presentation of the synagogue, which might have seemed an ancillary matter, was a crucial issue in that the formal perception of the building induced a certain view of Judaism. Other historical styles could have transmitted the message of emancipation and integration, but without the same significance on the religious plane. It is revealing that once again Austria-Hungary was the scene of these endeavours.

Other historicist forms: Renaissance and Baroque

Since the architectural forms of the Renaissance and the Baroque readily lent themselves to ecclesiastical building—although on a much smaller scale than the medieval models—there seemed to be no reason not to use them for synagogues as well. The examples, however, are extremely few: Rabbi Grunwald loathed imitations of a Renaissance style he saw as aristocratically-tainted and revelatory not of the striving towards God but of mere self-assertion. Pure Renaissance examples are rare: a handsome serliana or 'Venetian window' serves as the principal door to the synagogue in Karlsruhe (1875), but this is in fact a playful gesture on the part of Josef Durm, architect and editor of an enormous architectural encyclopaedia, who also adds in Romanesque and Oriental motifs. Naturally enough, traces of Palladianism are visible in the English Neoclassical synagogues of the Regency period, notably John Davies' New London Synagogue (1838).

Yet it was once again in Central Europe that the use of these styles took on a more pronounced political edge, with Vienna and Bohemia—but also Poland—providing a series of remarkable examples.

Simultaneously with Fleischer's Neo-Gothic synagogues, other Viennese members of the historicist school were taking advantage of the potential of the Neo-Renaissance style as an instrument for integration. Karl König, a famous architect who had carried off the Town Hall competition and a practitioner of Viennese Neo-Baroque, was responsible for the Renaissance-style Turnergasse Synagogue; his most striking work of this kind, however, was the synagogue at Liberec (then Reichenberg) in Bohemia in 1889. The impressiveness of this building derives from its position in the city and the visibility of its tower, reminiscent of that of a parish church. In Germany the classical idiom was used in Frankfurt for the famous Börneplatz synagogue (1882).

A further variation on the Renaissance style, with two spires, is to be found at Vinohrady in the suburbs of Prague (1896-98). This is the work of Wilhelm Stiassny, a leading Viennese Jewish designer of synagogues who brings to all the historical styles a freedom and power of imagination drawn from his links with the Secession movement. The most extraordinary of his works is the Jubilee synagogue in Prague, which adopts the orientalist manner. In Vienna, where he was the architect for the Jewish community, he restored the Förster Synagogue and designed, among other buildings, the Rothschild Hospital (1870-75), the Blind Institute and the Polish Synagogue (1893). A committed participant in the life of the community, he was also the founder of the Society for the Preservation of Jewish Art Treasures (1895). It is interesting to compare his point of view with that of Fleischer, as he is a staunch defender of the orientalization of synagogue architecture and uses the approach in most of his work.

In Poland the Renaissance style was evoked in a slightly different spirit according to whether it was being used in the German-annexed or Russian part of the country. In the old, extremely Germanized Hanseatic city of Gdansk, then called Danzig, it was no accident that the Berlin architects Ende and Böckmann chose to build their enormous synagogue in a 'Baltic' version of German Renaissance (1887); in doing so they Germanized the Jewish community while at the same time matching the building to the city's other public monuments, which were in the same style. By contrast, the principal synagogues in Warsaw, on Tlomacka Street (1878, Leandro Marconi), Czestochowa and Lodz, on Spacerowa Street, were much more Italian in style, doubtless because the Polish Renaissance, coinciding with a period of real political influence for the country, had drawn heavily on Italian culture. In the nineteenth century the Baltic countries also created synagogues whose model oscillated between Jesuit-style façades and allusions to the rich Jewish heritage of Vilnius, Kaunas, Jelgava and other cities. The Great Synagogue of Grodno, on the other hand, shows a Baroque tendency.

Neo-Baroque synagogues were a rarity, but one of them—Potsdam—amply illustrates the role played by context in the choice of a meaningful style. In Frederick II's famous city with its profound Rococo influence, Kaiser Wilhelm rejected the Neo-Romanesque project of architect Otto Kerwien in 1899, imposing instead the Neo-Baroque style. Completed in 1903, the synagogue

Gruss aus Reichenberg. *Synagoge.*

Liberec (formerly Reichenberg),
Czech Republic, *View of the synagogue*
(1889, architect Karl König).
Postcard, private collection. This aerial
view shows how a monumental
Neo-Renaissance synagogue
was ultimately incorporated into
the town plan in the same way
as a parish church. As it happens,
the building resembles
the Holy Trinity Church in Paris.

Warsaw, *Synagogue on Tlomacka Street*
(1878, architect Leandro Marconi).

was a veritable Neo-Baroque lexicon: tripartite façade divided by pilasters with a slightly convex central part, cornice balustrades and flattened bull's eye. Inside, a semi-circular choir behind a curvilinear railing housed the Holy Ark, above which were an organ surrounded with Rococo openwork and a rayonnant aureole with, at its centre, the Tables of the Law. The outcome of a princely whim, this unique building is proof of the extreme flexibility of the synagogue, capable as it was of aping the Asam Brothers' St John Nepomucene in Munich.

Magyarization and the Hungarian style

With the advent of various versions of Art Nouveau, the Jugendstil and Secession, the close of the century brought a break with the language of the historic styles, but not, however, the end of the nationalist approaches, which in certain countries actually intensified. Armed with a new-found freedom and intricate interpretations, artists of many nationalities were working at inventing new creative languages drawing at once on the origins of national identity and the wellsprings of modernity. A hotbed of Slav, Hungarian and Zionist identitarian movements, Central Europe was the architectural crucible, especially between Vienna, with Otto Wagner and his students drawn from the four corners of the Empire, and Budapest, with Ödön Lechner. Their experiments were to influence the synagogue in two distinct ways: introduction of the language of the Secession movement or the invention of a specific, national affiliation-led vocabulary. The most fertile of the movements arose in Hungary, where Magyarization of the Jews accompanied nationalist challenges to Vienna and even, in a Hungary then stretching from the Adriatic to the Carpathians, a certain expansionism. Literature and art became the expression of aspirations that could not always be formulated in political terms, even if, for example, the ideological content of the celebration of the Millennium of the arrival of the Magyars in 896 was obvious to all. Ödön Lechner's goal was a new Hungarian architecture which, while drawing inspiration from the Hungarian Renaissance and the sources of popular art, would become a branch of European Art Nouveau.

Lechner himself built no synagogues, but a number of his students applied his principles and specifically Hungarian aesthetics to the field between 1898 and 1930. Notable among them was Lipót Baumhorn, whose twenty-four synagogues on the Hungarian territory of the time[22] make him Europe's most prolific architect in the domain. It is significant that this record should be held by a Hungarian. Lechner's other students who worked with Jewish communities were Béla Lajta, who like Baumhorn actually was Jewish, and the associates Marcell Komor and Deszö Jakab.

In 1888, Baumhorn had built an orientalist synagogue showing enormous brio in the interplay of its polychrome materials and Moorish motifs. Ten years later, however, he made a stylistic about-face in favour of the aesthetics advocated by Lechner, establishing with the synagogue at Szolnok the approach he was to pursue until the 1930s.

Die neue Synagoge in Danzig.

Gdansk (formerly Dantzig), Poland, *Synagogue*, (1887, architects Ende and Böckmann). Old photograph. Paris, Musée d'art et d'histoire du judaïsme.

Following page:
Szolnok, Hungary, *Synagogue* (1899, architect Lipót Baumhorn).

He had already used a Greek cross plan with a central cupola which, depending on the needs and financial means of the community, could be extended with annexes and towers or with secondary cupolas around the main one. The synagogue at Szolnok, however, was even more eclectic, with a dome that, while reminiscent of that of the Museum of Applied Arts Lechner had given Budapest in 1891-96, also suggested domes created by Oppler. The moldings had acquired finely ribbed motifs, but remained quite orientalist. As for its central plan, Baumhorn may have taken some of the ideas from the remarkable model created up by architect Károly Benkó at Gyór in 1860, a building whose handsomely octagonal, orientalist interior may also have inspired Otto Wagner in Budapest (1872).

The high point of Baumhorn's art was the Szeged Synagogue. In winning the competition, restricted to Hungarian architects, he bested Komor and Jakab although their efforts were not in vain, the project being used in Subotica in 1901. The Szeged community was a substantial one and its Rabbi, Immanuel Löw, became involved in the design process, suggesting the inclusion of certain decorative features, notably the stained glass windows. The actual plan is that of Szolnok augmented with large doors and angle turrets. Here the sheer sumptuousness of the decoration reached the astonishing proportions that recent restoration has highlighted anew. Outside, every one of the curved openings is accented with gables and white ribbing that recurs in the backing of the bays and on the flattened domes with their turrets and pinnacles. This distinctively shaped ribbing is one of the characteristics of Lechner's work. Inside, the vaults are also ribbed in the Neo-Gothic manner and covered with paintings and stucco work in the blue, white and gilt repeated in the stained glass. Covering the entire breadth of the apse, the Holy Ark is an excuse for a proliferation of arches, candelabra and pediments, with each section given symbolic value by inscriptions in Hebrew and Hungarian. Polychromy, tracery and scalloped blind arcades add an orientalist touch, yet there is no clash with Magyarization in that nationalist Hungarian architects also used these motifs to hark back to the Asiatic origin of their people.

After the completion of the Szeged Synagogue in 1903, Baumhorn was called to Cegléd (1905), where the moldings are obviously less elaborate, although he continued to work in the polychrome mode. His later work at Kaposvár (1906) and Makó (1914) is in the same spirit. He also worked on more modest synagogues in Budapest itself, in Aréna Street (1908), Csáky Street (1927) and Bethlen Square (1931), collaborating for the last-mentioned with György Somogy, his son-in-law. During the 1920s he built synagogues like that at Nyíregyháza (1924-32), in which he re-uses the central plan but—doubtless influenced by modernist theory—abandons decorative overstatement in favour of greater formal simplicity. The remarkable handling of the volumes of the Gyöngyös Synagogue (1929-31) shows Baumhorn turning towards a kind of Neo-Byzantine then in vogue throughout the Jewish world.

Baumhorn worked all over the Hungary of the time. In 1899 in Transylvania, now part of Romania, he built the Fabrique Synagogue in Timisoara, a brick and stone replica of the Szolnok synagogue and among the most magnificent in the country[23]. The Brasov Synagogue (1898) is of the same type but on a more modest scale. In Slovakia he built two Reform Synagogues—also considered among the country's most impressive[24]—at Nitra (1911) and Lucenec (1925): both use the same plan and volumes, yet the building at Nitra is more ornate and features two of the little angle domes found at Szeged. He also took part there in the competition for Zilina in 1928, which saw his now rather fusty notions doing battle with those of Josef Hoffmann and Peter Behrens, the eventual winner. In Yugoslavia Baumhorn designed synagogues for Zrenjanin in 1895 and Novi Sad—then called Ujvidék or Neusatz—in 1906-09. The latter follows the central-dome, angle-turrets-for-the-façade model with pillars supporting the pendentives inside and a choir with a balustrade housing a large Holy Ark, as is customary in Reform temples. Baumhorn's work took him to the gates of Italy, to Fiume—now Rijeka in Croatia—where he built a Szeged synagogue in miniature.

With the Szeged Synagogue Baumhorn had given Lechner's Hungarian style one of its masterpieces, but when faced with financial constraints he was quick to come up with a more unadorned personal language. Other students of Lechner's contributed to the Magyarization of Jewish communities, even outside Hungary as we now know it. Komor and Jakab built the synagogue in Subotica in 1901-03: working from a plan closely resembling those of Baumhorn, they produced a result—curved gables, decorative friezes accenting the openings and volume articulations, onion domes, folklore-derived decorative motifs—more influenced by the Lechner approach. These two architects brought the same aesthetics to bear on the Subotica city hall in 1907. It should be pointed out that while a distinctly Hungarian style was developing here, it was doing so in parallel with a German movement using curved gables and a central plan marked by a dome. Using this style, Eduard Fürstenau built the synagogues in Dortmund (1900)

Szeged, Hungary, *Synagogue,*
old postcard.

Subotica, Yougoslavie, *Synagogue*
(1901-1903, architects Jakab et Komor).

Szeged, Hungary, *The dome
of the synagogue*
(1903, architect Lipót Baumhorn).

and, especially, Bielefeld (1905), following at the same time a trend related to the German Renaissance as already noted in Gdansk.

In Hungary, Komor and Jakab worked in Budapest and in Marcali, where they built in 1906 a synagogue notable for its combination of a square plan and curved forms. Nor were they the only ones to work thus in Hungary, the Hungarian style still being used by Gyula Müller in Hódmezövásárhely (1906), by Schönteil in Budapest-Köbánya (1907-10) and by József Doborszky in Kunszentmárton (1912). It could even be said that the Baumhorn style was imitated by József Stern in Zalaegerszeg (1903), and perhaps also by Olschläger and Boskó, designers of the Orthodox synagogue at Kosice (1927) in Slovakia.

Béla Lajta was led to pare down the language of his master by his contact with functionalist models and the brick-based architecture of the north, gradually moving towards the modernism he would apply to the Budapest community's charitable and educational establishments. The Blind Institute (1905-08) was one example, but there were also the private chapels and the Abony Street boys' school (1923). Nonetheless his early works retain a taste for decoration drawn from popular sources.

Thus the national styles, whether revivals or innovations, played a fundamental role in the integration of Jews into nineteenth-century society. Their use, however, depended on a perception of Judaism as essentially a faith, with the synagogue an active participant in the process of national affiliation of the various communities. On the other hand—as much for certain Jews consciously concerned with saving their identity from assimilation as in the imaginary of non-Jews incapable of dissociating Judaism from the palm trees of the Mystic East—another vision was emerging: a racial vision of Judaism, the race being one some would see as irremediably 'other' and even hostile. Initially this strangeness, or extraneousness, took shape innocuously enough in symbolic terms, via the Temple of Solomon and its inevitability as a reference for anyone seeking a specifically Jewish architecture. Then, as the period's changed anthropological structures received the scientific seal of approval, this differentiation was exacerbated by a process of Semitization, a tendency to accord everything Jewish an Oriental, racial connotation that was doubtless fascinating at the start but which rapidly veered into the discriminatory.

Orientalism: from Temple to Semitism

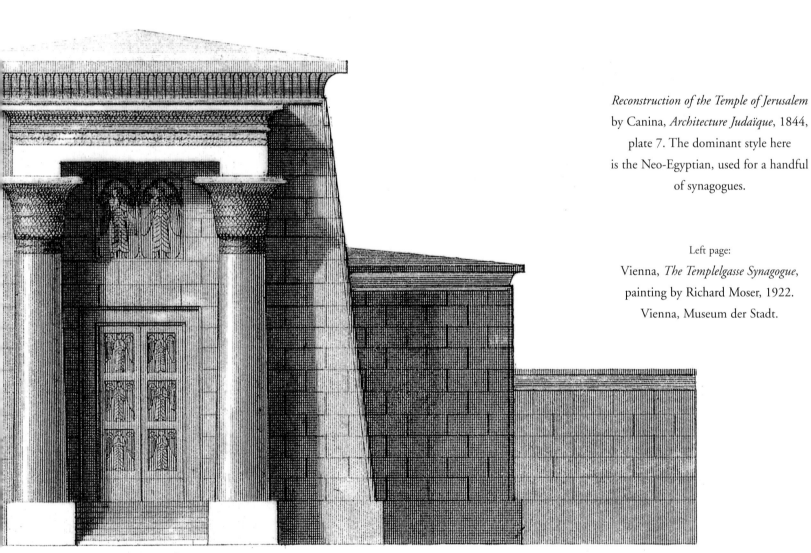

LEVAZIONE DI PROSPETTO

Reconstruction of the Temple of Jerusalem by Canina, *Architecture Judaïque*, 1844, plate 7. The dominant style here is the Neo-Egyptian, used for a handful of synagogues.

Left page:
Vienna, *The Templelgasse Synagogue*, painting by Richard Moser, 1922. Vienna, Museum der Stadt.

Kaiserslautern, Germany, *Synagogue*
(1886, architect Ludwig Levy).
Elevation published
in *Architektonische Rundschau*, 1891.

SYNAGOGE IN DORTMUND.

Dortmund, Germany,
Project for a synagogue (not built),
1895 competition, drawing by
architect Constantin Uhde.
Braunschweigisches Landesmuseum.
An evocation of Moorish Spain.

Once the process of Jewish emancipation was under way, the notion took shape that the synagogue should be not only a functional space but also, in terms of the historicist logic then governing architecture, an expression of Israelite identity. There were two ways of pointing up this coupling, the first being the evocation of Jewish history's one and only architectural monument— the Temple in Jerusalem—and the other the orientalization of the synagogue so as to spotlight the history of the Jews themselves. With its invention of Semitism, early nineteenth-century anthropology constructed a new vision of Jews and the Orient, a vision reinforcing the contrast between East and West and, especially, between a Christian Europe perceiving itself as Aryan on the one hand and the Jewish-Muslim world on the other. Thus Semitism justified recourse by the synagogue to the borrowing of Arabic motifs. This moment in Jewish history, in the same way as what, in the light of the rediscovery of the *Mudejar* synagogues in Toledo, was coming to be seen as the golden age of Hispano-Moorish Judaism, began to

nourish an orientalist imaginary. This was the case both among non-Jews, for whom it represented further justification of the notion of Jewish difference, and among Jews themselves, occupied as they were with forging a national identity that would soon find expression in the Zionist ideal. Assertion of Jewish orientalism has never been more clearly expressed than by the philosopher Martin Buber in a lecture given in 1912[1]: 'For the Jew has remained Oriental. Driven out of his country and dispersed throughout all the countries of the West, he has had no choice but to live under foreign skies, on ground he had never tilled. He has lived a veritable martyrdom, and worse still, a life of degradation. He has been influenced by the nations among whom he has lived and has spoken their languages. And in spite of all of this, he has remained Oriental.' Buber concludes with a summons to take root in the land of birth: 'It is on this manifest or latent orientalism, on this very foundation of a Jewish soul that has survived in the face of all these influences, that I base my faith in a renewal of spiritual and religious

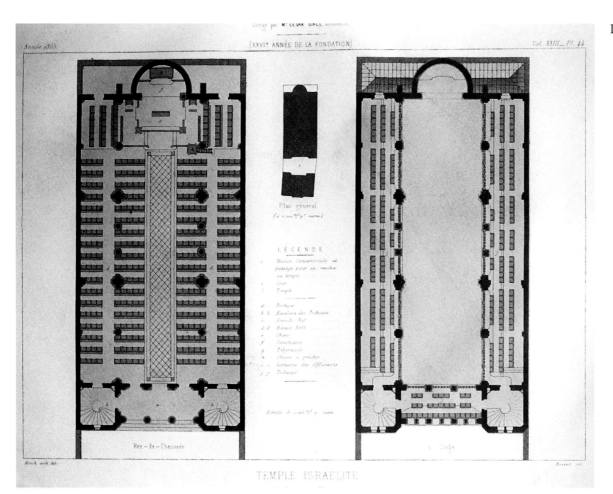

Lyon, France, *Israelite* Temple, plans by Abraham Hirsch, published in the *Revue Générale de l'Architecture,* 1865.

creativity within Judaism.' Thus through a somewhat troubling convergence of the Zionist ideal and a more or less conscious anti-Semitism, synagogue architecture, as the product of these 'influences' and in addition to the experiments already described in this book, testifies to another level of orientalism. This could be seen as a form of Semitization, that is to say a quest for a Jewish character that is not merely symbolic but which embodies historical references experts and architects discover in the Semitic world as explored by Ernest Renan and Max Müller. It is readily understandable that Jewish architects themselves were divided as to the use of Oriental references. Most of them, as we have seen in the preceding chapter, advocated integration via national styles; some dreamed of contributing to the shaping of a stronger Jewish identity, but all of them quickly came to understand that orientalism was fraught with dangerous racial implications.

The Temple of Solomon or the impossible model

References to the Temple of Jerusalem have always been part of the synagogue and Jewish art, functioning in symbolic terms via direct representation or allusive motifs. Thus ceremonial objects such as the *tass* and the spice containers, like the murals in Eastern European synagogues, provide actual images of Jerusalem and the Temple, with the emphasis in the nineteenth century becoming architectural when not frankly archaeological. Thus the use of the Neo-Egyptian style, almost exclusively limited to the period 1800-1840—the years of emancipation—can be explained, over and above such external contributing factors as freemasonry, by the fact that the Temple of Solomon could only be imagined in terms of the Egyptian temple model[2]. Moreover Neo-Egyptian, seen as a step towards Greek Classicism, served as a transition between abandonment of the Greek temple model common to all religions and adoption of other, more markedly Oriental models. It is revealing that in some cases Egyptian motifs were the only ones to be used as decoration within globally Classical compositions. An example is the synagogue whose building in Bordeaux in 1809-12 opened the

Rome, *Ceiling
of the synagogue (1904).*
Opting for an Assyrian-
Babylonian approach
suggestive of the Temple
of Solomon, the architects
based the ornamentation
on the notion of a palm-filled
Paradise. It is possible that
the paintings on the cupola
adapt the multicolored wings
of cherubim—known to have
been of Assyrian origin—
or of the *Checkhina*, a divine
manifestation said by the Sages
to possess protective wings.

period of emancipation in France, after the creation of the Consistories by Napoleon I. In his correspondence the architect, Arnauld Corcelles, expressly indicates his concern to introduce 'ancient Egyptian' ornamentation.

With the coming of emancipation the Temple took on a new role in Jewish culture. For centuries it had been represented[3] in any number of architectural styles and shapes, including Gothic in the fourteenth century, circular during the Renaissance and as being inspired by the Dome of the Rock. What counted above all was its spiritual and messianic significance, its value as a symbol of exile; and if its measurements were an ongoing preoccupation—as in the Talmudic treatise *Middot*—the intention was solely to aid interpretation, not to suggest some precise reconstruction. The positivist influence of nineteenth-century archaeology having made the Temple a historical monument, communities for whom the notion of a concrete return to Zion had been supplanted by emancipation as the equivalent of the flight out of Egypt, strove to restore its architectural veracity; and given the lack of Jewish monuments they borrowed the necessary elements firstly from Egypt and then from Phoenicia or Assyria. The Temple was no longer so much Judaism's one and only holy place as a testimony to a glorious historical moment:

in other words it had been secularised. The sacredness of the Temple was then transferred to the synagogue[4], with radical architectural consequences: thenceforth described as a 'temple', the synagogue was categorized as another 'sacred' building along with the church and the mosque. Furthermore, this trend was to become part of the move towards Reform and the famous Reform synagogue at Seesen, created by Israel Jacobson in 1810, was specifically an "Israelite temple". There can be no doubt that in the minds of the architects—non-Jews for the most part—the synagogue was a harking-back to the 'majesty of the Temple of Solomon', as Henri Labrouste put it in his disappointed commentary on Jean-Alexandre Thierry's project for the rebuilding of the synagogue in Paris' Rue Notre-Dame de Nazareth in 1851.

Lacking a trustworthy stylistic model, many architects continued, as in the preceding centuries, to make their synagogues part of the symbolic lineage of the Temple by using two Jachin-Boaz columns or two pylons on the façade. These arrangements favoured the inclusion of towers, until then rejected by Judaism as being without ritual significance. This was the ploy adopted by Ludwig Förster, architect of synagogues in Vienna and Budapest, and the justification for a proliferation of minarets.

The connection could also be established via the ground plan itself. In spite of the conflict between the plan of the Temple—tripartite and based on a mounting degree of sacredness culminating in the Holy of Holies—and that of a synagogue centred on the *bimah* to which all the faithful had access, some architects strove to establish a correspondence between the two by juggling with courtyards, annexes and even naves. Friedrich Weinbrenner's synagogue in Karlsruhe (1798), for instance, is a clear example of a succession of spaces—peristyle, worship area, sanctuary—inspired by the layout of the Temple. In some cases architects put their theories on paper, among them Ludwig Förster, who explained the tripartite character of his plan for the Vienna synagogue[5] as reflecting the Temple model. In 1865 Abraham Hirsch was to present his synagogue in Lyon in practically the same terms[6]: 'In respect of maintaining the link with tradition this temple, like that of Solomon, takes the form of a rectangle preceded, in the West, by a porch and a courtyard or forecourt. It is divided into three naves, the middle one of which recalls the *Holy*, with the sanctuary or *Holy of Holies* at its eastern end. The lateral naves and the galleries occupy the place of the chambers built against the side walls of the Temple of Jerusalem.'

Opened in 1833, the Copenhagen Synagogue[7] is an excellent example of a monumental building coming to supplant the earlier private chapels in apartment blocks. To celebrate this relinquishing of anonymity, Gustav Friedrich Hetsch drew on a mixture of Classicism and Egyptian references within a scheme—façade with pylon, interior pillars with palm-leaf capitals—apparently inspired by the Temple.

The ultimate factor in favour of the Temple model was the impact of Masonic culture on both the political and architectural scenes during the emancipation period[8]. The Neo-Egyptian style so dear to the Freemasons became an unequivocal symbol of emancipation, the Bordeaux architect Corcelles describing himself as a 'modern Hiram'; there was no doubt, in his opinion, that he was building a new Temple. However, the most famous examples are found in the United States and Australia, scenes of a veritable 'Egyptian revival'[9]; but in its use of distinctive capitals, painted pylons and even hieroglyphs and symbols, the movement lacked the discretion found in Karlsruhe and Bordeaux. The series began in 1824 with the Mikveh Israel in Philadelphia, designed by the renowned William Strickland: the columns supporting the dome were intended to suggest the Egyptian temple at Denderah, in a style that would be taken further in the Crown Street Synagogue (1849)

in the same city, with its hefty, lotus-capital columns flanking the main door. The Masonic influence is clearest in Australia[10], where all the early synagogues are in this style and where in Sydney in 1842, James Hume included a pylon and pyramidions. While links with Freemasonry in that city remain a matter of conjecture, in the case of the Hobart synagogue in Tasmania (1845), with lotus-capital columns either side of its main door, it is known that the architect John Alexander Thomson was a lodge member; and in Launceston (1846) the first stone of a synagogue notable for its pylon was laid in the presence of members of the Lodge of St John in full ritual regalia, with a band playing Masonic airs! In 1850 it was Adelaide's turn to inaugurate a synagogue with flared openings, the design being that of William Weir. Brought to Australia by the British army, itself there to control the convict population, the Masonic lodges played a key role in the shaping of the new country and the social integration not only of convicts who had served their sentences but also of Jews. A shared fraternal ideal and a common culture based on the Temple of Solomon may have favoured use of the Neo-Egyptian style and a similar interpretation may be valid for other countries as well: in Bayonne, in France, the plan for the reconstruction of the Saint-Esprit Synagogue in 1837 was defended in openly Masonic terms. Most of the members of the building committee belonged to the Parfaite Réunion Lodge, as did the mayor and, doubtless, the architect Capdeville; since the eighteenth century the lodges had provided Bayonne Jews with a means of entering local society and acceding to positions of responsibility.

Neo-Egyptian remained widely popular from the 1820s through the 1840s. In Munich (1825, J. B. Metivier) and for the renovation of the synagogue in Hamburg-Altona (c. 1832) palm-leaf capitals were used, while in Strasbourg, where a former church was reworked by Auguste Fries (1834), the Holy Ark was surrounded by columns and pillars supporting a palmette-decorated architrave. In Canterbury (1848) the small synagogue designed by Hezekiah Marshall has lotus-shaped capitals and an Egyptian-temple feel to it. By contrast, in Kassel (1833) the relatively free Neo-Egyptian interpretation proposed by Bromeis—like the more orientalist plan put up by Ruhl—was rejected in favour of a Neo-Romanesque proposal from Schuchardt and Rosengarten. After all, was not Egypt also the land of slavery? A similar conflict arose in 1847 in Metz, where the community had asked county architect Nicolas Derobe for an edifice in the 'Oriental style'. Declaring himself incapable of producing a design 'Hebrew in character', he proposed an 'Egyptian' alterna-

Verdun, France, *The pillars
of the synagogue doorway*
(1875, architect Mazilier).
There is an allusion
to the Temple in the form
of the two Hebrew inscriptions
on the capitals.

tive; however, this turned out to be a mix of genuinely Egyptian decorative motifs and such other elements, borrowed mainly from the Arabic tradition, as horseshoe arches and knotwork. The upshot was that a local commission turned down what it saw as excessive exoticism and imposed a Neo-Romanesque approach. So although the arrangement continued to show the influence of the Temple, the Metz Synagogue represents a style then regarded as more appropriate to its religious function and as a gesture of recognition towards the nation's history.

While Neo-Egyptian allusions tended to fade after the 1840s, references to the Temple continued, often in conjunction with use of Moorish moldings. An extreme case is Mazilier's Verdun Synagogue (1875), which follows an arrangement described by its creator as 'Arabic' and including horseshoe arches, merlons and colour work. In his estimate Mazilier overtly resorts to the vocabulary of the Temple: the apse is occupied by a raised space described as a 'holy place or *Hechal*' and a Holy Ark that is the 'Holy of Holies or *Debir*', wood panelling being employed throughout. The façade has an antechurch perhaps meant as reminiscent of the Dome of the Rock and whose capitals bear the Hebrew inscriptions *Jachin* and *Boaz* in an unequivocal reference to the Temple of Jerusalem.

The versions of the Temple of Solomon produced during the first half of the nineteenth century were inevitably Neo-Egyptian, but fresh archaeological discoveries in the East were to generate new hypotheses and building approaches. Ferguson[11] thus established a link with India, while Perrot and Chipiez[12] looked towards Assyria. A synagogue that testifies unambiguously to this shift is that of Rome, where demolition of the ghetto meant replacing its private chapels. In the competition for a synagogue in 1889, the proposals oscillated between the Moorish style and borrowings from the ancient East, both approaches being intended to symbolize the Jews' new-found status in the capital of the Kingdom of Italy. Architects Costa and Armanni set about incorporating a host of Biblical geographical allusions they then reinforced with 'archaeological' motifs, ultimately emerging victorious with a project mingling Assyrian, Egyptian and Moorish references. The actual construction process, delayed until 1901-1904, saw increased emphasis on the Assyrian-Babylonian aspect of the ornamentation, as on the capitals in the loggia, whose motifs recurred on the interior pilasters. The paintings, especially on the inside of the metal dome, provide an image of paradise in the form of symbols and the flora of Mesopotamia. This central-plan synagogue is topped with a square dome whose height nearly brought

fatal retribution under Fascism, when it was seen as 'clashing' with the landscape on the banks of the Tiber. The exoticism of the building was complemented by the planting of palms in the surrounding garden.

The quest for a Semitic architecture

As with Neo-Egyptian, it was in the 1830s that the first signs of a more assertive orientalism appeared in the form of recourse to Arabic or Moorish motifs; however its development, in parallel with that of Semitism in anthropology, was to continue for the rest of the century. A similar spirit now informed research in linguistics, anthropology and archaeology and it was not uncommon to find Oriental references in conjunction with reminders of the Temple. Ludwig Förster, for instance, expressly evokes the columns of the Temple and minarets in his explanations of his use of towers on the façades of his synagogues in Vienna and Budapest, buildings that were to play a major role in the spread of the style. Yet here no archaeological influence dictates the choice of forms, for what we are witnessing is rather a shift tied to the ethnological categories of the time: the Jews had no architecture of their own, but their Semitic cousins the Arabs did; and not only was this heritage a remarkable one, it was also unambiguously different from that of Christians and the West in general. Chosen in the first instance as a reminder of the Oriental origins of the Jews and a sign of Jewish identity, orientalism—just as certain Jewish architects had sensed at the outset—soon fell victim to the same ambivalence as the actual role of the synagogue itself. And so, with the unleashing of anti-Semitism in Western Europe during the 1890s, the Neo-Moorish style faded from view. 1893 saw the rise of the last orientalist wave, from Antwerp (Bouwmeesterstraat, E. Stordiau) to St Petersburg (I. Chapochnikov and L. Bachman) and including Pforzheim (L. Levy) and Bratislava (Dezsö Milch's new-look synagogue).

The widespread success of orientalism in synagogue architecture is only surprising if we forget the perceived relationship between Arabs and Jews: in the absence of Jewish models, Arabic or Moorish architecture could fill the gap. Of course this orientalist view of Judaism has more to do with Western fantasy than historical reality, as one critic has ably shown in her examination of the portrait of a great Jewish lady[13]; and as long as it did not become a basis for segregation, certain Jews were ready to subscribe to this imaginary, to accept this Semitization.

Like the Jewish woman, that supreme target of Western orientalist fantasizing via the inevitable combining of jewelry and rich colours, of sensuality and languor, the synagogue decked itself with all the colours of the East, with decors whose complexity and refinement were designed to stimulate the interplay of light and shade. There exists a secret relationship between Walter Scott's Rebecca (*Ivanhoe*, 1819) and the profusion of Alhambra-style colonnettes, stucco lacework and vividly coloured decoration in the synagogues in Dresden, Besançon and Florence. In such a context the metaphor employed by Oscar Mothes in his *Building Dictionary*[14] hardly surprises: 'Moorish architecture is the bride of Gothic.' Recounting the inauguration of the Neo-Romanesque synagogue in the Rue de la Victoire in Paris, a journalist from *Le Gaulois*[15] still cannot resist the temptation of the Orient in his portrait of the ladies taking up the collection: 'It is in the features of these young, beautiful Jewesses that the Chief Rabbi could observe the faithful transmission of the proud line of the daughters of Israel. Not a single one of these visages is less regular than the others. Here one finds the same purity of contour, the same dark eyes, the same Oriental nose…'

Breaking with the monochromatic austerity of its Western equivalent, be it in a Greek or a Gothic vein, synagogue architecture—now become an odalisque, or a bride taken directly from the Song of Songs—introduced a polychromy that was never really accepted in spite of the campaigns of Hittorff and Semper, a plethora of architectural motifs which rationalist observers and the general public alike saw as the purest kitsch. Thus we can sympathize with the misgivings of certain Jews regarding an assimilation that called for a stylistic choice between a place of worship and show-business glitter.

This new approach to the synagogue had two major stylistic sources: Egypt as described by Pascal Coste in his *Architecture arabe ou Monuments du Caire, mesurés et dessinés de 1818 à 1826*, published in 1837 and the Moorish Spain whose most famous monument was the Alhambra in Granada as publicized by Girault de Prangey (*Choix d'ornements mauresques de l'Alhambra*, 1837; *Monuments arabes et moresques de Cordoue, Séville et Grenade*, 1841) and Owen Jones (*Plans, Elevations, Sections and Details of the Alhambra*, 1842-1845). These were not the first works to appear on the subject, but their success coincided with synagogue architects' infatuation with the Orient. As for the model established by the Hispano-Moorish synagogues of Toledo—the Cordoba synagogue was only rediscovered in 1884—these latter had substantially less architectural influence than direct evocations of the Alhambra in Granada or the Alcazar in Seville.

Germany under the Moorish spell

In Germany the movement was launched by highly reputed architects. The first synagogue to be given a façade with horseshoe arches and colonnettes with cushion capitals was designed for Ingenheim in 1832 by Friedrich von Gärtner, who also built the Ludwigskirche in his native Munich. It was no coincidence that use of these Moorish features should be pioneered by architects working or trained in Munich, a city that, under the historicist influence of Ludwig I of Bavaria and his architect Leo von Klenze, had become a veritable encyclopaedia of architectural styles. Ingenheim was in the Palatinate, a dependency of Bavaria, as were the synagogues built by August von Voit, a pupil of Gärtner's, in Kirchheimbolanden (1835) and Speyer (1837). The fashion then spread to other parts of the country. Among the major architects experimenting with the Moorish style was Gottfried Semper, who had succeeded in reconciling, as already noted, a Romanesque exterior and an orientalist interior. The Moorish style made itself abundantly felt all over Germany, not only in towns like Heidenheim (1853, Eduard Burklein) and Landsberg (1853, Hähnel), but also in such large cities as Mainz (1853, Ignaz Opfermann). In 1855 in Leipzig Otto Simonson, a Jewish pupil of Semper's, proposed an entirely Moorish design characterized by horseshoe, multifoil and blind arches. Here again, in the published version of the project, reference is made to the Temple of Solomon in respect of the overall arrangement. Simonson saw it as appropriate to express the notion of Jewishness via recourse to the Moorish style, since every facet of Judaism was reminiscent of the Orient; thus he was able to draw his decorative elements from both Spain and the mosques of Cairo. Gustav Breyman, whose project was posthumously completed by his pupil, Adolf Wolff, had been commissioned to design the Stuttgart synagogue in 1858: here the emphasis was on the Moorish, Breyman adopting merlons for the street façade—the eastern end, with the projection of the Holy Ark—and covering the building with cupolas. The doors are borrowed from the Courtyard of the Lions in Granada. The interior had its own splendidly Oriental look, with its cupolas, and its arches decorated with stucco and knotwork. For the Holy Ark he chose a cupola-shaped canopy, an idea also used in the new Berlin synagogue on the Oranienburgerstrasse.

Ernst Zwirner, the architect charged with completing Cologne cathedral—ultimate symbol of the German national dream and celebration of the Gothic style as a supremely Christian, Germanic art form—also won the

Berlin, *Oranienburgerstrasse Synagogue*
(1859-1866, architects Knoblauch and
Stüler).

Köln, *Interior of the Glockengasse
Synagogue* (1861, architect Ernst
Zwirner), Chromolithograph by
Y. Hoegg after the watercolor by Conrad.
Köln, Kölnisches Stadtmuseum.

commission for the Berlin Synagogue. In 1861, in striking contrast with his vision of the ideal cathedral, he produced a building modelled on the Vienna Synagogue, to which he added a lofty cupola.

With its generous proportions and frank assertion of identity, the Berlin synagogue was the supreme triumph of the orientalist approach. Its ribbed onion dome rises some fifty meters above the vestibule and its worship area, 57 meters deep, has room for 1,800 men on the ground floor and 1,200 women in the galleries. Apart from the blue, red and gilt decoration covering the entire structure, its Oriental character is principally established by the metal cladding of the corbelled trusses set on enormous cantilever beams, and its cupolas with roundels. The apse, embellished with blind arches worthy of the Alhambra, houses a miniature temple with an openwork cupola. The architect, Eduard Knoblauch, died in 1865 and the project was completed by Stüler for its inauguration in 1866. This synagogue was imitated—especially in terms of its cupola, its central plan and the angle turrets this latter implied—in several other buildings in Cologne (1861), Weisbaden (1869, Philipp Hoffmann) and throughout Germany's sphere of influence: from Delme in annexed Lorraine (1881, Otto Saupp), where it is miniaturized, to Cernovcy in the Ukraine (1877), where Julian Zachariewicz's design includes an Indo-Islamic dome, and Basle (1868, H. Gauss, renovated in 1892). Certain architects showed a real predilection for this model, among them Adolf Wolff in Ulm (1873), Nuremberg (1874), Karlsbad (1877) and Heilbronn (1877), and Ludwig Levy in Kaiserslautern (1886) and Pforzheim (1893). All these structures display an eclectic use of Oriental references, especially in respect of their domes, whose models are drawn from Mogul India (the Taj Mahal as reinterpreted by Nash's Brighton Pavilion), Andalusia and Turkey's Seljuk tradition. Is it pure chance that the impact of this sheer monumentality—but also, probably, of the Oriental exoticism of the synagogue in Nuremberg, sanctum of German culture and homeland of Dürer and Hans Sachs—drove the notoriously anti-Semitic Richard Wagner[16] to rage against its 'insolent luxury' and damn it as being 'in the purest Oriental style' when in fact it also presents Neo-Romanesque features? Wagner would later suggest 'banning Jewish holidays…and pretentious synagogues'.

But then the Moorish style was not to the taste of all Jews, either, witness the reaction of a writer in a French magazine after a visit to the newly finished synagogue in Knoblauch[17]: 'One can understand the choice of the generous, grandiose Oriental style for a monument designed to put us in mind of the Temple of Solomon. But why this imitation of Moorish floweriness and the arabesques

Entwurf für das in der Leopoldstadt in Wien zu errichtende israelitische Bethhaus

von Prof. L. Förster, k. k. Architect.
April 1858.

Vienna, *Tempelgasse Synagogue* (1858),
handcolored drawing by the architect,
Ludwig Förster.

of the Alhambra, too often indulged in here?' The message here is that evocation of the Temple can justify orientalism, but not the Moorish style, rejected as artificial and unsuited to the religious function. Nonetheless the association between the Temple and 'Moorish floweriness' was to remain a constant until the 1890s, when the style was abandoned. A competition in Dortmund in 1895 gives a clear idea of contemporary disaffection: of the twelve prize-winning projects, ten were Neo-Romanesque; yet a magnificent Moorish proposal had been made by Constantin Uhde[18], the originality of which lay in its circular plan and its combining of motifs drawn strictly from Hispano-Moorish art. This architect had a predilection for the Moorish style he had discovered on a visit to Spain in 1888. His Braunschweig Synagogue dating from 1874 is largely Neo-Romanesque, even if a few orientalist features have crept in; but the more highly coloured Wolfenbuttel Synagogue (1893) with its Giralda-style towers has a distinctly Oriental tone that becomes more pronounced around the Holy Ark, the apse being covered with arabesques. An interesting point here is that in his presentation of the Dortmund project, Uhde makes specific reference to the *mudejar* style, which appears in the drawings in his *Baudenkmäler in Spanien und Portugal* (1892); but at the time *mudejar* and Moorish were both considered inappropriate.

Ludwig Förster: Oriental models

The driving force behind the success of orientalism in Austria-Hungary was the famous architect Ludwig Förster, who was commissioned to build the synagogues of the Empire's two capitals—the one on Vienna's Tempelgasse (1854) in the Leopoldstadt district with its substantial Jewish population, and the other on Dohány Street in Budapest—each of which became a model in its own right. For the historicist Förster, one of the designers of the monuments on Vienna's Ring and much concerned with the fit between style and function, the synagogue should be identifiable by its mingling of Hebrew elements drawn from the Temple of Solomon and meaningful Oriental references. The result in one instance is the use of towers in the form of minarets, reminiscent of the columns of the Temple. Förster explained his approach in an article in the *Allgemeine Bauzeitung* in 1859, a tactic that gained his work a wide reputation.

The most striking individual feature of the Vienna synagogue is its tripartite façade. The taller central section contains a round-arched doorway and is topped by the Tables of the Law. Each crenellated section is accentuated

The poet Ludwig August Frankl comes to Jerusalem in search of the first stone for the Vienna Synagogue, lithograph. Vienna, Historisches Museum. Author of a famous 'Nach Jerusalem!', Frankl made his visit in March 1856. The lithograph represents a fashionable pre-Zionist association of Orientalism with Jewish identity.

Szczecin, Poland, *Synagogue* (1875). The building is based on the Vienna model.

Budapest, *View of the towers of the synagogue* (1853-58, architect Ludwig Förster).

Bielsko-Biala (formerly Bielitz), Poland, *Synagogue.* The building is based on the Budapest model.

BIELITZ   Kaiser Franz—Josefsstrasse

Aufnahme Photograf. Atelier „Helios". Verlag: B. Loinger, Biala.

by angle turrets bearing little lanterns and decorated with quatrefoils set with roundels. Borrowed from Arabic decoration, these motifs recur inside the building, where the vaults, the rear wall and the Holy Ark are covered with paintings and polychrome stucco work. This façade and certain decorative elements can also be found in Germany at Giessen (1878), in Poland at Szczecin (then Stettin, 1875), in Bohemia at Karlin, near Prague (1861) and in Slovakia at Senica (1864), Vrbové (1883), where the synagogue has just been magnificently restored, nearby Hlohovec (1890) and Precov (1898). In the last-mentioned of these, the architects Kólasek and Wirth embellished the Viennese model with a central tower imitated from Budapest. Förster's influence was also felt in Zagreb in Croatia (1867), in Hungary—Vac (1864, Abis Cacciari), Szekszárd (1897, Johann Pestchnik) and Barcs (1899)—and in Romania in Bucharest (1857-1867, Enderle and Freiwald), Carei (1870) and Cluj (1886). The faithful imitation of the Vienna synagogue in Romania is evidence of the Jewish community's aspiration to the emancipation already granted to their coreligionists in Austria-Hungary, for their situation was extremely precarious and was to remain so well into the twentieth century, some Jews only being granted civil rights in 1921. Begun in 1856, the Bucharest synagogue was almost complete in 1866 when it was sacked by rioters. Some features of the rebuilding of the Altschul synagogue in Prague by Vojtech Ignác Ullmann and Josef Niklas (1868) may be due to Förster's Vienna synagogue, whose Moorish decor had earned it the nickname Spanelska. Förster himself built a synagogue with a tripartite façade in Hungary, at Miskolc in 1861-63, but on this occasion he opted for Neo-Romanesque external moldings, while the interior, with its little cupolas, is more Oriental in flavour.

Förster's design for the Budapest synagogue made it even larger and more sumptuous than that of Vienna, from which he borrowed the curved openings. The nave is 55 meters long and the octagonal towers topped with onion domes are more than 40 meters high. Lack of funds meant the use of relatively light materials, but the painted cupolas, stucco work, woodwork and terracotta, together with the use of blue, red and gilt ensure a warm atmosphere for the vast nave whose apse houses a Holy Ark in the form of a small temple. The pride of Hungarian Jews, this synagogue was imitated in other cities, notably Szombathely (1880) where, in a gesture of stunning disproportion, Ludwig Schöne crowned the Vienna model with the towers from Budapest. Symbols in their own right, these towers were reproduced in Székesfehérvár (1862, Bernardin Commetter) and Békéscsaba (1893,

Lipót Langer) in the context of compositions that were more Neo-Romanesque than orientalist. A few examples were to be found in Romania—the so-called Citadel synagogue in Timisoara (1865) is one of them—and in Poland at Bielsko-Biala, where the towers are pushed to the back of the structure.

The most astonishing of all the imitations, however, is to be found in the heart of New York, on Lexington Avenue. In 1870 the Shaaray Hashomayim congregation, in conjunction with Ahavath Chesed, commissioned Henry Fernbach to design what became known as the Central Synagogue (1872). Attentive to what was going on in the field in Europe, Fernbach designed a replica of the Budapest synagogue; but while the façade is an exact reproduction of the original, the interior is more sober, the triumphal arch giving onto the choir is pointed and the gallery arches are horseshoe-shaped. Onion domes were to become a common feature of American synagogues, even in such Neo-Gothic compositions as Emanu-El in San Francisco (1866, W. Patton) and Beth Israel in Portland (1887).

Budapest became home to a host of synagogues, one of which—the Orthodox synagogue on Rumbach Street—was very much a continuation of Förster's work. Its architect, Otto Wagner, was to become a master of the Secession approach. This is a youthful work of a type Wagner did not include in albums devoted to his work, doubtless because he felt it to be insufficiently modern and too imbued with a traditional stylistic language. Having just joined Förster's agency, he reused the latter's tripartite façade and angle turrets, adding the three doors of the Berlin-style synagogue in Knoblauch. The interior, on the other hand, is much more original in its use of an octagonal plan perhaps derived from the Dome of the Rock and decorated in the Alhambra manner. However, it is possible that a Hungarian model was used, that of the synagogue of Györ (1866, Károly Benkó), with its handsomely orientalist octagonal volume.

New York, *Central Synagogue*
(1872, architect Henry Fernbach).
One of Manhattan's
finest synagogues,
it imitates that of Budapest.

Florence, *Exterior view of the synagogue*
(1882, architects Treves,
Falcini and Micheli).

Orientalism: successes and ambivalences

The Moorish variant of orientalism was thus a force to be reckoned with in Central Europe, but its influence was felt throughout Europe and in the Unites States as well, to an extent that varied according to historical factors and differences of mentality. In Italy, for example, it virtually became the living symbol of emancipation, while in France it found acceptance only in the east of the country, Paris rejecting it as too kitsch. Nor was it uncommon that oriental features be more marked inside than outside the synagogue, the façade remaining the showcase for a community concerned to demonstrate its integration. Yet everywhere the fascination with the East that marked the collective imaginary was so strong that the synagogue seemed to present as a focal point; and the road from fascination to hatred was to be very short indeed.

WESTERN EUROPE

Förster's influence was to extend as far as Italy: very marked in the German-rite synagogue at Vercelli (1874-1878), with its façade ordered by the turrets and serrated cornices of Vienna, in Florence (1874-82) it went no further than re-use of the Budapest towers. In both cases the architects—Locarni in Vercelli and Treves[19], Falcini and Micheli in Florence—had opted, like Otto Wagner, for the triple door and a mode of construction based on alternating courses of stone of different colours; this latter figures in both the Oriental and the Italian tradition, its best-known example being the cathedral in Sienna. Similarly, inside the synagogue, the walls were covered with Moorish knotwork, while the coloured marble-mosaic floor is very Italian. This approach nicely illustrates the search for a compromise between the local roots of people whose status as citizens was in some cases quite recent and the actual assertion of identity. The green dome that rises against the Florence sky may not be a serious rival for Brunelleschi's, but at least it calls attention to a hitherto concealed Jewish presence. As in Turin, the scope of the project was determined by the role as capital the city was briefly to enjoy.

In Italy the Moorish style truly was the symbol of an emancipation won in the Kingdom of Sardinia in 1848 but in Tuscany only in 1859, after the annexation of Sardinia. In the Papal States the ghetto was not done away with until Italian unification was achieved... It is also significant that after Alessandro Antonelli's project had been abandoned, the Turin Synagogue (1880-84)

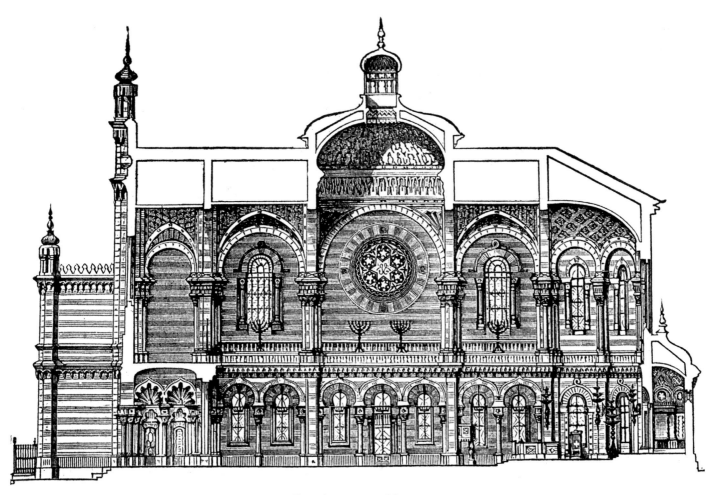

Vercelli, Italy, *Section of the synagogue*
(1878, architect Giuseppe Locarni),
drawing.

was designed by Enrico Petiti in the Moorish style, with horseshoe arches, polychromy, onion domes and so on. The decision to build a synagogue dated from 1859: eager to celebrate its emancipation and to contribute to the beautification of a city now capital of the Kingdom of Italy, the Jewish community held a competition whose results were judged unsatisfactory. It then consulted the engineer Antonelli, who proposed a Renaissance-style project with a metallic structure whose height rapidly got out of control. At ruinous expense he began accumulating story upon story of a synagogue that would have been the tallest building in Turin—the cupola was to be topped with a *Menorah* beginning 90 meters up—if the community had not decided to sell it to the City to be turned into Turin's flagship monument. On completion in 1889, the 'Mole' had passed the 160-meter mark. In the same year Rome's Jewish community, eager to celebrate its emergence from the ghetto, launched its own competition; Attilio Muggia's winning proposal, like sev-

eral of the others, was largely Moorish, in spite of certain Gothic features and an Antonelli-style dome. However, Muggia's project never came to fruition and the Moorish style vanished from Italian synagogues. Rome finally opted for a design evocative of the ancient East.

Although the Moorish style was much used in Western Europe, nowhere did it enjoy the sheer breadth of success that awaited it in Germany. Initially rejected in the French city of Metz in 1847, it was later accepted in Paris for the synagogue in the Rue Notre-Dame de Nazareth (1852, Jean-Alexandre Thierry). There, in a globally Neo-Romanesque setting, a patio, colourful decoration and metal supporting elements created an Oriental note. However, this experience was the source of widespread misgivings and the Moorish style was finally banned from Paris in favour of an extremely discreet Neo-Romanesque. It would seem, also, that this stylistic choice was dictated by the demands of on-site rebuilding with metal pillars. The diffusion of the Moorish style in

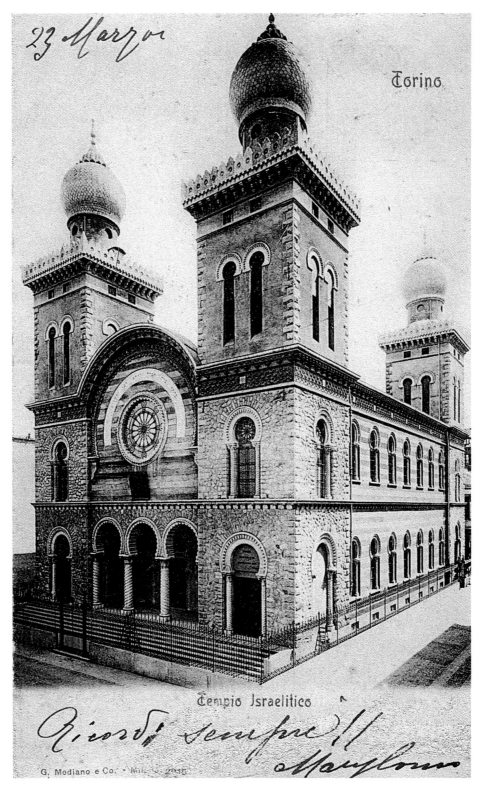

23 Marzo

Torino

Tempio Israelitico

G. Modiano e Co. · Mil...

Turin, *Synagogue*
(1884, architect Enrico Petiti).
Color postcard, c. 1925.

Turin, *Mole Antonelliana* (1862-1889).
Antonelli's project swelled to
such proportions that the Jewish
community ceded the partially built
structure to the City, whose best-known
monument it became.

Besançon, *Interior view*
of the synagogue near the Holy Ark
(1869, architect Pierre Marnotte).

France was perhaps linked to the nearness of Germany, since it was limited to the east of the country, from Besançon (1869, Pierre Marnotte) with its mosque silhouette, to Verdun, already mentioned and Sarreguemines (1862, Charles Desgranges). True, an example is to be found at the gates of Paris, at La Ferté-sous-Jouarre (1891, Edmond Fauvet), but this is in fact a copy of the synagogue at Châlons-en-Champagne (1875, Alexis Vagny). Sometimes a single motif is enough to give a synagogue an Oriental character, an example being the multifoil arch of the door at Toul (1862, Mangeot). The choice made at Besançon is revealing: an initial, highly integrative project had been prepared by Lyon architect Abraham Hirsch for a site in the Old Town; but when a public petition obliged the community to withdraw to the other bank of the Doubs, the new—non-Jewish—architect opted for a deliberately Moorish scheme.

The Bordeaux synagogue is a good example of a widely shared hesitancy as to the choice of style. After the synagogue at Corcelles was destroyed by fire in 1873, the municipal architect Charles Burguet made an interesting proposal using the Romano-Byzantine style successfully introduced into the region by Abadie, future designer of the Sacré-Cœur in Paris. Burguet's successor Charles Durand opted for an eclecticism embellished with hints of the Oriental: a façade with windows that could have come from a mosque in Cairo, an interior with a handful of discreet horseshoe arches, and most notably a metal-frame roofing system suggestive of Berlin but excluding the Alhambra colour scheme. Paradoxically the Jews of Bordeaux, originally from Spain, were disinclined to evoke a past that at the same period was so cherished in Germany. This reserved attitude may be explicable in terms of Judaism's status in France, where it was considered a religious and not an ethnic allegiance—a conception that made it difficult for Zionism to gain a foothold. Moreover all French Jewish architects adopted the integrative Neo-Romanesque and Romano-Byzantine styles, leaving the Moorish free for the fantasizing of their non-Jewish colleagues.

Another factor behind the interest sparked by orientalism in the French context—but one that may also have limited its scope—was the country's colonialist expansion into North Africa. Since 1830 the French in Algeria had been living with Islamic architecture and with the need for a style in harmony with its setting, whether they were building cathedrals or government offices. Nonetheless, many of the synagogues built in small towns at the instigation of the Consistories set up by the French are strikingly European in aspect (Lalla Marnia, Tiaret) and Neo-Romanesque projects went ahead in Constantine

(Temple Algérien) and even in Algiers itself (Belcourt). However the two most monumental synagogues are Moorish: the Great Synagogue in Algiers (1845-1865, Viala du Sorbier), built to a central plan and featuring a dome with stepped merlons; and the Oran Synagogue (1880-1918), the largest in North Africa: its façade is perhaps more indebted to the work of Förster than to the surrounding mosques, but at the same time does not appear at all out of place. The interior, with its imposing arcades, is also European in character, the traditional galleries for women obviously being unknown in the local synagogues.

Belgian Jewry also acquired a remarkable orientalist synagogue in the form of Shomre Hadass in Antwerp (1893, Ernest Stordiau and Joseph Hertogs). Where the synagogue in Liège (1898, Joseph Rémont), with its Oriental two-colour scheme and handful of horseshoe arches, is in fact Romano-Byzantine in the style used in France and Brussels, its equivalent in Antwerp is intentionally Arabic and may even have been largely based on the mosques of Cairo. An early drawing signalled by Jo Braeken[20] went so far as to propose authentic minarets. The decorative motifs are taken from Coste or from *L'Art arabe d'après les monuments du Kaire*, by Prisse d'Avennes (1869-1877). Hertogs' definitive proposal has a column each side of the door in a clear transposition of those in the Temple; the gambit is repeated on the Holy Ark. Other decorative features are *Mudejar*. The Jews of Antwerp thereby opted for pushing differentiation and particularism to the limit, in reaction both to the Belgian context generally and to the attitude of their doubtless more assimilated coreligionists in Brussels.

Switzerland, where Alsatian Jews made a major contribution to the growth of local communities, has several orientalist synagogues, of which the most interesting, in Geneva, may well have influenced the others. Once again the synagogue became a symbol of emancipation, Switzerland being reluctant to grant civil rights to Jews. Emancipation took place gradually during the 1850s and 1860s, but canton by canton and always subject to numerous restrictions. Nonetheless, as soon as civil rights were accorded in Geneva, architect Jean-Henri Bachofen set about raising a remarkable synagogue (1857-58): his central plan earned the praise of Léon Vaudoyer who, correctly, drew the parallel with the synagogue in Algiers, then under construction. Both the structure and the decoration are resolutely Moorish, a style that was also to be used in Basle (1868, H. Gauss), Porrentruy (1874), Saint-Gall (1881) and Zurich (1884, Chiodera and Tschudy).

Oran, *Early view of the synagogue.*
Postcard. Borrowed from European synagogues, this kind of monumentality is uncommon in North Africa, where the faithful usually prayed in (usually private) oratories. As a consequence of the radical change this kind of architecture represented, the Oran Consistory's project, begun in 1880, was not completed until 1918. After the departure of the Jewish community in 1962, it became a mosque.

Edmond and Jules de Goncourt, *Manette Salomon,* (1867)

Edouard Moyse,
Hagbaha (1896), detail.
Musée d'art et d'histoire
du Judaïsme, Paris.

Coriolis, the painter hero, suspects his model Manette of being unfaithful to him; following her through the streets of Paris, he sees her enter a building:

'She disappeared through a doorway hung with the Tricolor, which Coriolis in his haste failed to see. As he plunged in after her, several steps brought him to strange little courtyard, an Oriental *patio* or a kind of cloister as in the Alhambra. Manette was not there.

He felt himself abruptly cast into a nightmare, a hallucination in the very heart of Paris, only a few steps from the boulevard. Descrying further in a door limned with traces of light, he advanced and passed through: there in a shadowy room he discerned a great candlestick around which men wearing hats trimmed with bands of lace chanted over enormous books, their nocturnal voices intoning darkly.

He was in the synagogue of the Rue Notre-Dame de Nazareth.

A feeble light flickered in an open gallery: and the first woman he saw there was Manette.

He sighed with relief. Filled with the joy of a suspicion discarded, his heart light within him, he felt a sudden happiness replace the baneful thought that had fled; and as he let all that was pacified and liberated within him founder into the half-dark, the unflagging murmur of a people at prayer, the elusive, caressing mystery of these half-sounds and half-lights met and crossed and intermingled, seeming to permeate the synagogue with the low tones of a sighingly reverent twilight melody.

His gaze surrendered to the crepuscular dimness descending from above, blue-tinged by the stained glass windows, and he scanned the dying, multicolored shimmering of the sombre, dark-drowned walls, the fire-pink reflections of the candlesticks that glimmered here and there in the gloom, the sudden touches of white that sprang to life on the wool of a *talith.* And he began to lose himself in something resembling a Rembrandt painting come to life and itself quickening the tawny, golden night. He turned again towards the gallery, towards the shapes of the

women whose countenances, under the great splashes of darkness, were no longer those of Parisiennes, but seemed to withdraw deep into the Old Testament. And from time to time, in the muttering of the prayers, he detected the guttural ruggedness of syllables that filled his ear with the sound of distant lands…

Then, little by little, amid the sensations awoken in him by this ceremony and this language neither of which were his own, and by these prayers and chants and faces, by this abode of a foreign people, so far from Paris yet within Paris itself, there arose in Coriolis the consciousness, initially vague and confused, of something that had never before given him pause, something that had until then never existed for him nor been aware of its own existence. This was the first time he had felt this perception of Manette as a Jew, yet he had known her to be Jewish from the very first day.'

Bordeaux, *Interior view of the synagogue*
(1882, architect Charles Durand).
Especially remarkable for its volume
and distinctive, metal-framed roof.

GREAT BRITAIN AND THE UNITED STATES

In Great Britain where assimilation was as high a priority among the Jewish officials at the United Synagogue as it was in France, not a single synagogue was given an authentically Moorish façade, orientalism being restricted for the most part to the interior decoration of mainly Classical or Gothic arrangements. Examples began to appear in the 1870s, Nathan S. Joseph's Central Synagogue (1870) being the most obvious, with its horseshoe arches and knotwork. On the other hand neither the West London Synagogue in Upper Berkeley Street nor the East London Synagogue in Stepney Green (1870 and 1876 respectively, both by Henry D. Davis and Barrow Emanuel) reveals more than a few traces of orientalism in terms of decoration. The former was a Reform synagogue whose statement of intent was a lofty façade topped with an attic and Romanesque blind arches; the latter, designed for the Orthodox community and the only East End synagogue to belong the United Synagogue, used its monumental character as a symbol of anglicisation. The New West End Synagogue in St Petersburg Place, Bayswater (1879, N. S. Joseph and W. and G. Audsley) was intended as an 'Anglo-Jewish cathedral'. Significantly, the basilica plan and two-tower façade are accompanied by decorative features reminiscent of Moorish Spain or the Middle East: of Neo-Romanesque design, the great rose window on the façade is set in a multifoil arch and the door arch is horseshoe-shaped. The interior, and notably the Holy Ark with its cupolas, has a distinctly Oriental feel. All these elements were in fact borrowings from the synagogue the Audsleys had built in Princes Road, Liverpool in 1874: there the Oriental atmosphere is due to the colours used throughout, from the gilt capitals to the vaults and the Holy Ark. In the same year Manchester's Sephardic community established its synagogue at Cheetham Hill: here Edward Solomons who, together with Nathan Joseph, had brought a relative eclecticism to bear on the first Bayswater Synagogue (1863), took the bold step of introducing a Holy Ark with an extremely Classical curvilinear pediment under a horseshoe arch doubtless intended to suggest the community's origins. The upper openings on the façade are intended to be Oriental. In Glasgow, John McLeod's Garnethill Synagogue (1879) combines Neo-Romanesque elements, Corinthian columns, a Byzantine dome and Moorish galleries.

It is interesting that this trend to the eclectic, which restricts the Moorish presence to decorative and symbolic features, is also to be found in the United States, where no thoroughly Moorish project of the type met with in Italy was ever brought to fruition. Identity and emancipation not being major issues there, the Moorish style found few takers and the rare experiments actually put into practise always involve a Gothic basilican plan with Moorish decoration. The first Islamic-inspired synagogue was built in Cincinnati in 1886 by James K. Wilson for the B'nai Yeshurun congregation: named after the famous reforming rabbi who headed the community, the Isaac M. Wise Temple has three naves whose volumes are signalled by pointed arch openings, its Oriental motifs being mostly restricted to the upper part of the building and the interior. The two slim minarets flanking the entry and the thirteen flat cupolas covering the naves seem inspired by Mameluke Egypt, while the interior, with its colours, blind arches and colonnettes is reminiscent of the Alhambra. This latter reference, as it happens, was a favourite of Rabbi Wise, who expressly commended the choice of a style borrowed from Moorish Spain for his 'Alhambra temple'. More heterogeneous still was the Emanu-El synagogue in New York, built in 1868 by Eidlitz and Fernbach for a Reformed congregation at the corner of Fifth Avenue and 43rd Street. When the community moved in 1927, the building was demolished. With its Gothic silhouette set between its two towers, the building was orientalized by the use of polychrome materials, notably red and black tiles. Once again, however, the overall impact comes from an interior reliant on the splendours of the Alhambra. Eidlitz was in fact a specialist in this domain, having already designed Phineas Barnum's famous Iranistan in Bridgeport (1846-48). Other traces of orientalism were to be found in New York, but were systematically restricted to decoration. An example is the celebrated Kahal Adath Jeshurun Synagogue (1886), built by a congregation of Eastern European Jews on Eldridge Street on the Lower East Side. The architects, the Herter brothers, retained a Romanesque façade, but added serrated horseshoe arches supported by colonnettes, a feature that recurs in the handsome wooden Holy Ark and was much used in later synagogues built by Central European congregations. Examples of this latter trend are Park East (1890, Schneider and Herter), whose complex moldings make its façade one of the most astonishing in New York, and Shaare Zedek in Harlem (1900, Michael Bernstein).

While orientalism was not a dominant feature of American synagogue architecture, it made its presence felt in the last great historicist project, the new Temple Emanu-El on Fifth Avenue, designed by Robert D. Kohn, Charles Butler and Clarence S. Stein and opened in 1930. The arrangement may be that of a paleochristian basilica, but the decoration and the interplay between the materials incline more to the Oriental and the side chapel

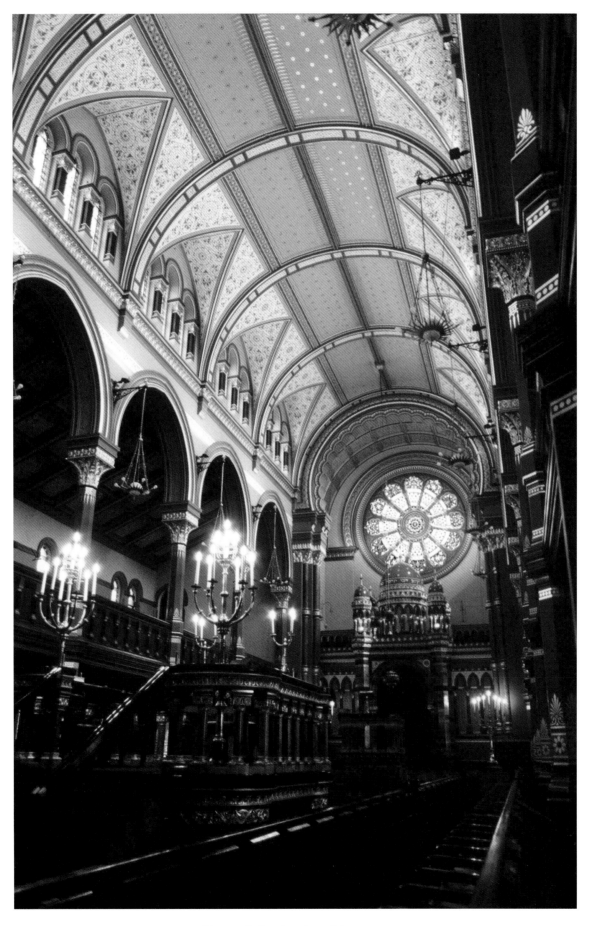

Liverpool, *Interior view of the synagogue*
(1874, architects W. and G. Audsley).

New York, *Temple Emanu-El*
(1868, architects Eidlitz and Fernbach).
Engraving courtesy of the American
Jewish Historical Society.

Manchester, *Exterior view*
of the Sephardic synagogue
(1874, architect Edward Salomons).

is Byzantine. In an article[21] for the *Architectural Forum*, Clarence Stein relates that after many changes of mind and preliminary drawings testing all sorts of solutions in all styles—especially domes—the architects plumped for 'the Romanesque as used in the south of Italy under the influence of the Moorish, because it was a expression of the intermingling of Occidental and Oriental thought.' It hardly needs to be said that adherence to this kind of vision of the synagogue in 1930 reveals a total incomprehension of the changes that had taken place as much in Judaism as in architecture.

AUSTRIA-HUNGARY AND RUSSIA

For reasons to do with their specific histories, several countries had other reasons for building orientalist synagogues. In Austria, for instance, where the struggle against the Turks had long been a founding issue, the configuration of certain synagogues can be explained by the presence of Jews from countries on the Lower Danube still under Turkish domination. In Vienna, with the notable exception of Förster's project, most synagogues were neo-Gothic or Neo-Renaissance, as if the primary need were a rootedness in a deeply Western, Christian frame of reference. One of the rare synagogues to feature overtly Oriental decoration—but only in the interior, the exterior being quite unremarkable—is the Türckische Tempel designed for the 'Türkisch-Jüdische Gemeinde' by Hugo von Wiedenfeld in 1887. As a reminder of the Sephardic origins of the faithful here, the architect appears to have taken the octagonal volume and the decoration directly from Otto Wagner's synagogue in Budapest. The onion domes Jakob Gartner was so fond of adding to his Neo-Romanesque synagogues—Humboldtplatz (1896-1909), Kluckygasse (c. 1900) and Siebenbrunnengasse (1908)—can be explained in terms of the local Baroque tradition. By contrast, the onion dome topping community architect William Stiassny's 'Polnische Schul' (1893) is associated with the markedly more orientalist tripartite façade already used for the synagogue in Malacky, Slovakia in 1886-87, which in fact has two domes. At the same time there is nothing particularly surprising about this, given that Stiassny, one of Austria-Hungary's foremost synagogue architects, would go on to restore Förster's building in 1898. Taking a stand against the anti-Semitism of the time, he justified his choice at the inauguration of the Polish Synagogue: 'The shapes and colours of this building are used here to remind us of centuries long past, of a time when our co-religionists lived as free citizens among their non-Jewish fellows, in peace and on good terms and as useful, respected

members of the community. Of a time when the Jews knew the pleasure of acceding to high office, competing equally in the noble contest for places in the arts and sciences. Of a time when the Jews were demonstrating imperishable abilities in mathematics and astronomy, in physics and the natural sciences, in medicine and ethnology, in poetry and the arts. And now? Together with our memory of times past there lives on in us the hope of a future that will bring us better days.'

Stiassny went on to build a succession of synagogues in Bohemia in which he helped to maintain the orientalist tradition: Teplice Sanov (1882), Caslav (1899) and Jablonec nad Nisou (1892), but first and foremost in Prague itself, where his immense two-towered Vinohrady Synagogue (1896-98) was in the Renaissance style but with Moorish touches to its decoration. He also drew up the plans for what was to be the last display of this style in Central Europe, the Jubilee Synagogue on Jeruzalémská Street (1906). Actually built by Alois Richter, it was situated in the Old Town where it replaced three earlier synagogues demolished in the course of neighbourhood renovation. Strangely, the sixtieth anniversary of

Franz-Josef's accession to the throne was celebrated by the Jews of Prague with a building that was a veritable anthology of Islamic arches, from its enormous projecting horseshoe arch under the gable to Mogul and Hindu versions.

In Russia, where there was little justification for Arabic or Moorish styles, it is interesting to note that the Hispano-Moorish St Petersburg synagogue (1879-1893) was built by Ivan Chapochnikov and Lev Bachman after authorization was granted by the Tsar Alexander II in 1869. It appears that the choice of style was influenced by the critic Vladimir Stassof, a student of Jewish art who had come to the conclusion that the synagogues of Spain represented a striking synthesis of Jewish and Arabic culture and were capable of providing the Russian synagogue with the model it needed. For him it was clear that the Jews were a nation and that the synagogue should express this identity in national terms.

This last example is an excellent illustration of how orientalism found its primary *raison d'être* in a vision of Judaism 'as race', to quote Renan[22]. Jews concerned with assimilation would soon take issue with this definition

St Petersburg, *Interior view*
of the synagogue (1879-93, architects
Chapochnikov and Bachman).

Prague, *Exterior view*
of the Jubilee synagogue
(1906, architect Wilhelm Stiassny).
Stiassny used this polychrome building
as an excuse to explore the gamut
of Oriental arches.

and its aesthetic implications, yet some Zionists, Buber among them, saw it as a stimulant to rejudaization. Be that as it may, Jews—even those who had long since lost the sense of exile—still retained a certain fascination with orientalism; many the Jew who, raised on a combination of prayer in the synagogue, traditional literature and the ambient culture, created for himself what Anatole Leroy-Beaulieu in his *Israël parmi les nations* (1893) called an 'orientalism of the mind'. 'And so,' Leroy-Beaulieu continues[23], 'we sometimes feel we detect something Oriental in them. Speaking for myself, I would be grateful if they brought a ray of Eastern sunshine to our gloomy skies. But this Oriental gleam we are so ready to see in the eyes of their daughters—how many sons of Jacob have it in their soul?

'What you see in us as a racial trait, an Israelite once said to me, is mostly no more than the mark of an education. Books have more to do with it than blood. We were for so long turned towards the hills of Jerusalem that the Orient is still an image before our eyes and its voices a shimmering in our ears. When we are only twenty and still have time to dream, those dreams are filled with palm trees, with more palm trees, perhaps, than have ever existed in the whole of Palestine. But in actual fact we are scarcely more Oriental than we imagine ourselves to be.'

The architecture of the nineteenth century made a substantial contribution to this imaginary.

Kassel, *Exterior view of the synagogue*,
(2000, architect Alfred Jacoby).

Page 204:
Darmstadt, *Project of synagogue*,
drawn by Alfred Jacoby.

IV

A MODERNIST ARCHITECTURE

If the emancipation years were crucial in terms of the changes brought to the conception of what the synagogue and its architecture should be, the other major period of change can be situated between the two World Wars. The reasons for this were increased emigration, the Zionism-induced emergence of a Jewish homeland in Palestine and a radical shift in architectural theory. In the wake of the transition marked by Art Nouveau, architecture abandoned for the first time the strictly historicist approach that had dominated the entire nineteenth century, one result being a redefinition of the synagogue in terms of both function and form. The notion of exile was rekindled in certain communities, the role of the synagogue changed to take account of social as well as religious needs and the first signs appeared of a community centre that also included a place of prayer. The abandoning of the old historicist forms and stylistic languages was accompanied by the end of a blinkered approach to religious symbolism that had so often seen synagogues decked with towers, spires and domes. The advent of new materials also contributed to this spirit of renewal. Obviously, these innovations did not appear everywhere simultaneously, as local factors continued to have an influence. The United States, which was to play a major role in the revival of synagogue architecture after the Second World War, was still in search of the compromise it would ultimately find in Neo-Byzantine, while Europe was developing modernist models drawing on the theories of Loos, Le Corbusier and Gropius.

This, then, was the period of what, in 1932, Henry Russell Hitchcock and Philip Johnson christened the International Style—a not particularly illuminating term in that the movement had actually grown out of the break with the stylistic process. But it was also a time when the synagogue lent itself, perhaps more readily than the church, to the experiments advocated by the modernists of, notably, the International Congress of Modern Architecture—even if, as was clearly the case, synagogues were not one of their central concerns. The synagogue would certainly have fitted with the 'cultivating oneself' function, but could hardly have been turned into a 'prayer machine'. Nonetheless the modernist influence began to make itself felt as early as the 1920s: foreshadowing the community centre notion that would become commonplace after World War II, the synagogue was resuming subsidiary activities necessitating changes in spatial organization to which Modernist divisions of function were more architecturally appropriate. In Israel, pioneer builders had brought with them methods of construction learnt at the Bauhaus or from Le Corbusier, at the same time taking care to develop a 'Hebrew' style that incorporated local elements. This quest for synthesis was to leave a deep and lasting mark on Israeli architecture.

However modernity as a concept—as quintessence of the Occidental model and basis of the emancipation process—underwent an irremediable suspension with the Holocaust. Emil Fackenheim, a young rabbinical student imprisoned the day after the Kristallnacht, could find no

reply when a fellow-prisoner asked him what Judaism had to say there and then. The answer he tried to formulate fifty years later begins as follows[1]: "The very soul of Germany's Jewish community was murdered in the course of that single night, with the burning of places of worship where the prayers of innumerable generations of the faithful had been offered up to God." With those synagogues, and even before the systematic destruction of a people, there vanished a civilization thousands of years old. And while modernity as such cannot be held responsible, a shadow is cast over an entire historical period. Other age-old Jewish civilizations also disappeared during that barbarous century, at the hands of a culture which, while not driven by Western modernity, made use of its most dangerous concepts: Arab nationalism put an end to 2,500 years of Jewish presence in Egypt, the Jews later having to flee the Middle East and North Africa and many more synagogues being destroyed. Nor was it easy for Israel to protect its heritage, even on its own soil, where the synagogues of Jerusalem were wiped out by the Jordanians in 1948. The need then, for European as for Israeli Judaism, was to rebuild.

Only American Judaism, benefiting from a climate of prosperity and renewed dynamism, was able to develop new architectural forms in the post-war period, through the efforts of great architects like Mendelsohn, who had fled Europe, or the native-born Frank Lloyd Wright. The American synagogue—250 were built between 1945 and 1955!—evolved into a community centre, most often in a suburban setting. This was the beginning of a new, modern Judaism, still reeling under the impact of the Holocaust, but conscious of its role as keeper of the European flame and as a focal point for Jewish identity.

Nonetheless, with the arrival of refugees from North Africa, certain European countries witnessed a revival that was not only spiritual but also communitarian. France was particularly fortunate in this respect, the outcome being a Judaism no longer limited to the old confessional boundaries laid down by the Napoleonic Code. In this changed context the Jewish experience found expression in synagogues combining the functional and the symbolic. In Israel, with the notion of exile abolished, the synagogue had to be given a new role; yet the Diaspora remained a cardinal influence and Chagall's stained glass windows are an eloquent illustration of how the modern art of the West could help revitalize a venerable institution re-established on its native ground.

Buffalo, New York, *Beth Zion*
(1967, architects Harrison and Abramowitz).
The stained glass and the motifs
from the Decalogue are by Ben Shahn.

Functionalist Changes 1

Paris, *Framework of the synagogue
in the Rue Chasseloup-Laubat*
(1913, architect Lucien Bechmann).

Left page:
Josef Hoffmann, *Sketch for the Zilina
synagogue competition* (1928).
Published in *Menorah*, February 1929.

*T*hus the years 1900-1920 were to see the emergence of a new architecture, born of the challenge to the hitherto accepted stylistic languages and of increasing pressure from the functionalist camp. In a remarkably apt convergence of ideas, functionalism allowed for a close match with the specific social values the church model had tended to exclude during the previous century. Moreover, it was just at this time that Judaism, reacting against Christian architectural prototypes, was finding itself increasingly in phase with the claims of the modernist camp. Writing in the Zionist review *Ost und West* in 1906, Ernest Hiller opened his 'Thoughts on the Architecture of Modern Synagogues'[1] with the observation that 'We are surprised when, entering a synagogue, we have the same impression as when entering a Christian church. The construction, use of space and formal approach seem absolutely Christian.' Going on to condemn the spires and campaniles of the synagogues in Little Rock, Arkansas and Albany, New York, he called for buildings free of extravagance, ornamentation, bright colours and monumental doorways. This is hardly the language of Adolf Loos, but the stress is on rejection of gratuitous, assimilationist decoration and Hiller was delighted that in the final analysis Judaism had no stylistic tradition of its own: this left the way open to the truly creative artist.

Architectural avant-gardism did not preclude various relapses into past practice, yet most striking of all was that in its acceptance of modernist aesthetics, the synagogue returned to a simplicity much more appropriate to Tradition than were the styles borrowed from various ambient cultures. This was doubtless why Jewish circles—especially Orthodox communities, who had never really concurred in the aesthetic values advanced as an aid to integration—so readily entrusted their religious buildings to modernist architects, a step Christian groups were much more hesitant to take.

Paris, *Interior of the synagogue*
in the Rue Pavée
(1914, architect Hector Guimard).

Art Nouveau and the challenge to the monumental

With the advent of Art Nouveau and its break with earlier stylistic languages, architects and Jewish communities found themselves facing a choice that called into question the most fundamental aspect of nineteenth-century building practice: the Christian ecclesiastical ground plan. It is hardly astonishing then, that the early 1900s were a period of transition during which archaic pastiches rubbed shoulders with new, experimental approaches. Orthodox circles frequently showed themselves much more modern, being unencumbered by the aesthetic preconceptions of Reform Jews.

The architectural value Jews had most difficulty in abandoning, especially in the case of such well established communities as those of Berlin, Paris, Amsterdam and certain American cities, was monumentality. This had become both the symbol par excellence of Judaism's social function and its integration into civic life and a characteristically emancipist assertion of its religious values. While undermined by pressures for a more functional approach, monumentality, like the formal impressiveness it entailed, was never to be completely abandoned: for the Liberal synagogue on Berlin's Printzregentenstrasse (1930), Alexander Beer designed a façade with a lofty triangular gable and colossal pilasters, while the dome covering the immense, circular worship area—room for 2,400 people—provides a silhouette whose proportions, while gigantic, remain true to tradition. At the same period, Beer was working on another, geometrical design for the synagogue on the Agricolastrasse. In some cases continuity with the nineteenth century cannot be ignored: in Detroit, Albert Kahn (1869-1942), renowned as the creator of the Ford automobile factories, designed in 1922 a monumental temple with an Ionic portico for the Beth El congregation; earlier, in 1903, he had offered the same group a miniature Paris-style Pantheon. United States communities were most reluctant to give up the monumental approach: whatever the actual style—and America was home to all of them—what really seemed to count was sheer size. Nowhere else were there so many towers, spires and Babylonian domes, while Art Nouveau refinement only succeeded in making its presence felt in decoration or the occasional inclusion of a Tiffany window.

The output of an architect like Arnold Brunner illustrates perfectly a monumentalist tendency still very much alive around the turn of the century. In 1891 he built one of New York's largest synagogues, Beth El on Fifth Avenue, and topped it with a gigantic square dome; for the Spanish & Portuguese Synagogue (1897) on Eighth Avenue, opposite Central Park, he resorted to the Corinthian colossal order; and at the Temple Israel in Harlem (1907), the colossal order used was Ionic. Brunner had plumped for Classicism after an eclectic period that included Shaaray Tefila on 82nd Street in New York (1894) and Mishkan Israel in New Haven, Connecticut (1897). Recent archeological discoveries had led Brunner to the realization that Classical architecture as practiced in ancient Palestine was the perfect foil to his dreams of grandeur, a point of view shared by many other architects. It is understandable, then, that given architectural ambitions wholeheartedly approved of by the client congregations, America was not yet ready to adopt a more modern vision of things, nor even to rethink the synagogue in terms of Art Nouveau.

This latter style, however, had made a notable contribution to the renewal of domestic architecture in Europe. It is significant that the synagogues that adopted this new aesthetics in most cases rejected the ecclesiastical approach, more closely resembling houses or apartment blocks. This change was in line with community aspirations which were themselves of two orders: increased discretion in a context of anti-Semitic outbreaks and the wish to return to a form that was more functional than symbolic.

Naturally enough there was also a search for compromise: symbolic forms are not readily abandoned. In Antwerp the Machsike Hadass synagogue (1910-14, Jules Hofman), built on Oosten Street by a Polish-Russian congregation, is a three-level structure whose street-side windows could be those of a normal apartment block—except that two little onion-domed towers signal the building's function. At exactly the same period, in Paris, another Polish-Russian group, the *Agoudath Hakehiloth*—not averse, as noted in the previous chapter, to modern conveniences and a degree of gallicization—commissioned a synagogue from Hector Guimard. Guimard worked fast and the building was inaugurated on 7 June 1914. Once again the façade combined slenderness and a use of curvature in a way that retained the look of a religious edifice—squeezed into a tiny street in the Marais neighbourhood, this synagogue looks much taller than it actually is—and reconciled them with a series of horizontal divisions corresponding to the stores. In fact the street side of the building is given over to offices and classrooms, while the worship area is set in back and is unrelated to the façade. The decoration—all Guimard's work—is of impressive quality and achieves a high degree of originality, despite the incorporation of prefabricated elements.

Art Nouveau—or Jugendstil—was to be found principally in the modest synagogues of cities like Ostend (1910, Joseph DeLange), Tours (1908, Victor Tondu) and Baden in Switzerland (1913, Dorer and Füchslin). The large windows used to light the worship area in Baden reflect the architectural practice of the city's thermal baths. Other examples were Lucerne (1912, Max Seckbach), Peine in Germany (1908), which resembles nothing so much as one of the Darmstadt School's enormous houses, and Thionville in France (1913), where Ludwig Levy dropped his Neo-Romanesque and Neo-Moorish penchants in favour of an experiment in Baroque.

Vienna's Secession movement left little trace in terms of synagogue architecture, but Hradec Králové (1905, V. Weinzettel) deserves mention for the oddness of a composition associating a traditional apartment-style structure with a façade whose geometrical pylon and decoration are suggestive of both Secession and Biblical approaches. In ascending order its central section comprises the door, a pointed arch, a Phoenician-looking story bearing an inscription in Hebrew and a square dome. Topped with crenellations, the pylon's uprights bear plane sculptures of stylized palms, a motif copied directly from Chipiez's reconstruction of the Temple of Jerusalem, with its Phoenician pylons at the entry to the Temple forecourt[2]. Thus at the very moment when Costa and Armanni were bringing a still markedly historicist vocabulary to bear on their Assyrian-style dream in Rome, Weinzettel succeeded in retaining the reference to the Temple by showing just how rich in modern creative potential was the magnificently imaginative reconstruction then being carried out by archeologists working from the description in Ezekiel. In the same year similar palms and pylons appeared on the façade of the synagogue in Adly Street in Cairo, a magnificent version of Chipiez's Temple. Like Otto Wagner, Weinzettel had shown himself capable of reinterpreting an antiquity that was no longer Greek, but Semitic.

Cairo, *Synagogue in the Rue Adly*
(1905).

Hradec Králové, Czech Republic,
Present-day view of the synagogue (1905).
Weinzettel, the architect,
doubtless sought to give his building
a distinctively Jewish character
by drawing on the reconstruction
of the Temple of Jerusalem proposed
by French architect Charles Chipiez
in 1889. Curiously, the palm-tree
motif used for the entrance
recurs on the façade of the Rue Adly
synagogue in Cairo,
built in the same year.

Los Angeles, *The Wilshire Boulevard Temple*
(1929, architect A.W Edelman).

Neo-Byzantine:
a pathway towards modernity

While Neo-Byzantine can quite justifiably be classified as simply one style among many, it also possessed distinct potentialities in terms of synagogue architecture. In particular it was the source of models recommended by rabbis themselves: as far back as the eighteenth century mention is made of a *responsum* by Ezekiel Landau, in Prague, proposing an octagonal ground plan. The interest of the Neo-Byzantine, then, lay not in its character as a historical style, and one that could be combined with Romanesque to provide an Orientally-tinged aesthetic variant, but in its capacity to match the specific character of the synagogue. Its use, then, indicates a shift towards functionalism. Reversing the historicist approach and its tendency to subordinate function to forms dictated by existing models—temple-style synagogues were almost all basilican—it seemed to fit with Sullivan's famous dictum that 'Form follows function'. Gradually stripping itself of its decorative elements, Neo-Byzantine approached, most notably in Peter Behrens' synagogue in Zilina, the formal austerity of modernism.

The Neo-Byzantine model owed its appearance in France to the prevailing spirit at the Ecole des Beaux-Arts in Paris, as revealed in the prize-winning work of Emile Ulmann in Neuilly (1878) and Emmanuel Pontremoli in Boulogne-Billancourt (1911), and equally in the monthly competitions for students[3]. It is evident that what appealed to architects about this model was not only the central plan so perfectly suited to the synagogue, but also, as we have already seen, the triumphant progress of a stylistic variant of Romano-Byzantine through France in the second half of the nineteenth century. The Byzantine reference was unambiguous, as when Baron Edmond de Rothschild termed 'St Sofia' the synagogue he commissioned from Lucien Bechmann on the Rue Chasseloup-Laubat in Paris (1913). An interesting connection sprang up between the Ecole des Beaux-Arts and the United States: Gustav-Albert Lansburgh, who had come from America to study there, decided to base his degree submission in 1906 on the synagogue, using—yet again—the central plan and Byzantine cupola. In 1926 we find Lansburgh working as a consultant on the Neo-Byzantine Emanu-El synagogue in San Francisco… Moreover, he was far from being the only American to have trained at the Ecole des Beaux-Arts and clung to the stylistic preferences thus acquired up until the 1930s.

The United States, where recourse to all the historical styles had sometimes resulted in an utterly zany eclecti-cism, continued down the same road in the twentieth century. One example is the paleochristian Temple Emanu-El (1929, Kohn, Butler and Stein) on Fifth Avenue in New York, which was even copied in Toronto (Holy Blossom, 1938, Chapman and Oxley). It should, however, be pointed out that in their preliminary projects the architects had proposed a domed plan, ill-suited to the small, deep building block, and that the side chapel was itself roofed with two small domes. After 1920 the style that ultimately won out in practical terms was the Neo-Byzantine, although much earlier examples already existed. Buffalo's Temple Beth Zion (1889, E. A. and W. W. Kent) offers a central plan, a cupola and Byzantine moldings and was accorded the signal honor of being used by the *Architectural Record*[4] to illustrate an article on the choice of styles. Other synagogues based on this model and its variants include Shearith Israel in San Francisco (1904) and Rodef Shalom in Pittsburgh (1907, Palmer and Hornbostel). Nonetheless a building like the Touro Synagogue in New Orleans (1908, Emil Weil) provides evidence of an ongoing compromise: a Byzantine exterior with a flattened dome encloses a Neoclassical interior, doubtless a reflection of the desire to retain the pre-existing Holy Ark. The main point about the Neo-Byzantine, however, is that the 1920s would simplify it and use it as a functional solution.

In 1939 Bruno Funaro[5] noted that having made its appearance at the turn of the century, 'the central dome takes its place as a typical feature of American synagogue design and, with variations, is still characteristic of today's trend.' His article is illustrated with a sketch of the Buffalo synagogue.

By 1925 Lewis Mumford was wondering[6] just where American synagogue architects should go next. Critical of the American grab-bag approach to styles and taking as an example the recent Temple Beth El in Detroit—it could just as easily have been a library or a courthouse—he concluded that the solution was a return to basic architectural principles via modernism's key 'form and function' notion combined with a revival of Judaism's Palestinian roots. Thus the dome seemed to him a perfect answer, both technically, in that it lent itself to the use of concrete and symbolically, in terms both of unity and its inherent reference to Middle Eastern architecture. In support of this approach he mentions the Temple Anshe Chesed (1924, I. L. Lehman and T. Schmidt), the Temple Tifereth Israel (1924, C. R. Greco) in Cleveland and the Temple Emanu-El in San Francisco (1926, Bakewell, Brown and Schnaittacher).

Before the crash of 1929 and the subsequent halt to building came Beth Israel in Portland (1926), whose

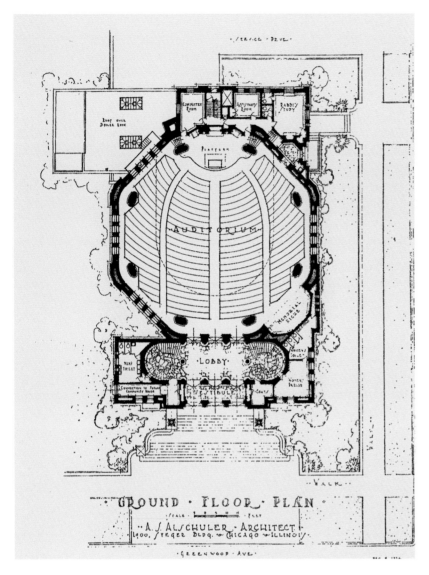

Chicago, *Isaiah Temple*
(1924, architect Alfred S. Altschuler).
A typically Byzantine plan.

New York, *Emanu-El*
(1929, architects Kohn, Butler and Stein).

architects, M. H. Whitehouse and H. Brookman seem to draw on Beth Zion in Buffalo; Ohabei Shalom in Brookline-Boston (1928, Blackall, Clapp and Whittemore); and Bnai Brith on Wilshire Boulevard in Los Angeles (1929, A.M. Edelman), mainly remarkable for Hugo Ballin's frescoes and their figurative recounting of Jewish history.

In Canada the synagogue of the Shaar Hashomayim congregation in Montreal (1922, Melvin Miller) adopted several Byzantine features and became a model for, among others, Shaar Hashamoyim in Windsor and Shaare Zion in Montreal (1939, Milton Eliasoph, Greenspoon and Berkovitz).

Many of these synagogues included truly remarkable stained glass windows and decorative sculpture. One example, the Isaiah Temple in Chicago (1924), is interesting for the way its architect, Alfred S. Altschuler justified his aesthetic choices[7] on grounds similar to those put forward by Mumford: not only had he resorted to the Byzantine model as a means to re-using the plan of San Vitale in Ravenna (already applied to the synagogue in Essen), he also included references to archeological fragments recently discovered in Palestine which, in his view, contained motifs resembling those of Byzantine architecture. Somewhat more startling is the use of a minaret as a chimney, Altschuler considering a 'prayer tower' as more aesthetically pleasing and picturesque than a factory-made pipe! This succession of surprises is capped by the enormous stained glass Moses inside.

As Rachel Witchnitzer observes[8], the United States provided 'no new ideas during the 1930s'. Nor were any to be forthcoming until the end of the Second World War and the arrival of architects of the modern movement.

Just as the United States had gone overboard for Neo-Byzantine, Europe seems to have made the great leap forward into modernity fairly rapidly. The choice of Joseph Delange's Neo-Byzantine proposal by the board of the Van den Nest Avenue synagogue in Antwerp after the competition in 1923 perhaps betrays an enduring timidity regarding much more inventive proposals. Yet certain other countries still showed real affection for the Byzantine and we have already seen Lipót Baumhorn produce something similar in Gyöngyös (1929-31). Slovakia is home to a number of central-plan synagogues more or less inspired by Byzantine approaches: in 1913 Trencin acquired a synagogue with an enormous dome on arches and in Kosice both the Orthodox synagogue (Olschläger and Boskó, 1927) and its Reformed equivalent (Lajos Kozma, 1925) drew on this model. Most famous of all is the synagogue built in Zilina by competition winner Peter Behrens: this is a perfect illustration

of how the Byzantine central plan and dome that were expressly called for by the specifications could be reconciled with functional spaces and geometrical forms. Hósöle Temploma, a small synagogue in Budapest dedicated to the memory of the Jewish fallen of the First World War, was built as an annex to the larger synagogue on Dohány Street by architects Lázló Vágó and Ferenc Faragó (1929-1931). The arrangement opted for was that of a very plain miniature temple topped with a cupola. In Genoa, in one of the rare synagogues to be built in Italy after the First World War, architect Francesco Morandi,

although working in concrete, still chose in 1935 an arrangement similar to the Byzantine, with a large dome surrounded by four small ones. The resultant silhouette is quite Classical.

Despite its reminders of a now doomed historicist architectural language, the Byzantine model found fresh acceptance in Israel. In the name of the need to anchor architecture in the vernacular traditions most forcefully symbolized by Rachel's tomb—a reference used by architect Georges Wybo for the Palestinian pavilion at the 1931 Colonial Exhibition in Paris—and amid praise for

Trencin, Slovakia, *Synagogue*
(1913). Old photograph.

Antwerp, *Project for a new synagogue*,
competition drawing
by Joseph De Lange, published
in *L'Emulation*, 1923.

2 16

the modernity taken for granted by new arrivals at the Bauhaus and in Russian Constructivist studios, the domed roofs and Byzantine models already used in Jerusalem in the nineteenth century—for the Hurva synagogue (1854-64), for example—found a new lease of life. Best known of all is the Great Synagogue in the new city of Tel Aviv (1922, Yehuda Magidovitz). There too, as in Afula, the forms were simplified to the extreme and while remaining Oriental, merge perfectly into the modern context.

Competitions and the formal explosion

One consequence of the break with historical styles advocated by the modernists was an unfettering of the architectural imagination, with the 1920s simultaneously marked by the emergence of a geometrical, sometimes minimalist aesthetics and all sorts of highly individual approaches that left no lasting trace. The new trends frequently found expression in competitions although, regrettably, the preference of the communities putting up the money most often went to proposals that were frankly backward-looking. The competitions were also a chance for innovative architects to make themselves known: thus Wagner's students were frequent participants as were such future key members of the Austrian Werkbund as Oskar Strnad in the Trieste competition and Josef Frank in Antwerp.

Except in Germany no great use had been made of competitions in the nineteenth century, Jewish communities mostly preferring the services of State architects. In the twentieth century, more independent[9] and, like their American counterparts, formally organized as associations, they set out down the tricky road of the competition. Already, before the First World War, the 1903 Trieste competition, held in an Austro-Hungarian Empire whose dying years were marked by all sorts of daring architectural innovations, had shown historicist approaches having to prove themselves against highly imaginative exercises, even when these latter fell short of any radical modernism. Thus projects showing the influence of the Otto Wagner school rubbed shoulders with others still firmly committed to imitation of Assyrian and Oriental styles. With its curvilinear pediments and decorated façades, the proposal made by Wagner's pupils Emil Hoppe and Otto Schöntal would have created a real link between Trieste and Austro-Hungarian culture. Also of interest was the proposal submitted by the Hungarian Franz Matouschek, a gigantic elevation soaring above a

low door in the manner of the imaginary architectures of the symbolist period. Of the some forty proposals entered—one of them by the Zionist architect Oskar Marmorek—not one convinced the judges, who finally turned to the Triestino Ruggero Berlam. Working with his son Arduino, Berlam designed a massive structure whose exterior harked back to the austerity of ancient Syria, while the decoration of the interior drew more on the contemporary Italian Liberty style. The building was completed in 1912.

Modernity loomed larger in the proposals for the competitions in Antwerp (1923), Vienna-Hietzing (1924), Zilina (1928), Hamburg and Berlin Klopstockstrasse (both 1929). Moreover, when competition was not restricted to Jewish architects, such major figures as Josef Hoffmann and Peter Behrens sometimes participated. Concerned to defend a new conception of the synagogue, the critic Max Eisler became the chronicler[10] of competitions and modernist projects and published many sketches, notably of Hoffmann's Zilina proposal. These latter consisted of a series of variants in which the synagogue resembles a desert tent, or Oriental allusions emerge, or the architect explores the potential of an enormous hemispherical dome. Compared to Behrens' more Classical gambit, the ensemble is richly poetic and evocative. It is true that the specifications called expressly for a cupola and thus induced to a greater or lesser extent a resort to the Neo-Byzantine. A neat illustration of this confrontation of ideas in the 1920s is the fact that Hoffmann and Behrens often found themselves competing not only with each other but also with the influential Hungarian Lipót Baumhorn.

Surviving material from the Antwerp competition includes the proposals of local architect Joseph DeLange and the Frenchman Germain Debré, who shared second place. Both plans achieve a harmony between Neo-Byzantine arrangements and more modern forms. Other entries included Gruenberger's frankly eccentric pyramidal project and Josef Frank's systematic use—except for the immense Tables of the Law—of plain, strictly quadrangular forms.

The competition in Hietzing, in the Vienna suburbs, attracted more original contributions. Hugo Gorge had entered an initial competition in 1912 and published drawings of an arrangement combining simple modernist lines and a traditional wrought-iron *bimah* worthy of comparison with those in the synagogues of Prague and Krakow. His new proposal, a simplified version of the same project, earned him second place. Third place went to Fritz Landauer for a design whose volumes were relatively traditional. The most innovative

Zilina, Slovakia, *Project sketch*
by Josef Hoffmann (1928). Published
in *Menorah*, February 1929. In addition
to Hoffmann's highly innovative
proposal, the German architect
Peter Behrens, a fervent rationalist,
provided a competition entry that was
an exemplary modern interpretation
of the Byzantine model, with central
plan and cupola.

Vienna-Hietzing, *Project for a synagogue*,
competition drawing by Richard Neutra
(1924). Published in *Menorah*,
November-December 1929.

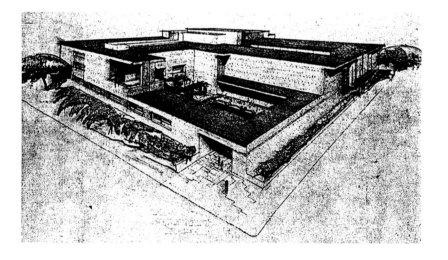

proposal came from Frank Neutra, who had emigrated
to the United States a year earlier and was then working
with Frank Lloyd Wright. Totally committed to modernity, he suggested a drawn-out complex in which the
actual synagogue would merge into groups of low buildings with roof-terraces. Nothing remained here of the
religious character or impressive monumentality still to
be found in the work of most of his 1920s competitors,
for what Neutra had done was anticipate certain community centres of the post-Second World War period.
Hardly surprisingly, first prize went to Gruenberger's far
less radical proposal, a simple cube embellished with
graceful serried arches, whose character was to be reinforced by architect Adolf Jelletz's supervision of the
actual building.

Nor was it surprising in Germany, where architectural
debate was being led by such energetic avant-gardes as the
Bauhaus, to see rivalry between the most retrograde monumental forms—typified by Augsburg (1917, Fritz
Landauer and Heinrich Lömpl) and Berlin-Prinzregenten
(1930, Alexander Beer)—and schemes inspired by the
Modern Movement. As it happened, victory in the competitions in Hamburg and Berlin-Klopstockstrasse went
to innovative proposals. In the case of Hamburg's Liberal
synagogue there was an outright convergence between
the proposals of winner Felix Ascher, and those of second
and third place-getters Fritz Landauer and Robert
Friedmann, all of which were based on a simple rectangular form. The building erected in 1931 by Ascher and
Friedmann working in association, involved setting an
antechurch annex each side of the main volume that
housed the worship area. The façade is characterized by
the absence of windows, a single oculus filled by a *meno-*

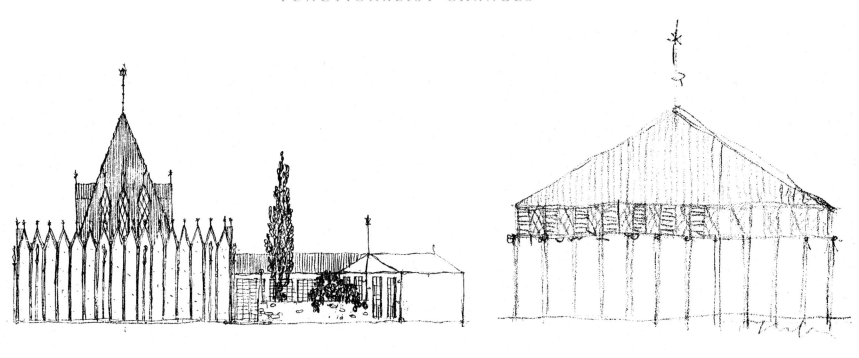

rah interrupting the high central wall and breaking with the right angles. All the other openings are cut into the lateral façades.

Attracting exactly the same kind of proposals, the competition for the Berlin-Klopstockstrasse synagogue was won by Gusti Hecht and Hermann Neumann, other prizes going to Sokolowski, Wiener and Jaretzki, Leo Nachtlicht and Moritz Lesser. The winning entry consisted again of a substantial volume preceded by two stepped antechurches meeting over the door.

The first modernist projects

Undeniable leaders within the Modern Movement, France, Holland and Germany became focal points for experiments aimed at creating a new kind of synagogue. In addition to the plans or actual buildings by Neutra and Behrens already mentioned, the latest innovations were to be found in several other synagogues. Even Fritz Landauer, prone to conservatism in this field, set his 1930 Plauen synagogue on pilotis and introduced lengthwise openings into its bare walls, borrowing the massiveness of volume from Le Corbusier's Citrohan House (1922) or his own houses at Weissenhof (1927). Avant-garde tendencies moved quickly through Central Europe, examples including Otto Eisler's 'international style' synagogue at Brno (1936), the rebuilding—on pilotis—of the Smichov synagogue in the Prague suburbs by Leopold Ehrmann (1931) and the straightforward cube at Velvary, near Prague, where each wall is pierced by a large oculus containing a Star of David. For his Orthodox synagogue in Bratislava (1923) Artur Szalatnai combined a tradi-

tional approach—going so far as to include a metal baldachin over the *bimah*—with a plain concrete structure. In Paris Lucien Hesse, working with Germain Debré whom he would succeed in 1929 as architect to the Paris Consistory, designed a functional synagogue characterized by modern spareness; this had been made possible by the fact that while the building was financed by Baron de Rothschild, it was to be used by immigrants in the working-class Belleville district. Debré pressed on in the modernist spirit, however, even in Neuilly (1937). The new architecture and functionalism generally were supported by many rabbis, who felt that Judaism, lacking a rigid architectural tradition, enjoyed greater freedom in this respect than other religions. At the inaugural ceremony for the Plauen synagogue a rabbi was able to remark that 'The Jewish religion demands a modern setting because it is at one with life.'

In Holland, where a specific form of modernism arose in the late 1910s with the famous 'Amsterdam School', several synagogues were to reveal the best of the movement in their combination of rationalism, local references—notably the use of bricks—and bold, even symbolic forms. The Dutch community seems to have been particularly dynamic at this time and the result was a plethora of synagogues, the most remarkable of which is beyond doubt Harry van Elte's Jacob Obrechtplein (1927-28). In this combination of geometrical volumes dominated by a tower apparently borrowed from Dudok with a narrow-windowed façade reminiscent of Wright's Unitarian Temple, Elte achieved a thoroughly intelligible articulation of worship area and community section. With his parabolic openings above the main door and, especially, the large pierced arch over the Holy Ark, he

succeeded in investing the structure with near-mystical dimension. Inaugurated at the same time, Jacob Baars' Linnaeusstraat synagogue is more traditional in spirit: its layout and high gables suggest church architecture and in this context the parabolic arches in the interior look more like Gothic throwbacks. The Enschede synagogue, also completed in 1928 from plans drawn up in 1919 by Karel De Bazel, associates a contemporary layout with volumes emphasized by polygonal domes and the use of traditional materials and decorative motifs. Since the late nineteenth century De Bazel had been a pioneer of regionalism and a model representative of the Amsterdam School. Overall, then, several synagogues of this period draw directly various conventional models while others, like Abraham Elzas Lekstraat (1936-37) resort to the lines of the 'international' style.

This latter trend found a reflection in the only synagogue to have been built in Europe by Erich Mendelsohn, in Tilsit (now Sovestk) in Eastern Prussia (1925-26). Here the eminent avant-garde architect, who

was later to play a key role in the renewal of the American synagogue, proposed a very simple structure whose virtues lay in the match between form and religious and community functions. In aesthetic terms Mendelsohn played on contrasts between materials and openings in a way that emphasized the shape and articulation of the different parts.

Of the number of synagogues built in England —mostly in the London suburbs—at the same period, very few adopted modernist principles, the enduring conservatism of the United Synagogue imposing the use of models from the Victorian era. Only engineer Owen Williams' synagogue at Dollis Hill (1937), to quote Edward Jamilly[11], told 'the world Judaism was a modern religion and alive in England.' Williams covered his vast nave with a veil of concrete whose saw-tooth pattern determined the placing of hexagonal openings set with Stars of David. Less tall, the annexes have U-shaped windows decorated with *menorot*. Jamilly's assessment is rather harsh in that several other architects also introduced modernist principles into their designs, among them Fritz Landauer, who pursued his career in England. Landauer's English synagogues include Willesden Green (1938), a sober, wide-angle, brick-built volume articulated with its entry and featuring a projecting window.

The 1930s too were a difficult time, marked as they were by renewed exile from Central Europe. Hitler's coming to power drove many Jews to leave their home countries, but the migratory movement, notably out of Russia, had already begun. Thus Palestine became the new home of several architects of the Modernist Movement, among them Mendelsohn, who opened an agency in Jerusalem in 1935; his friend Richard Kauffmann, trained, like him, in Munich; Arieh Sharon from the Bauhaus; and Zeev Rechter, late of Paris avant-garde circles. Zion then saw the appearance of buildings reflecting a Bauhaus or Le Corbusier-derived aesthetics that found astonishing counterparts in local traditions: whence the wedding of the cube and the sphere in both a Neo-Byzantine and a modernist spirit, and the combining of concrete and broadstone. Jerusalem, a city whose religious architecture included every imaginable pastiche, saw its first example of modern architecture in the form of a synagogue: Jechurun, designed in 1934 by A. Friedmann, M. Rubin et E. Stolzer.

Exile was even to become the source of new architectural approaches. German-born Rudolf Joseph, who in 1928-29 had built in Deiburg a simple synagogue featuring a striking interplay between its openings, was driven into exile in 1934. Moving to Paris, he played a part in the anti-Nazi movement and is said to have renovated an Orthodox synagogue. With the Fascist threat looming, he conceived in 1935 a symbolic 'Community Centre' that would have included a 700-seat hall, conference rooms, offices, a restaurant and an art gallery. In the same spirit Joseph suggested for the 1937 Paris World's Fair—scene of monumentalist rivalry between the German and Russian pavilions—a Jewish pavilion that could later be converted into a synagogue. Continuing his exile in the United States, he also proposed this pavilion for the 1939 World's Fair in New York.

Thus European Jews found themselves living through a new era of emigration, as did other opponents of fascist ideologies and their backward-looking aesthetics. Thus it was that the United States saw the coming of major figures who were to get its domestic architecture out of the rut, with some of them contributing to the reinvention of the synagogue. The most notable of the new arrivals were Gropius in 1937, Mies van der Rohe in 1938 and Mendelsohn in 1941.

Rudolf Joseph, *Project for an Israelite Pavilion for the Paris World's Fair in 1937*. As envisaged in 1935 by this exiled, militantly anti-Nazi German-Jewish architect, the pavilion uses the forms of Germany's geometrical synagogues, the intention being that it should later be re-used as such.

Amsterdam, *Obrechsplein synagogue* (1928, architect Harry Elte). A fine example of the application of Dutch forms and rationalism to synagogue building.

New York, *The Jewish Centre*
(1919, architect Louis Allen Abramson).
The worship area is once again
part of an flat building,
like the immigrants' *shtibl.*

The development of the community centre

The major change in the conception of the synagogue in the twentieth century remains the shift from the vision of an impressive confessional structure—whence the resort to Christian ecclesiastical forms—to that of a community centre including a flexible worship area and social spaces. This radically different view of the synagogue's function had the effect of restoring its role within Judaism as a whole: now more functional than symbolic and representative, the synagogue space could become multi-purpose. Stylistic symbolism was thus rendered pointless, since the synagogue was no longer restricted to the category of religious architecture; it was now a hybrid, and as such closer in spirit to local domestic architecture. As we have seen, this change had been under way since the beginning of the century.

A reflection of the lifestyle of an exiled minority, the community centre was an ancient mode of organization and one still to be found in traditionalist Jewish contexts in Central Europe. Its revival, after a nineteenth century profoundly marked by the monumentalist approach, can be traced to New York in 1919. Concerned to avoid mixed marriages and assimilation, Rabbi Mordecai Kaplan set out to help young Jews meet in clubs and activity groups that would complement the synagogue. The first Jewish Centre, mingling religious, social, cultural and sporting activities, was built by Louis Allen Abramson on 86th Street in Upper Manhattan; naturally enough, it was a building of several stores with no distinguishing external features. In 1920 the same architect built the Brooklyn Jewish Centre. The specifications did not exclude a certain taste for visible quality, while the interiors were handled in the Classical manner.

In the course of the between-wars period architects became acutely conscious that new needs would have to be met and even the highly Classical synagogues of Philadelphia architect William Tachau always incorporated complementary functions. His designs include the famous Mikve Israel, built for the Philadelphia community in 1909, with its colleges; the Sinai Temple at Mt. Vernon, New York, with its adjoining building housing an assembly room, classrooms, library and so on; and the B'nai Israel Synagogue in Elizabeth, New Jersey, whose community spaces were laid out behind the main building. It is nonetheless significant that Tachau, trained at the Ecole des Beaux-Arts in Paris and a pupil of Victor Laloux, abandoned neither the prestigious façades bequeathed by the Classical orders nor the impressive

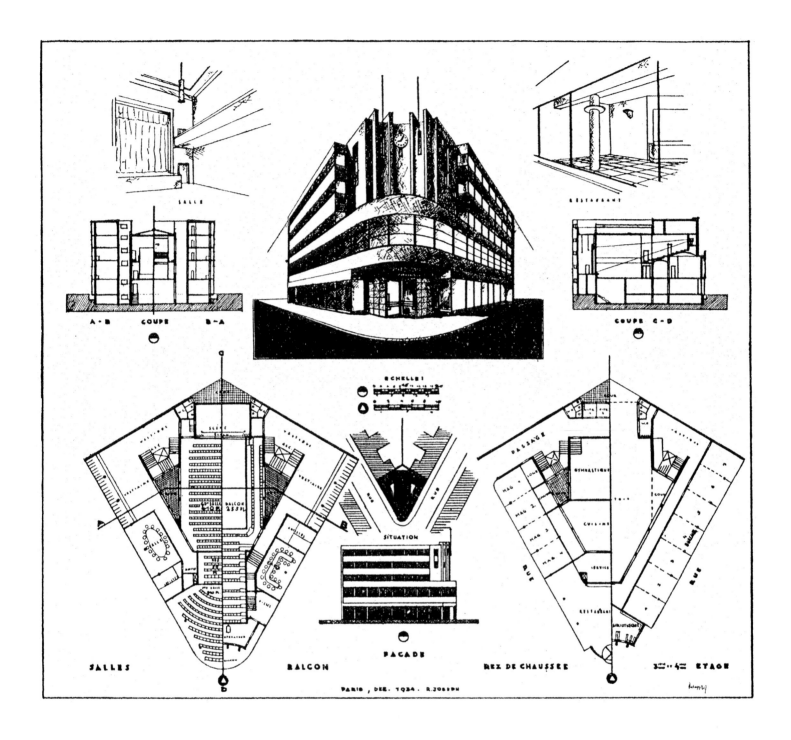

Rudolf Joseph, *Project for a Community House for Paris*, 1934. The architect planned a kind of community centre with facilities including a hall with seating for 700, another for 200, offices and a gallery for exhibitions.

worship areas; but as he explained in an article[12], 'A very interesting development in synagogal plan that had confronted the architect in the last few years is the establishment of a «social centre» in connection with houses of worship.' He had grasped perfectly the transformation of the synagogue into a 'centre for the community in respect of everything relating to Judaism': the auditorium, initially used for Sabbath classes, also served as a theatre, cinema and dance centre, while the ensemble was rounded off by gymnasiums, swimming pools, workshops and, not uncommonly, a chapel. In New York and other big cities each storey had a special function, since worship required only one or two floors. For several decades, then, there existed the community complex housing a synagogue that was often independent. In a context where the historic styles still ruled supreme, architects thus reconciled a new internal function with an exterior firmly set in the past.

In Europe too the community centre made its appearance between the two World Wars, but in a much less comprehensive and elaborate form than in the United States. However, the new approach was quick to take advantage of modernist aesthetics. European community centers were basically educational facilities attached to the synagogue, yet in 1930 the Belleville temple in Paris provided the kind of innovation rare in a United States still bogged down in Classical architectural thinking: 'cubic' forms, as they were then termed, fitted readily with the multi-purpose spatial ideal and the use of terraces as playgrounds. Lucien Hesse and Germain Debré included movable partitions to enable enlargement of the worship area, itself laid out like a cinema, on feast-days.

In the United States it was 1946 before a synagogue was built in a modern style free of all extraneous references and containing such features as roof-terraces, a social room and sliding doors. This was Anshei Israel in Tucson, Arizona, designed by Cecil Moore. At the same time Erich Mendelsohn, commissioned to design a synagogue in St. Louis for the B'nai Aimoona congregation, opened a new phase in the architectural history of the synagogue—something quite different from what had been taking place in Europe since 1945.

Paris, *Interior view of the temple
at Belleville,*
Fondation Baron de Rothschild
(1930, architects Hesse and Debré).

American and European Experiences 2

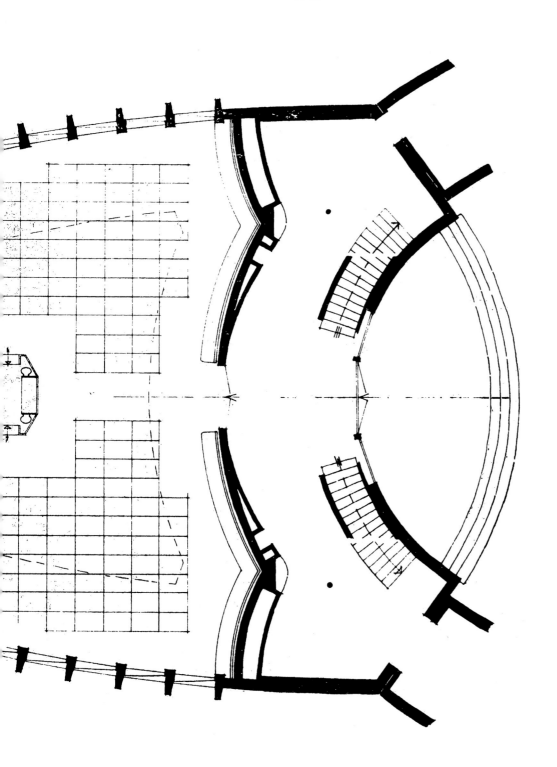

Hanover, *Plan for a synagogue* (1963).
Guttmann, the architect,
devised a distinctive parabola-based
language that also informs the arches
and openings.

Left page:
Cleveland, Ohio, *Park Synagogue*
(1946-1952, architect Erich Mendelsohn).

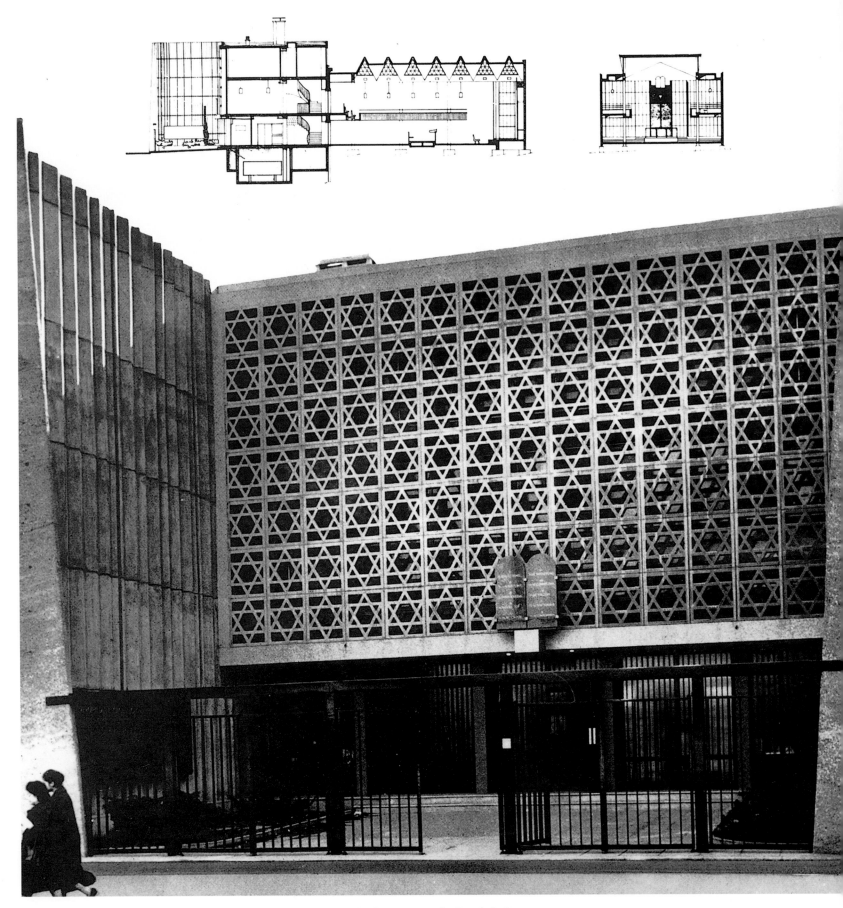

Paris, *Synagogue in the Rue de la Roquette*
(1962, architects Heaume and Persitz).

Europe:
From ruins to reconstruction

In 1945 Europe was still reeling from a catastrophe that had wiped out a form of Judaism born with emancipation, a Judaism living in symbiosis with post-Enlightenment European culture. By 1948 two new focal points had emerged, in the form of Israel and American Judaism; and yet, in one of those swings that have so frequently marked Jewish history, migration by hundreds of thousands of Jews driven out of the Muslim countries was to bring new life and energy to communities decimated by the Holocaust. This was notably the case in France in the 1960s, its Jewish community developing into Europe's largest as refugees flooded in from Algeria and elsewhere in North Africa.

Not only had the Holocaust wiped out entire communities and dispersed the survivors, it had also caused the destruction of countless synagogues. In some cases traces of a Jewish presence going back thousands of years were totally obliterated; and in the course of this desecration the Nazis had not shrunk from destroying the oldest synagogue in Europe, in Worms. Even now calculation of the losses due to Nazi and Soviet havoc is no easy matter. The Kristallnacht—9 November 1938—was only a paroxystic symptom of a process of annihilation already well under way and destined to endure until 1944. In the communist countries other factors continued to take their toll, lack of worshippers meaning that the synagogues still standing were expropriated and sometimes razed or radically altered. Nor was the West immune to the kind of devastation so systematically practiced in certain Eastern European countries: in Alsace and Moselle dozens of synagogues were lost, not only to the fury of Nazi Germany or wartime bombing, but because already weakened rural communities eventually died out, leaving their places of worship ownerless and abandoned. In Germany, the extinction of such rural communities before the war had in fact saved old synagogues, but none of the monumental examples survived. Burning might have been too dangerous in certain contexts, but demolition proved just as effective and we should not be deceived by the dome of the Oranienburgerstrasse synagogue in Berlin: left symbolically in ruins throughout the lifetime of the German Democratic Republic, it is now splendidly restored—but beneath it remains only the original vestibule, the rest having been totally destroyed.

In heritage terms, then, the future of synagogues is now a major issue in regions or countries that no longer have a Jewish population. The governments concerned

Livorno, Italy, *Exterior view
of the synagogue*
(1962, architect Angelo Di Castro).

are not always willing or able to find them a use compatible with their dignity and the preservation of their past glory. In countries like Austria, the equivalent of post-1492 Spain, near-total annihilation means the question does not arise. Germany, by contrast, has adopted an approach combining heritage preservation and reconstruction: legacies of the past can become symbolic focal points, a notable example being the inclusion of the door of the Fasanenstrasse synagogue in the façade of the Jüdisches Gemeindehaus, built in 1959 by architects D. Knoblauch and H. Heise. As the fiftieth anniversary of the outbreak of war drew near, the period around 1988 saw an increased awareness of the crimes of the past and a concomitant proliferation of museums and restoration ventures.

Throughout Europe the Holocaust left an enduring mark on synagogues and synagogue construction. Some, built to replace those razed by the Nazis or heavily bombed, have a monumental character more expressive of their symbolic function than of any real community need. Bombed in May 1940, the 1,727 synagogue in Rotterdam was replaced by a building designed by Jacob Baars, who had survived the war, and Jan van Duin in a near-brutalist style much starker than that of the synagogues of the 1930s. Their design also introduced the widely imitated concrete motif based on the Star of David. Absent from Baars' earlier synagogues, the Star, as symbol of the State of Israel and the Holocaust, now became a frequently used element. It is part of the façade in Strasbourg, where the synagogue on the Quai Kléber, razed by the Nazis, was replaced by an extremely tall building on a new site on the Avenue de la Paix. Competition winner Claude Meyer-Lévy, while opting for a modern approach—even if he had initially hoped to use Vosges sandstone—sought to retain a certain ecclesiastical feel in a basilica-plan building reminiscent of one of the most famous of all concrete churches, Auguste Perret's Notre-Dame du Raincy (1923). In Strasbourg twelve concrete pillars, two of them part of the façade, support the concrete vault that gives the nave its sheer immensity. The Holy Ark, the work of iron craftsman Gilbert Poillerat, is a tent and as such an unequivocal symbol of exile. Inaugurated in 1958, the Synagogue de la Paix is the voice of a Judaism renascent after the bid to exterminate it. Indeed, the architect was probably guided more by this message than by the building's religious function, which was then in a period of transition. Be that as it may, his approach did not fail to strike home and André Neher, one of French Judaism's leading postwar thinkers, was to write of it[1]: 'While excluding all forgetting of the past, it is architecturally totally different from the past and, in style and conception oriented towards a still unknown future. While a synagogue it is also a community centre, and while a community centre it is also a synagogue—for there still exist in France and around the world synagogues that come to life only twice a year, or once a week or once a year, as well as community centres possessing all the trappings of Jewish life except an oratory. For these reasons, this avant-garde structure, within which the sacred and the profane coexist, offers us the hitherto inconceivable hope that tomorrow may see a fundamental recasting of our shattered Jewish unity.'

England may have escaped occupation, but in May 1941 the Blitz had cost it two veritable jewels in the form of the Great Synagogue and the Central Synagogue, dating from 1809 and 1870 respectively. The former was to be replaced by the Marble Arch Synagogue (1962, T. P. Bennett and Son). Rebuilt in an extremely sober style by Edmund Wilford in 1958, the latter contains a single distinctive note in the form of a sequence of large arched windows; here we are a long way from the striving for symbolism that mark Strasbourg and Livorno. Liverpool, another victim of German bombing, saw its Orthodox synagogue rebuilt as a community centre in 1956.

Completed in 1962, Livorno is one of Italy's few modern synagogues. The brief inclined towards a community centre, but architect Angelo di Castro was bent on a highly symbolic worship area, the result being a ribbed structure whose heavily accentuated bays with their octagonal windows convey the impression of a tent with an external framework. It has also been likened to Noah's Ark.

In England, the spread of cities and communities led to the building of suburban synagogues, examples in the London area being Woodford (1954, Harald Weinreich) and Finchley (1966, Dowton & Hurst), and institutional synagogues such as the one at Stepney Green Hospital (1958); the last-mentioned of these was the work of Ernest Freud, son of the founder of psychoanalysis, who had come to London with his father in 1938. Further population shifts led to the construction of some sixty synagogues around London in the 1960s, while the one in Hove, Sussex (1966, Derek Sharp) was indicative of what was taking place in other parts of the country.

In the 1950s West Germany had begun a building campaign aimed at providing small, reconstituted Jewish communities with their own synagogues, even if this was small consolation for the destruction of pre-war communities and their property. The Berlin community, for example, which had had 160,564 members in 1933, was still Germany's largest in 1989—numbering 6,000. Each year now saw the appearance of synagogues whose architectural quality, in contrast with the makeshift buildings of the immediate postwar period, bore witness to a concern with discreetly consolidating a Judaism whose rebirth in Germany was little short of astonishing. It should be pointed out, however, that these regenerated communities were largely made up of refugees from Eastern Europe.

Building a synagogue in Germany at the time was, then, no simple matter and it is readily understandable that the architectural approaches used should put the emphasis on sobriety and prudent symbolism. In some cases Jewish architects contributed, among them Ernst Guggenheim (Stuttgart, 1952), Helmut Goldschmidt (Dortmund Community Centre, 1956; Bonn, 1959; restoration of the Roonstrasse synagogue in Cologne, 1959; Münster, 1961) and above all Hermann Guttmann[2]. Guttmann, whose first synagogue in Offenbach (1956) shows him already in search of a formal approach capable of expressing a mystical dimension, was to find his fundamental expressive line in the parabolic arch[3] used to such effect in his windows, Holy Arks, galleries and, in Hanover, in the plan itself. His entry for the Essen competition (1959) included three lofty parabolic arches, a feature he likewise used with great skill for funerary monuments. He was also the creator of the synagogues in Düsseldorf (1958), Osnabrück (1969), Würzburg (1970) and in a retirement home in Frankfurt (1978), where he combined an elliptical ground plan with a parabolic space for the Holy Ark. For the worship area in the new Essen synagogue Knoblauch and Heise used a circular plan that drew on the original 1913 building and on Mendelsohn's synagogue in Cleveland, by then an international model. Other architects resorted to the octagonal plan: Backhaus and Wolf Brosinsky in Karlsruhe (1971) and Fleischmann and Kasperek in Nuremberg (1984). Among more recent work, that of Alfred Jacoby stands out for its use of such traditional elements as a dome on a square ground plan in Darmstadt (1988) and a rotunda in Heidelberg (1991). In most of the cases cited the degree of emphasis on the synagogue itself seems to suggest a fear on the part of the architects that it would be overshadowed by the adjacent community centre.

In France little rebuilding took place after the war except in Alsace-Lorraine, where a handful of communities were re-created. The synagogues of Thionville (1957, Roland Martinez) and Sarreguemines (1959, Robert Mayer) were rebuilt on the original sites; in Sarreguemines the community centre surrounded a central worship area, while in Thionville non-religious activities were restricted to the basement. In the Bas-Rhin *département* rebuilding and restoration were in many cases overseen by Lucien

Cromback, president of the Strasbourg Consistory, who had already rebuilt, among others, the synagogues at Bischheim (1959), Lingolsheim (1959) and Wissembourg (1960). All are marked by the austerity of the 1950s, as seemed only fitting in terms of establishing a post-Holocaust style.

The first synagogue to be built in Paris after the war opened a new chapter in the history of French Judaism. This was the Sephardic Association synagogue in the Rue de la Roquette (1962, A. G. Heaume and Alexandre Persitz). The profusion of Stars of David on the façade and a serrated concrete shell reminiscent of the tent in the desert eloquently symbolize a renewed sense of exile. As both a religious and a community centre—complete with lecture theaters, conference rooms and classrooms—this was also the first synagogue to welcome recent immigrants from the East. Since 1956 repatriates and refugees from Egypt and the Maghreb had been finding a foothold in France via the Association; and every year since 1962 saw new synagogues spring up on the Côte d'Azur, in Provence, in and around Lyon and in the suburbs of Paris. Initially makeshift affairs, they went on to become more permanent.

In the Paris area the need was such that in 1959, inspired by the 'Cardinal's building projects' model[4], the Consistory under Alain de Rothschild began its own 'Consistory building projects'. Five years later, in addition to the necessary emergency facilities, the movement had created four new synagogues in areas now housing substantial numbers of North African Jews: these were Villiers-le-Bel (1962), Massy (1964, Louis Sonrel), and Sarcelles (1965), together with Fontainebleau (1965, Stern and Pietrasanta), where the synagogue had been destroyed during the war. Establishment of synagogue-community centres continued apace[5], in most cases with the stress on necessity at the expense of aesthetics; however, the centres undeniably played a key part in structuring the new communities, which were often readily incorporated into the Consistory system. Integration of North African Judaism was a crucial issue for French Jewry, and although it inevitably involved a certain amount of conflict the then president of the Consistorial Association of Paris, Alain de Rothschild, was able to acknowledge[6] in his inaugural address at the community centre at Villiers-le-Bel, that 'You have brought with you a new religious momentum, something pure, fresh and profound. Thanks to you our old communities will take on a new lease of life as new blood and new energy begin to circulate.' The movement eventually spread throughout France, with community centres springing up in cities as far apart as Caen, Valence and Toulouse.

Strasbourg, *Façade of*
the Synagogue de la Paix
(1958, architect Claude Meyer-Lévy).

Le Perreux, France, *Interior view*
of the synagogue
(1996, architects Herzberg and Aubert).

The dynamism of the Sephardic community brought marked change to Jewish life in the Paris area, in Southern France and around Lyon. This took the form of an entirely new culture and the revival of an identity gravely impaired by assimilation and the Holocaust. Moreover it found further expression in the fact that many of the synagogues in question were the work of such Sephardic architects as Tunisian-born Jacky Sarfati, designer of a number of buildings for Jewish bodies in Paris.

The 1980s saw the beginning of a new phase in synagogue building, as the feeling of urgency declined and a concern with quality and symbolism returned. And yet—doubtless for lack of finance—very few projects showed the inventive, innovative spirit then so much in evidence in the United States. The *hiddur mitzvah* was subjected to a number of experiments such as the commissioning of stained glass windows from the painter Théo Thobiasse for the Synagogue de l'Esplanade in Strasbourg (1992, Pierre-Henri Hermann), a project that clearly harked back to Chagall's contribution. A symbolic gesture had already been made in Strasbourg when the stained glass windows from the demolished Barr synagogue were re-used by the De La Meinau congregation (1985).

Paris saw a handful of innovative undertakings, as when the Liberal movement commissioned a synagogue from Ionnel Schein (1981), the result being a tile-covered volume two of whose levels are beneath the slab of the Seine embankment. Thus the synagogue is buried, as in the Middle Ages, although its presence is indicated by a *menorah*. At Le Perreux Max Herzberg, working in association with Joel Aubert, used handsome volumes of white concrete combining sharp edges, curves and asymmetry and roofed them with copper to make them stand out against the surrounding townscape.

It is worth noting here that the modern notion of functionalism, expressed in the ascending order of the various activities—communal rooms, classrooms, place of worship—follows the system used in certain medieval communal houses. One interesting example has survived in Carpentras, in France: naturally the synagogue is topmost, but the oratory is symbolically crowned by the women's mezzanine[7]. In their synagogue-community centre in Paris' 12th district (1993) Herzberg and Aubert defined the volume with a gracious curve that subtly resolved the issues of unequal access for men and women and the siting of the building on a tricky plot. At Le Perreux (1996) the character of the worship area has to do with the height and the changes of level of the roof, but more so with the wood-lined ceiling and south wall, the latter providing an agreeably warm light through its nine openings.

It would seem that the trend, even if institutional communities were still drawn to a symbolic monumentalism, is now towards more intimate spaces for the faithful; in parallel with the more elaborate buildings typified by the vast naves of Strasbourg and the United States, we are now witnessing a proliferation of oratories and the return of the *shtible*. The optimal solution would seem to lie in harmoniously combining community centre and place of worship and giving the ensemble a sufficiently distinctive character to avoid its being confused—as one community leader expressed the hope it would not be!—with a superette.

Southfields, Michigan, *Shaaray Zedek*
(1962, architect Percival Goodman).

Suburbanization and the vitality of American Judaism

While not directly touched by the Holocaust, American Judaism, as we have seen, was nonetheless profoundly affected; and it is now to America that we look for the Ashkenazy focal point and the essence of a certain kind of Yiddishness. This shift, however, also took place in conjunction with two other ongoing changes: the first was architectural, as American synagogues—notably under the influence of European architects—ultimately cut free of stylistic pastiche, and the second was sociological, being rooted in the phenomenon of suburbanization. It is true that American congregations have always been migratory, but since 1945 the majority of synagogues have been built well away from the traditional centres. In all, the last three decades have seen the appearance of more than five hundred new synagogues.

For American congregations frequent changes of premises for reasons of expansion or merger are part of the tradition; once the character of a neighbourhood begins to change, the buildings are sold off to African American or Hispanic churches. One illustration is the itinerary followed by the Shaarey Zedek congregation in Detroit[8]: opening its first synagogue in 1861, it moved in 1864 to the deconsecrated wooden church of St Matthew, then built its third synagogue between 1877 and 1880. Continuing its wanderings, the congregation moved to a fourth synagogue in March 1903 and to a fifth in December 1915. In January 1932 it occupied a new building by Albert Kahn on Chicago Boulevard, before coming to rest, a century after its founding, in suburban Southfield (1962, Percival Goodman).

Analysis of such itineraries provides a sociology of American Judaism marked by phases of integration and social advancement, centrifugal tendencies, neighbourhood specialization, regroupings and other phenomena. The route followed by the oldest congregations in a city like Baltimore is most instructive: founded in 1830 the Baltimore Hebrew Congregation built its handsome Neoclassical temple (1845, Robert C. Long) on Lloyd St, then the downtown neighbourhood. Har Sinai, founded in 1842, set up not far away on North High St (1849, Niernsee and Neilson). After a few years spent on North Gay St, Oheb Shalom, a Reformed congregation founded in 1853, took over a former church on Hanover St, a little further west. And when Chizuk Amuno, an Orthodox congregation dating from 1871, built its first synagogue (1876, Henry Berge), Lloyd St was again chosen.

In about 1890 a westward mass-movement began towards a neighbourhood around Eutaw Place and McCulloh St. Some of the synagogues then became monumental in style, one example being Oheb Shalom with its towers and domes (1893, J. E. Sperry). The Baltimore Hebrew Congregation had opened its temple (1891, C. L. Carson) two years earlier on nearby Madison Avenue, while Har Sinai, using the same architect as Oheb Shalom, arrived in the same district in 1894.

The third migration coincided with the spread of suburbanization. Beyond Eutaw Place and further northwest lay the immensely long Park Heights Avenue, where new synagogues—Shaarei Zion, for example—were established in the 1920s. With the passing of time the associations that built them gradually moved further out along Park Heights Avenue until, in the 1960s, they became concentrated in Pimlico, a suburban neighbourhood with all the accoutrements of a Jewish city: Jewish hospitals and schools, community centres and synagogues of all persuasions. It was here that Oheb Shalom built its enormous temple and community centre (1960, S. J. Leavitt and Walter Gropius) next-door to that of the

Baltimore, Maryland, *Oheb Shalom*
(1960, architects Gropius and Leavitt).

Baltimore, Maryland, *Chizuk Amuno*
(1876, architect Henry Berge).

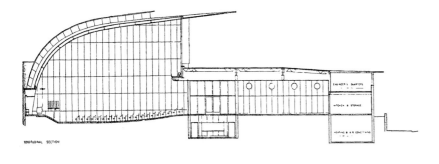

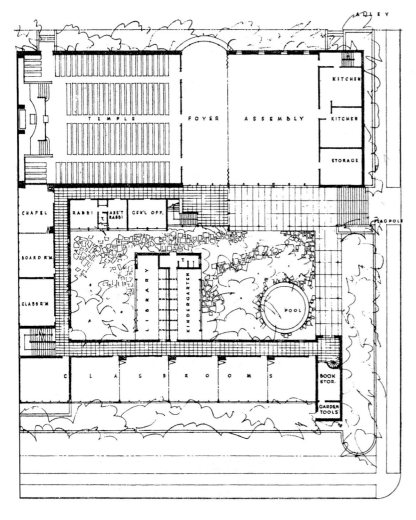

Erich Mendelsohn, *Plan for a synagogue
in Saint-Louis, Missouri.*
While exploiting the modernist forms
and the latest materials to the full,
Mendelsohn returned to the original
significance of the synagogue,
writing in 1946: 'Today's religious centres
should be in three parts:
the Worship area/House of God,
the Meeting room/House of the People
and the School for child education
and leisure/House of the Torah.'

Baltimore Hebrew Congregation (1951, P. Goodman). The former premises were either passed on to new congregations, African American churches, Masonic lodges or other bodies. Nonetheless the sense of heritage led to the preservation of the Lloyd St temple, by then the property of the Jewish Historical Society of Maryland. The adjacent Chizuk Amuno synagogue has been restored and is still used by the B'nai Israel congregation that took it over in 1895. Similar analyses could be carried out in Chicago, in Boston where the synagogues are scattered along Beacon St and concentrated in Brookline, and also in Montreal with its Jewish neighbourhoods in La Côte-Sainte-Catherine and La Côte-Saint-Luc.

This suburbanization of Jewish communities was to have major architectural consequences. For reasons of plot size the synagogues of New York—like those of Paris and London—were mostly built to the basilica plan and squeezed between other buildings, giving directly onto the street. The move to the suburbs allowed for horizontal expansion as a community centre, whereas the communal part of Emanu-El in New York (1930) was situated in the tower over the temple! Suburban communities offering space for gardens, courtyards and a residential-style layout generally provided architects with an opportunity for more subtle designs.

At one point the coalescence of the functionalist approach with a wartime economy seemed to point to a synagogue ready to accommodate such new notions as interconfessional centres or settle for minimalist modular arrangements. However this was to bargain without each confession's desire for its own centre and the prestige still adhering to actual synagogue design. At the same time rational, economically justifiable use of space became an imperative: not only did synagogues continue to provide a week-day oratory, the worship area also became more flexible as parts of it were partitioned off for other purposes. The principle had been formulated in September 1944 by Ben C. Bloch[9], who proposed a synagogue separated from its 'social hall' by a movable partition; each room would have its own function, but the two could be readily amalgamated for feast days.

Faced with this building fever, Jewish institutions set about organizing committees and publishing manuals. In its 1946 publication *Synagogue Building Plans*, the Union of American Hebrew Congregations, a Reformed body, provided plans by Harry M. Prince, head of its Synagogue Architects Consultant Panel. In the same year the conservative United Synagogue of America released its *Manual for the Synagogue Building Committee* complete with plans, one of them by Percival Goodman. Goodman was to become a recognized specialist and issued his own guide[10]. Other publications concerned with the historical and artistic aspects of the question included *An American Synagogue for Today and Tomorrow.* The *Guide Book to Synagogue Design and Construction*, published in 1954[11], also monitored new buildings: first in line was Mendelsohn's B'nai Amoona, followed by Goodman's B'nai Israel at Millburn.

Opinion was by now unanimous and was backed up by current ventures: use of historical styles had led nowhere and modernism alone was appropriate to synagogue building. Recalling the notion of 'meshugothic'[12], Rabbi Kline declared that 'A minaret on a synagogue is no less incongruous an appendage than a belfry. Both are functionally out of place. And a synagogue having the appearance of a Moorish mosque is no more appropriate than one that looks like a Greek temple. Architecture must somehow express the spirit: it must be the embodiment of an idea as well the outgrowth of a function.'

A further outcome was that historians who had fled Nazi Europe also became involved in the invention of a modern synagogue. Rachel Wischnitzer, architect, art historian and former curator of the Jewish Museum in Berlin—her classic work *The Architecture of European Synagogues* appeared in 1964—was one contributor to the preservation of the pre-Holocaust world. In 1947, while she was working on the study of American synagogues finally published in 1955 the review *Commentary* asked for her point of view[13] on the current wave of building. She too offered a negative assessment of the historical styles as lacking the ancient, venerable character so often attributed to them, and called for an approach allowing for close community involvement. While still falling into the trap represented by the notion of style, Wischnitzer sensed the extent of the coming change and was putting her faith in Erich Mendelsohn.

The great architects step in: from Mendelsohn to postmodernism

There can be questioning Erich Mendelsohn's key role in the evolution of the American synagogue. He paved the way for the great architectural experiments: approaching the synagogue with his European background, an avant-garde vocabulary acquired in Germany and Russia in the 1920s, and the dual experience of exile and the return to Palestine, he achieved a remarkable synthesis of a newly rediscovered expressionism and total mastery in technical and organizational terms. The utter commitment he brought to his work made each of his synagogues unique: 'Sleepless night,' he noted when the B'nai Amoona com-

mission came in. 'Too excited by the possibility of doing something out of the ordinary: a new religious structure for a new religious significance!' Bursting with the imaginativeness Judaism sparked in him, his lean, edgy sketches reveal a Mendelsohn returning to the sculptural forms of his youth. Cited at the very beginning of this book, Mendelsohn is imbued with a quest for the sacred—or at least for a form of modern sacrality that unifies man's aspirations as they have always been expressed by religious architecture, 'the highest art form of which man is capable'[14].

The B'nai Amoona community center (1946-1950) in St Louis, Missouri contains three main areas—a place of worship for 600 people, a lobby and an assembly hall—separated by movable partitions that allow them to be combined for feast days and thus provide room for 1,500. Mendelsohn was concerned, however, with symbolic as well as spatial considerations and the actual synagogue is marked out from the other, lower areas by an immense cantilevered roofing system whose full meaning can only be appreciated from inside. Its graceful curve is divided along the middle by a band of light obtained by cutting the vault in its course from the Holy Ark to the clerestory supporting the concrete shell at the other end. Here both symbolism and dynamics are emphasized by the light that seems to emanate from the Holy Ark itself. The ensemble also contains educational buildings and annexes set around a patio.

In Cleveland, Ohio the community centre (1946-52) adopts the tripartite synagogue-lobby-assembly hall plan, but using a fan-shaped arrangement radiating outwards from a circle defined by an enormous dome resting on a glassed-in drum. Two wings containing classrooms and offices run along the fan-shape, whose central space is occupied by a garden. The symbolism, then, flows from the setting of a concrete hemisphere over a worship area whose thousand seats face a podium on which a kind of blue and gold tent covers the Holy Ark. The architect also designed the ceremonial objects, lamps and chandeliers.

Mendelsohn continued his exploration of the synagogue-community centre model for the Emanu-El Congregation in Grand Rapids, Michigan, commissioned in 1948. His decision here was to create a single large space set within a triangle and, given the presence or absence of the Holy Ark, able to serve equally as a synagogue or an assembly hall. If necessary, the area could also be divided lengthwise by a folding partition. The school and various annexes are to be found in wings to the right of the main building, to which they are linked by a patio and galleries. The temple volume is pointed up by a clerestory in the façade and a roof comprising two concrete slabs sloping slightly towards the centre and suggesting the internal division. The entry is set on this axis.

In the case of St Paul, Minnesota, a distinction must be drawn between the project begun in 1950 and the building completed in September 1953, after Mendelsohn's death. At the outset the architect had clashed with the Mount Zion congregation, which turned down his roofs for the worship area. Mendelsohn's plan set the community centre spaces in two wings linked to the usual synagogue, itself an extension of the lobby and the assembly hall. His goal, this time, was a symbolism founded on the contrast between the high roof and the low wings: but where his model proposed a tent-inspired volume, the final rendering provides rigorous parallelepipeds, the weekday chapel, set in one of the wings, having been given a miniature version of the roof of the main sanctuary. This synagogue is dominated by vertical lines, in terms not only of its volumes but also of its decoration: the Holy Ark, at the top of twelve steps, is framed by vertical striations that cover the entire wall.

This taste for the symbolic recurs in the 1951 proposal for the Emanu-El congregation in Dallas, Texas, a project never implemented because of the death of the architect. Mendelsohn repeated here the succession of spaces used in Cleveland, this time setting the synagogue itself at the centre and surmounting it with a tall, abruptly cropped volume. The horseshoe-shaped synagogue was to open onto a circular open area with, at its centre, monumental Tables of the Law. A gallery encircling this pivotal element would have given access to a weekday chapel aligned with the main sanctuary, the synagogue and school buildings laid out in slabs. Here, in a consummate interplay of curves, sequences, volumes and contrasts, Mendelsohn attains a stunning level of compositional plasticity in a building symbolically redolent of the tent and even of Mt Sinai itself. His ultimate intention, via resort to the metal framework roofed with vermiculite sheeting that Wright would soon use at Elkins Park, was to provide the enormous nave with translucent walls. And so, in a brief American career representing a radical break with Kohn, Stein and Butler's paleochristian Emanu-El of fifteen years before, Mendelsohn had realized an oeuvre of unrivaled quality and revolutionized synagogue architecture. Only Wright, Yamasaki and Kahn would ever attain such heights.

Mendelsohn and Wright—who had employed Mendelsohn before building his own synagogue—introduced a new poetics of the tent and the mountain. In doing so they evocatively pinpointed the two elements on which the identity of the Jews had been founded in the desert: the movable tabernacle that has so fascinated architects—even Le Corbusier came up with a version—and Mt Sinai, where Moses had accepted divine law in the name of the Jewish people. Here we sense, too, Mt Moriah, first refuge of the Ark of the Covenant. For these architects, then, the issue was one not only of symbolism, but also of a poetics: these were themes whose meaning depended on the context of the fundamental events of Jewish identity and religious practice, yet they also gave rise to artistic forms whose richness was enhanced by dialogue with the extraordinary potential of new materials and a vernacular imaginary. We have already seen this illustrated by the use of wood which, just as it had done in eighteenth century Poland and Lithuania, was to find fresh significance in America.

Similarly light, always a fundamental aspect of religious architecture, was sometimes used to astonishing effect in American synagogues; these were synagogues striving to overcome the paradox of a monumentalism that in the name of movement, advance and aspiration to higher things was bogging Judaism down in the mire of exile. Their concrete foundations were sunk deep in the earth, but their thrust was upwards and towards the East.

Wright himself was certainly not imbued with Jewish culture, but the man who had revolutionized church architecture with his Unitarian Temple at Oak Park showed true genius in the multiple subtleties of Beth Sholom, his 'transparent Sinai'. In 1954 he was commissioned by the Beth Sholom congregation in Elkins Park to create a synagogue for the community centre already built in 1952. His complex plan combined hexagonal and triangular forms on different levels: each of the three base angles was marked by a concrete abutment rising to a point, while to the west the entry was topped with an enormous canopy. The abutments formed the supports for a pyramidal metal structure some thirty meters high covered with sheets of glass; these were later replaced with corrugated plastic, the aim being a translucent effect. The ridges of the ribbed pyramid bristled with aluminium spikes that reminded some observers of an Indian tent, although the reference here was clearly to the tent in the desert. Wright set the chapel and the communal rooms on the ground floor; the main worship area, which has no gallery, is on the next level, with access via lateral ramps. Situated in the corner facing the entry, the Holy Ark seems to extend upwards in time with the structure itself and its decorated uprights. What Wright had done here, in fact, was adapt a megalomaniac 1926 project for a steel cathedral in New York; but reduced to more human proportions—without any loss of impressiveness—the Beth Sholom synagogue still provides a unique architectural experience, especially in the evening when the light-

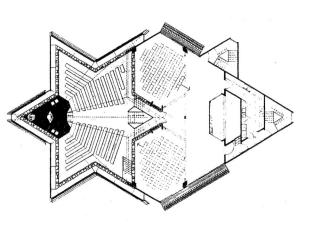

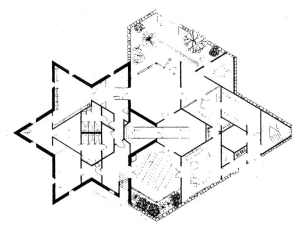

Elkins Park, Pennsylvania, *Beth Shalom*
(1955, architect Frank Lloyd Wright).

Harold Edelman and Stanley Salzman,
*Project for a synagogue for the Sinai
Reform Temple*, Bay Shore, New York.
While employing the most sophisticated
techniques, American architects
took pleasure in injecting a symbolic
dimension into their synagogues,
notably in terms of the ground plan.
Here Edelman and Salzman
set the worship area of their project
within a Star of David, a motif also
to be found in Belfast, Ireland and
Norwark, Connecticut.

Port Chester, New York, *Tifereth Israel*
(1954, architect Philip Johnson).

Projet Mikveh Israle, Philadelphie
(Pennsylvanie), (archives Kahn),
University of Pennsylvanie.

Livingstone, New Jersey,
Temple Emanuel
(1961, architect Peter Blake).

flooded sanctuary becomes reminiscent of the traditional notion[15] that the light of the Temple was brighter than the day.

On his own initiative Philip Johnson, another leading figure in American architecture—and one it is more surprising to discover as a synagogue designer—suggested a project to a congregation near his home, Kneses Tifereth Israel at Port Chester, New York State, in 1954. Was this because the idea interested him, or because he was seeking to compensate for a past tainted by Fascist tendencies[16]? Already in 1952 he had designed a highly unusual spherical structure set within a cube for a small synagogue attached to a community centre[17]. At Port Chester he used a long, modular, rectangular room roofed with an internal shell of concrete suggesting the tautness of a tent. The white concrete walls are slit with narrow coloured glass windows laid out in a regular pattern, the overall severity being broken only by the oval pavilion—a Baroque form Johnson was particularly fond of—set in front of the main volume and housing the entry and the lobby. The equally stark interior is reminiscent of the guest residence at his New Canaan home, a parallel reinforced by two bas-reliefs by Ibram Lassaw. The oval recurs in the dais of the Holy Ark. This synagogue marks the beginning of Johnson's break with the Mies van der Rohe functionalism and modernism he had until then advocated; doubtless the specific demands made by the synagogue as such—even if there is no great attempt at originality in this particular case—played a part in this change.

The 1950s, so rich in architectural innovation, also saw Louis Kahn receiving his first—abortive—commissions from Jewish congregations: in Philadelphia a synagogue and school for Adath Jechurun (1954-55) that never left the drawing board and in Trenton, New Jersey a community centre of which only the bath house was built (1954-59). With these projects he seized the chance to begin a meditation on assembly spaces he would pursue until his death. In 1961 he received another commission in Philadelphia, this time from Mikveh Israel, the city's oldest congregation, and in 1967 was charged with rebuilding the Hurva synagogue in Jerusalem. In spite of its modest scale, the Trenton bath house is often cited as typical of Kahn's work, for it illustrates to perfection two of his theories: firstly, that of the link between serving and served spaces and secondly, the entry of light via gaps between wooden roofs and walls.

Kahn made several proposals for Mikveh Israel and given the brief—study hall, social centre and place of worship—his choice is worthy of attention: while many architects were setting out to unite the different religious and social functions within a single, multi-purpose space, Kahn insisted on sharing them out among three separate buildings. For the synagogue itself, he opted for a square ground plan suited to the traditional ritual of this Sephardic congregation, with the *bimah* set in the central aisle opposite the Holy Ark; and while his theory was in large part based on notions such as the encounter, what is involved here—despite interpretations to the contrary—is an application not of any theory but simply of tradition. The project's originality lies more in the two 'window rooms' as they appeared in the plans dating from October 1962 and which Kahn introduces as follows[18]: 'The spaces are surrounded by "window rooms" six meters in diameter, with their own windows and interconnected by passages between the walls. These window rooms have glazed openings giving onto the exterior and larger, non-glazed arched openings giving onto the interior. These 'bright rooms' thus surround the inner space of the synagogue, serving as an ambulatory and a gallery for the women… The light drawn from the exterior into the cylinder reaches as far as the sanctuary without being dazzling. The whole idea is based on my observation that the contrast between walls in shadow and openings full of light renders the interior forms unintelligible and distracts the eye.'

The poetics of light and silence Kahn develops here is a central theme in his work and one for which the synagogues, even those not actually built, were a basic support. 'Window rooms' had also been planned for the community building, but on the inside. Their circular shape, their disposition within the plan—notably in the January 1964 version, in which a circle informs all the articulations—and the fact of there being ten of them (in the actual synagogue) raise the intriguing possibility that Kahn was inspired by the tree of the *sefirot*, a Kabalistic sign uniting all the emanations of the divine. It seems more than conceivable, even if the layout of Kahn's circles does not match that of the *sefirot* as they are now known, that their formal quality fired the imagination of an architect highly sensitive to fresh ideas but little inclined to submit to a symbolic straitjacket. Kahn, who wrote and spoke profusely about his conception of architecture, and who left poems on light, form and the spirit, seems never to have referred specifically to Jewish mysticism: for him a circular ground plan is first and foremost an allusion to the Pantheon or Shakespeare's Globe Theater. With the enduring support of certain influential congregation members, Kahn continued with his project until 1971, when a new committee decided that as the synagogue was to be situated in Philadelphia's historic district, it should be designed in the spirit of 'the synagogue of the

American Revolution' and complemented by a museum of American Jewish history. This meant a return to a lower, less costly building offering religious, cultural and social facilities—the standard auditorium, in other words. It also put paid to the subtlety and spirituality of Kahn's vision, with its separation of the sacred and the profane, leaving the little synagogue in Chappaqua (1962-72) as his only completed project, and even then in a reduced version.

More flexible than Kahn in terms of briefs, Minoru Yamasaki succeeded, also in 1964, in carrying through a truly extraordinary project for the North Shore Congregation Israel in Glencoe, not far from Chicago. The space is roofed with two series of eight concrete semi-funnel structures facing each other two by two, the intercolumnages are closed off with parabolic slabs and the interstices of the roof enclose skylights that fill the building with delicately diffused light. The lower part of the vertical slabs is broken by ogee-arched window openings. This combination of elements in white concrete provides a vault whose impressive purity approaches that of Indian Islamic architecture, as in the Gulbarga mosque (1367), for example. Inside, the Holy Ark is set in an ogival niche. The vigorously ribbed surfaces and the jetties and curved supports they give rise to seem inspired by the surrounding natural environment and the formal interplay of Art Nouveau. Here Yamasaki is concerned to incorporate his work into the natural setting and one commentator has even detected in his prefabricated structures a suggestion of lilies or Tiffany vases[19]. The link area between the Memorial Hall and the synagogue itself is enhanced by a repetition of the ogee-arch motif. This architect, who ten years later would become the creator of the celebrated twin towers at the World Trade Center, shows himself capable of inventing a space charged with a spirituality rising from the very roots of the Gothic or of Indian architecture, and of reconciling it with the most advanced technology of his time. The beauty of the building is further enhanced by that of the natural setting visible from its windows. This raises a crucial point in respect of the success of many American synagogues: often working in outlying suburbs, their architects enjoyed liberal amounts of space and plots on which they could retain trees, whereas their European counterparts found themselves for the most part faced with cramped, not to say residual building lots.

Among the significant synagogues of recent times Gates of the Grove at East Hampton (1989, Norman Jaffe) should be mentioned. Nor should we neglect those—of a totally different kind—of Harrison and Abramowitz: understandably synagogues are but a minor aspect of the work of this modernist pair whose impressive list of achievements includes part of the Rockefeller Center (1931-1940), UN Headquarters (1947-1953) and the Lincoln Center (1962-1968). Nonetheless they have succeeded in using a range of interesting plans and approaches, notably for Beth Zion in Buffalo (1967) whose elliptical shape features undulating, flared walls and is enhanced at each end by the stained glass work of Ben Shahn. Here too daylight slides over the walls and commentators[20] were right in drawing attention to the building's dramatic interplay of light and shade. Harrison and Abramowitz had a particular fondness for campus synagogues, interesting examples being the Evanston Congregation Hillel for Northwestern University (1948) and the Jewish Center in Champaign, Illinois (1952), both of which feature cylindrical chapels. Also worthy of note are the tri-confessional chapels at Brandeis University, Waltham, Massachusetts (1954) and the synagogue at West Point Military Academy, New York (1984).

Many other renowned architects have been called on in recent times, from the most exacting of the modernists to the driving forces of postmodernism. Thus Gropius contributed to Sheldon Leavitt's Oheb Shalom project in Baltimore (1960), an immense building roofed with transverse barrel vaults and which, united with its social hall, can provide seating for 2,000. Paul Rudolph, one of Gropius' students at Harvard and designer of the Yale School of Art and Architecture—an outright manifesto for building in concrete—added a less radical extension to the synagogue in New London, Connecticut. Aligning himself with the Johnson-Kahn challenge to the Modern Movement, Peter Blake provided the Temple Emanuel in Livingstone, New Jersey with a sloping roof worthy of a Japanese temple (1961). In his design for the Kol Israel synagogue in Brooklyn Robert Stern, another fugitive from Modernism, resorted—like Louis Kahn—to an evocation of the Sephardic past. Nor should we omit Stanley Tigerman, author of the though-provoking *The Architecture of Exile* (1988), who in 1989 presented in Frankfurt, as part of the historical exhibition *Die Architektur der Synagoge*, his project for Or Shalom in Chicago (1986). This minimalist, out-of-kilter building fronted by two high tubes—Jachin and Boaz—gives the impression of being a meditation both on exile and on the temples of Jerusalem. This return to Temple references could, of course, be taken as a postmodernist gesture; but its true function is to signal an undying flame, a quest—even among the most modernist synagogue architects—for symbolism and the expression of a specific spirituality, a specific human condition.

Glencoe, Illinois, *North Shore
Congregation Israel*
(1964, architect Minoru Yamasaki).

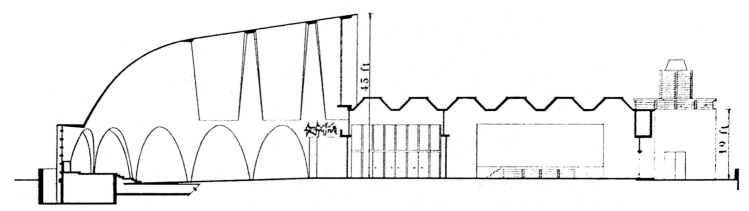

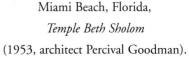

Miami Beach, Florida,
Temple Beth Sholom
(1953, architect Percival Goodman).

Parohet drawn by Adolph Gottlieb,
gift from B'nai Israel synagogue
in Millburn (New Jersey),
to The Jewish Museum of New York
(1951, architect Percival Goodman).

A new —sacred?—art of the synagogue

A major topic of debate in the postwar period, the revival of sacred art found an ongoing role in the Jewish context, all of Jewish art's deepest roots seeming to be religious. Many projects, even when functionalist in character, betray an aspiration towards the sacred for which synagogue-building was to become a principal avenue of expression. Granted, the synagogue is not the Temple, but as France's *Choulkhâne Aroukh* rightly points out[21], it merits at least partial application of the injunction in Leviticus to 'Revere my sanctuary'. And this sufficed to generate a dual approach in which a poetics of architectural forms and materials was accompanied by collaboration with creative artists.

A constant factor in synagogue architecture, the quest for symbolism found new status after 1945. Even the plan of a community centre could be given a religious significance: at the Temple Emeth (I. Richmond and C. Goldberg, 1948) in Brookline, Massachusetts, an unroofed circular courtyard serves as a link between two wings, one of which houses the synagogue and the other the school—both being set at the same level. Commenting on the courtyard and its surrounding portico, Rabbi Zev Nelson observed[22] that 'Religion embraces the whole round globe'; he himself saw the tree in the centre of the

Chicago, *Isaiah Temple,*
stained glass image of Moses (1924).
The taboo regarding depiction
of the human image was frequently
ignored in twentieth-century
American synagogues.

courtyard as the tree of life. Numerology was also a source of inspiration: the 10 openings represent the Commandments, the 39 square windows giving onto the courtyard correspond to the 39 books of the Bible, the 12 windows over the Holy Ark refer to the tribes of Israel. The numerous round and hexagonal ground plans all make play with the symbolism of the circle or invest it—often via the roof—with the six-sided star. Such is the case in Belfast (1964, Yorke, Rosenberg and Mardall), South Norwalk, Connecticut (1964, Oppenheimer, Brady and Lehrecke) and most of Pietro Belluschi's synagogues[23], which also include 12-part domes.

A number of motifs loom large in elevations: the hemispherical dome signaling the synagogue or chapel is omnipresent, from Mendelsohn's gigantic projects to the miniature Beth El in Providence, Rhode Island (1953, P. Goodman) and Darmstadt (1950, A Jacoby). Similarly the parabolic arch, given new prestige by Guttmann, was to find great refinement of expression with Sydney Eisenshtat: his synagogue in El Paso, Texas (1962) draws the eye with its use of a parabolic concrete shell whose considerable height is further emphasized by a hilltop location—as if the architect had paraphrased the name of the resident Mt Sinai congregation. This synagogue also draws enormous force from its desert setting, as does the same architect's Brandeis-Bardin Institute synagogue in Simi Valley, California (1964): again building on a hilltop, Eisenshtat created a *House of the Book*, a truly sculptural building whose concrete entry is stamped with a map of Jerusalem.

I have already drawn attention to the poetics of the tent, Mt Sinai and wood as a material, as well as to the symbolism inherent in the presentation of the Holy Ark and the eloquent suppleness of volumes and shapes made possible by the use of concrete. All these potent means of expression can be further enhanced by the introduction of a work of art, but debate continues as to what form this contribution should take and at what point its presence should be decided on. In many cases the outcome has been no more than an arbitrary addition, notably in France where, during the golden age of the 1% 'art tax' for public buildings, the 'art' took the form of a statue set haphazardly in a garden. Fortunately there have been attempts at more coherent use of the idea, in particular in the United States by Percival Goodman, a frequent figure in these pages.

Goodman's career, amid the building frenzy of the 1950s through the 1970s, is exemplary. The leading synagogue specialist, he built more than 50 all over the United States and was also called on by various Jewish bodies to provide not models—the notion had become unacceptable—but orientations. The sheer number of projects naturally allowed him to explore endless variations on the synagogue theme, but it was perhaps in aesthetic terms that his influence was most crucial. Moreover his career is indicative of the shift that took place in the American Jewish consciousness. Raised in an assimilated family, this brilliant architect who had trained in Paris and gone on to teach at Columbia was profoundly marked by the Holocaust and plunged into the study of Judaism. In 1947, with his philosopher brother Paul, he reacted to Rachel Wischnitzer's views on the creation of a 'Modern Synagogue Style'[24]: while for him the sole viable approach was founded on modernist, functionalist aesthetics, he remained intensely conscious of the need for formal expression of the symbolic dimension through the presence of works of art. The multi-purpose synagogue he built in Millburn, New Jersey, in 1951 is small and austere, yet the siting of the Holy Ark is overtly indicated by a break in the volume of the façade and a sculpture, *The Burning Bush*, by Herbert Ferber. The modesty of the ensemble is further counterpoised by works by such artists as Robert Motherwell and Adolph Gottlieb. Goodman's Temple Beth El in Gary, Indiana (1954), was even more severe: a long glazed façade worthy of Mies van der Rohe is broken only by a sculpture by Seymour Lipton and metal Tables of the Law. Goodman opts for symbolic volumes, resorting to the widely used poetics of the tent in the desert for the roofs of Fairmont Temple, Cleveland (1956), B'nai Israel in Bridgeport, Connecticut (1958) and most notably in Southfield, Michigan (1962).

The last-mentioned of these, built for the Shaaray Zedek congregation, is a fine illustration of his quest: aligned with a fairly classical community centre, the synagogue is a long building flanked by two equilateral-triangle 'social halls' with which it can be amalgamated. The pointed roof, a metal structure supporting sheets of concrete, is a perfect simulation of the tent and focuses attention on a Holy Ark set between stained glass against the sloping triangle of the wall. With its majestic proportions, the visual impact of the stepped roof and its siting pointed up on the exterior, the sanctuary is more than reminiscent of Mt Sinai. At Beth El in Providence (1953), the worship area is demarcated by an enormous, curvilinear concrete shell; the same form was used at Miami Beach (1953), but with its eastern side becoming a barrel roof with mesh-covered openings at its base. Miami suits architects with a liking for the organic and informal, as is shown by the Cuban Hebrew Congregation (1981, Oscar Sklar) and the Temple Israel's Gumenick Chapel (1969, Kenneth Treister), the latter a building worthy of a 1930s expressionist film.

El Paso, Texas, *Mount Sinai*
(1962, architect Sydney Eisenshtat).

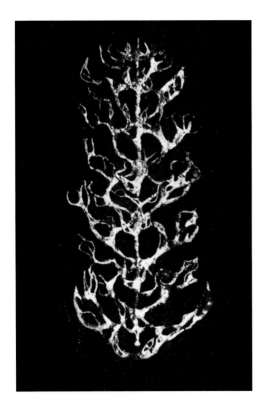

Springfield, Massachusetts, *Beth El*
(1953, architect Percival Goodman).
The façade features Ibram Lassaw's
sculpture *The Burning Bush*.

Yaakov Agam, *Paam*, 1991.

In 1951, then, the Millburn synagogue served as a manifesto for Goodman, who called in Ferber for *The Burning Bush*, Gottlieb for the curtain of the Holy Ark and Motherwell for the wall decoration. He pursued his campaign with the synagogue at Springfield (1953), where he worked with Motherwell and Lassaw, and in Providence (1954), where Abraham Rattner designed the tapestries and Lassaw provided a *Hanukah* candlestick and two sculptures representing the pillars of cloud and fire described in the Book of Exodus. These sculptures were so highly thought of that they were chosen to represent the United States at the Venice Biennale of the same year. In Albany, New York, Goodman used Robert Sowers for the stained glass, Nathaniel Kaz for the Holy Ark and Samuel Wiener for the wall decoration. Seymour Lipton, meanwhile, provided distinctive *menorah* for Beth El, Gary (1954) and Temple Israel in Tulsa, Oklahoma (1955). Goodman also called on goldsmiths: taking as his subject the 36 Just Men, Ilya Schor created for him the repoussé silver doors of the Holy Ark in Great Neck, New York (1955). Most of the artists employed by Goodman also worked for other synagogues, with Rattner designing an ambitious stained glass window entitled *Day of a Mystic* for the Loop synagogue in Chicago (1960, Loebl, Schlossman and Bennett) and Ferber the *Ner tamid* for the synagogue at Brandeis University (1955).

In addition to the ensembles created by Goodman, who appears to have had misgivings about using figurative art, we should mention such truly original works as Milton Horn's figurative low reliefs in wood for Temple Israel, Charleston (1960) and in stone for River Forest, Illinois (Har Zion, 1951, Loebl, Schlossman and Bennett). Other interesting work came from Luise Kaish in the form of an expressionist bronze Holy Ark in the Temple B'rith Kodesh in Rochester, New York (1964, Belluschi): the sculpture is a dramatic rendering of Moses receiving the Tables of the Law. A further example is Ben Shahn's mural interpretation of Malachi II, 10 in the vestibule of Oheb Shalom in Nashville (1959), this synagogue also being home to Jacques Lipchitz's *The Miracle* (1948). It is striking, however, that figurative work became rarer after the 1970s. In Europe, the handful of artistic works to be found in synagogues adhere to a strict abstraction, while in Israel Chagall limited himself to a half-realistic, half-symbolic bestiary.

Thus all this building was accompanied by vigorous debate[25] on Jewish art as applied to the synagogue, debate fuelled by the fact that the new artistic languages provided highly appropriate vehicles. These latter included lyrical and geometrical abstraction; kinetic art as advocated by

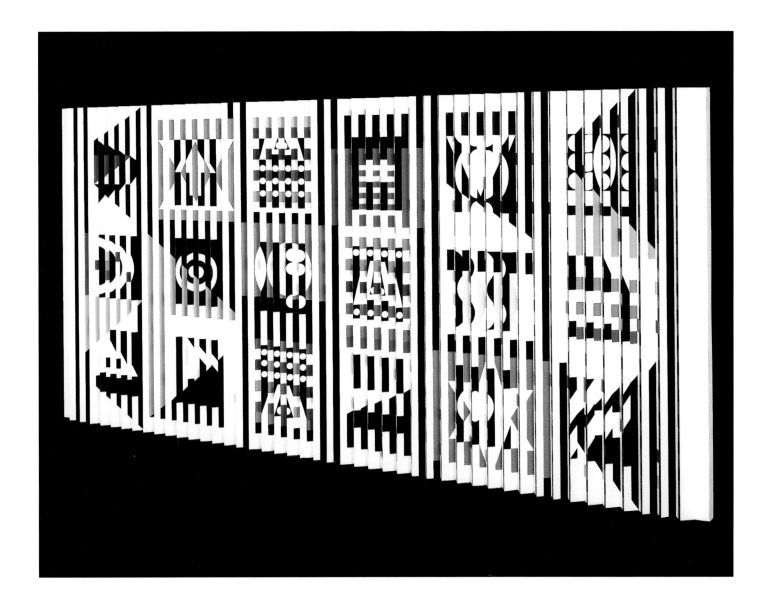

Yaakov Agam, son of an Israeli rabbi and one of Bezalel's students; and a form of expressionism that had developed with the return of figuration—although only in Reform synagogues—in the 1950s. Announcing his credo in 1964, Agam declared that 'the source of my inspiration is my determination to give sculptural and pictorial form to the ancient Hebrew concept of reality'; this explains his interest in kinetics, which incorporates the time dimension into works of art that often contain moving elements or are modified by the movement of the spectator. A spiritual heir of Paul Klee, Agam sought to 'make visible', examples of his work being a Plexiglas Holy Ark in the Park synagogue in Cleveland (1971) and the designs for the stained glass in the Hebrew Union College synagogue. More recently, he outlined[26] his personal view of the synagogue as a whole, with scattered Holy Arks and a rainbow-style use of colour.

In the 1960s artists began to specialize in what is sometimes termed Judaica: Jewish ceremonial objects, Holy Arks and decorative work. While there have been some successful ventures of this kind, the continuing influence of the traditional model has meant a fair degree of banality.

Art, then, was widely used, especially during the 1960s when synagogue construction was going strong. Later however, when the idea of the large synagogue with seating for hundreds came under fire, its role seems to have diminished in line with the quest for the sacred. As we have seen, the current trend is a return to simplicity and intimacy, a shift that had been anticipated in the United States, where large, modular halls are always accompanied by a chapel.

The Synagogue
in Israel

Tel Aviv, *Cymbalista synagogue*
(1998, architect Mario Botta).

Left page:
Marc Chagall, *Stained glass windows
at the Hadassah University Medical
Centre*, Jerusalem, Ein Kerem (1962).
Given Neufeld's use of twelve arched
openings, Chagall had little choice but
to incorporate the twelve tribes of Israel.
With considerable experience in French
churches, he employed here a very rich
colour range while respecting the taboo
on the representation of the human figure.
Breathing fresh, poetic life into Jewish
symbolism, he evokes the creation of the
world, the patriarchal realm of old and
the founding principles of Judaism.

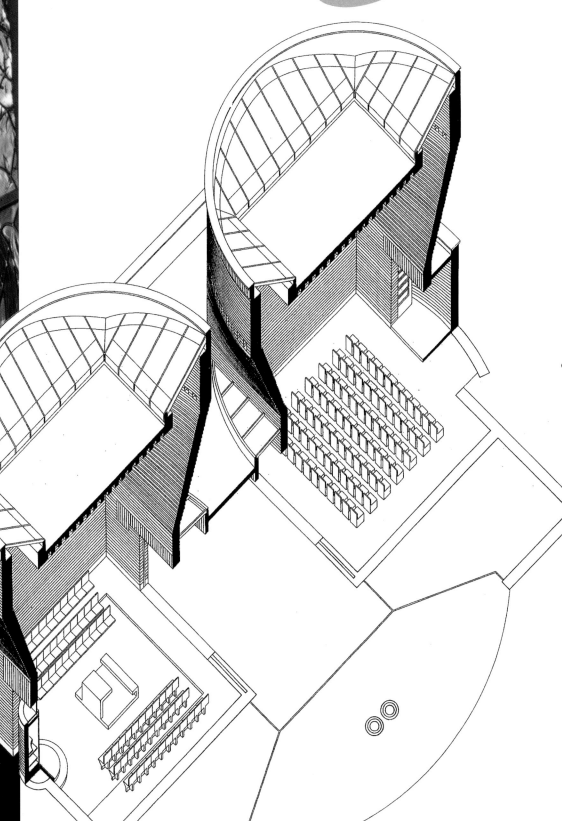

Beersheba, Israel, *Synagogue*
(1961, architect Nahum Solotow).

Jerusalem, *Synagogue*
on the Givat Ram campus
(1957, architects Rau and Reznik).

What future awaits the synagogue now that exile is no more, the ancestral home has been regained and the *Shemoneth Esre* prayer for the gathering of the exiles and the rebuilding of Jerusalem has been answered? Does this unique institution—born of exile and capable of adapting to all cultures and all historical circumstances—still have a raison d'être? For Judaism the birth of the State of Israel was a seismic shock, bringing with it the profound change that Gershom Scholem acknowledged in 1973[1] when he described the Jewish people as "in a time of beginning such as we have scarcely known since the destruction of the Temple." Was modernity as it then faced Jews in Israel simply a mode of normalization—a process of alignment with the Western model—or was it the beginning of a new phase of Jewish consciousness capable of radically challenging the function of the synagogue?

There exists a vein of Zionism for which the synagogue is far from a fundamental consideration, the ultimate goal being the restoration of the Temple. Nonetheless the synagogue has accompanied each new phase of the development of the State of Israel, from the arrival of the pioneers to the establishment of the university campuses and new cities that have proved such fertile ground for daring architectural experiments. It has also been the focal point of the quest for a symbolic dimension—but more in the official than the religious sense, for the Israeli synagogue, even though it can no longer lay claim to the same kind of representativeness, remains as protean as it ever was in the diaspora. Enjoying majority status, Judaism found itself in a totally new situation, but in 1948 Herzl's *Jewish State* became Israel, and for thinker André Neher this was a choice charged with meaning: after pointing out the nineteenth-century use of the term 'Israelite', he comments that[2] 'The adoption of the name «Israel» and its grammatical derivatives reflects this quest for life and honorability. In becoming Israel, Judaism freed itself from Exile.' The question that then arises is, has the modern synagogue succeeded in embodying this new emancipation or have other buildings taken over its traditional function?

The exiles' return

In his utopian novel *Old New Land* (1902), Theodor Herzl speaks of the theatres, factories, public buildings and houses of the new districts[3]: Jerusalem has become 'a twentieth-century metropolis' in whose heart the rebuilt Temple is a 'gigantic palace, all white and gold, its roof resting on slim marble columns, a veritable forest of columns with gilt capitals'. As for the synagogues, the novel relates that 'In addition to the great Temple, the Old Town and the new town contained many dwellings of the invisible God whose spirit Israel had breathed throughout the world for thousands of years.' However, it goes no further. Was not the synagogue, for Herzl, too closely connected with *galut*, with exile? In his idealized scheme of things the Temple, as a reflection of the messianic potential of his plan, had to be restored and the long parenthesis begun with its destruction closed; and indeed, 'it had been rebuilt, for the time had come to pass.' The synagogue clearly bears witness to another age, but Judaism will never be able to live without it. It

remains a discreet presence within the shadow cast by the symbolic Temple.

In a brief historical section of the same book, Herzl adds that 'The Jews had prayed in many temples throughout the world, some poor, some magnificent, with different degrees of fervour and in all the languages of the diaspora. Their omnipresent, invisible God was everywhere equally close and equally distant. The true Temple existed only in Jerusalem. But why?

'Because in Zion they had built a free society in which they had been able to realize humanity's most noble ideals. Formerly they had lived as a community, suffering persecution and oppression in the ghetto. Later, when civilized nations had granted them equal rights, they had come to know freedom. But in their *Judengasse*, their physical or spiritual ghetto, they lived without honour, without protection, without rights; and when they left it they ceased to be Jews. Jews need to live in community and as free men. Only then can they construct the house of the Invisible and the All-Powerful.'

Natanya, Israel, *Project for the World Centre of Tunisian Judaism* (1997).

Cochin, India, *Reconstruction of the synagogue*. Museum of the Diaspora, Tel Aviv.

Tel Aviv, *Hechal Yehuda synagogue* (1980, architects Toledano and Russo).

However, the Temple cannot be rebuilt by human hand and it was too delicate a matter to re-establish it on the mountain, on the site of the Dome of the Rock. In this context the synagogue could no longer act as a substitute; as in the time of the Second Temple, its role became a complementary one. Yet it was also to become an instrument of memory and of preservation, not of Jewish identity but of Jewish identities: thus the oratories maintain the traditions of the Yemenis, Russians, Italians and other national groups. As the generations succeed each other, the fusion into a single Israeli identity is taking its course; but the regular arrival of fresh migrants continues to nourish a complex relationship with the religious forms of the diaspora and the past.

The pioneers created synagogues in their colonies and in the cities they lived in, but these were for the most part modest affairs, small buildings indistinguishable from ordinary houses. A more impressive synagogue, its volume divided in two by an arcade, was incorporated into the first agricultural school, Mikveh Israel, established in 1870 by Charles Netter, one of the founders of the Alliance Israélite Universelle. Even in Richon Le-Zion, the colony founded by Baron Edmond de Rothschild in 1882, the synagogue is an enormous building with a hipped roof, as was customary in Alsace and Poland; two arched windows on the gable symbolize the Tables of the Law. In Jerusalem and Jaffa there appeared self-contained city blocks resembling ghettos, with a synagogue in their inner courtyard. Mea Shearim is by far the best known example of this spatial approach, in which the presence of the central synagogue did not preclude countless other places of prayer and study.

What better symbol of an emigrant community's attachment to a past lived in the diaspora than the departure for Israel accompanied by the oratory? True, the Talmud has it that with the coming of the Messiah the synagogues will return to Eretz Israel (*Megillah* 20); but many of the faithful preferred not to wait and simply transplanted their places of worship.

The most extreme case of this transfer of oratories is that of the 'emigration' of synagogues from Italy that began in 1952. With a structure depending essentially on internal organization, Italian oratories were readily transportable and since very early times their furniture had simply been moved from one building to another. One result was that after the Second World War many oratories abandoned decades earlier were taken to Israel: in all some forty synagogues and Holy Arks were thus transported as part of a movement that was doubly identitarian. At stake here were the concern with conserving one's Jewish heritage in the newly independent State of Israel—as witnessed by the transfer of the furniture of the Vittorio Veneto synagogue to the Israel Museum in Jerusalem—and the wish to maintain the Italian rite. In 1952 the Jewish community in Venice offered the Italian community in Israel the Conegliano synagogue, earlier entrusted to them for safekeeping; thus was born the Tempio Italiano, a combined synagogue and museum. The 1960s saw a somewhat startling redistribution take place at the instigation of Umberto Nahon: Holy Arks and entire sets of furnishings were dispatched to a number of religious institutions having no particular links with Italian Judaism: the Spanish Synagogue (1729) was given to the Grand Rabbinate of Jerusalem together with a Holy Ark from Mantua, the Scuola Grande synagogue from Mantua (1635) was reconstructed in the Yeshiva Ponivez at Bnei Braq and that of the Tempio Italiano in Pesaro (1650) in the Yeshiva Zanz in Natanya. Many synagogues were endowed in this way: three in Tel Aviv, two in Ramat Gan, one—recipient of the extremely handsome Holy Ark from Reggio Emilia (1756)—in Kiriat Shmuel near Haifa, and others in Rehavia, Bat Yam and elsewhere.

In 1983 Tangier's Jews dismantled Rabbi Mordecai Bengio's Etz Hayim synagogue (1880) and transported it to Israel with them. The Tunisian community, as noted earlier, was unable to do the same with its synagogue on the Avenue de Paris, and now plan to build a replica in Natanya.

Developments in the museum field underscore this enduring attachment. In addition to the Beth Hatefusoth, home to models of the diaspora's most historically significant synagogues, actual oratories have been re-created in museums. The nineteenth century had already seen the acquisition of Holy Arks and ceremonial objects by collectors like the famous Isaac Strauss[4], a practice that became a fundamental influence in developing a consciousness of Jewish art. The Israel Museum in Jerusalem is home to the Vittorio Veneto oratory already mentioned, a magnificent Cochin synagogue and paintings by the famous Eliezer Sussmann of the wooden synagogue in Horb, Germany (1735).

The departure abroad of Jewish heritage items can give rise to controversy when such material is also considered as part of the national heritage of the country concerned. In one instance the planned removal to Pisgat Peev, in the Jerusalem suburbs, of the façade and part of the interior of the Balbronn synagogue in Alsace (1895) was prevented by the French government's classifying the building as an Historical Monument.

Architecture: international or Sabra?

Architecture was a major concern for early Jewish settlers in what is now Israel, not only because towns and villages had to be built, but also because of the need for a mode of construction appropriate to a new identity. The first architects, in many cases trained in Berlin, in Paris or at the Bauhaus, were especially receptive to modernism in that it allowed them a symbolic expression of the break with the ghetto and chimed with their hygienist ideals. The 'Jewish style' they set out to develop thus emerged as very close to the 'international style' and brought with it a liberation from English colonial and Arabic forms. At the same time their modernism was adapted to the local setting, climate and materials, and as a result remained somewhere between European and Oriental models.

Some of the elements adopted—roof-terraces, for example—were common to the international and the vernacular styles, while others, such as pilotis, were characteristic of European Modernism. Moreover, the cubic volumes used came to be filled out with loggias, pergolas and other additions. It has already been remarked that some synagogues, notably that of Tel Aviv (1922, Magidovitz) followed the cupola model frequently applied in the West and readily amenable to the use of reinforced concrete. At the time Magidovitz was a town planning engineer in Tel Aviv, where he built the city's first hotel and its casino on pilotis. The Jeschurun synagogue in Jerusalem (1935, A. Friedman, M. Rubin and A. Sultzer) is a more typical example of the 'international style': initially designed as a library, it included a circular-plan worship area and a distinctive volume with narrow windows—doubtless an effective means of protection against the sun and terrorist attacks. The roofs were terraced. The Haifa synagogue, built in 1940 by Weinraub and Mansfeld, is in very much the same spirit.

Synagogue building really began to develop with the creation of the State of Israel. Two main trends were quick to appear: on the one hand relatively functional structures fitting with the local context and rejecting all ostentation in the name of tradition; and on the other synagogues with a marked symbolic value deriving from either their location or their experimental character. In the latter case, the architects were overtly asserting the synagogue's modernity and at the same time pursuing their explorations via resort to the most startlingly radical techniques.

In line with the trend that developed within the Judaism of the 1920s—a consequence of the return to tradition and rejection of the ecclesiastical model—many

Israeli synagogues were distinguishable from the buildings around them only by the presence of an inscription or special symbol. The forms were thus those of the domestic architecture. Moreover, synagogue construction was not emphasized by a new State with more urgent priorities, and Ministry of Public Works briefs focused on a standardized approach. Change came in the 1970s with the new interest in quality that marked Israeli architecture across the board. In Jerusalem the use of concrete and more especially stone brought increased aesthetic harmony and integration, the result being that synagogues in the new Orthodox neighbourhood of Har Nof are not readily distinguishable from other public buildings—notably the *yeshivot* with their rejection of architectural experimentation. The Har Nof synagogue (1972, David Cassuto) is part of a community centre, with only a small dome indicating its presence. Another synagogue by Italian-born Cassuto, also a historian of the genre in Italy, is to be found at Rehavia (1972); externally it shows great formal restraint, while the interior offers an exposed framework and an extremely subtle use of natural light. An oriental effect is obtained by the filtering of sunlight through openwork ceilings, a method widely adopted elsewhere.

The oriental influence is also to be found in the Yeshiva Porath Yosef, where Moshe Safdie's façade is covered with galleries whose arcades feature semicircular arches. The building sits well with its setting in the restored Old Town, but at the same time cannot be identified with any specific religious type.

The formal variety to be observed makes it clear that far from there being any fixed synagogue style, the genre now offers enormous freedom of choice in terms of merging into the context or assertion of the religious experience. The relationship with the natural setting has also come to loom large, the use of local stone going hand in hand with a search for integration into the landscape: the synagogue at Kiryat Yearim (1989, Baruch Baruch and Josef Salamon) is partially buried in a hillside, its presence being affirmed by a concrete shell in contrast with the Jerusalem stone used. Thus discretion is no longer a social tactic, but a kind of tribute to the setting and a striving for fusion of the natural with the spiritual.

On certain major sites—notably new towns and university campuses—the synagogue has reassumed its symbolic function. Nahum Solotow is a bold designer and a master of sophisticated techniques: in Beersheba a concrete shell with its corners embedded in the ground suggests the Tent of Meeting (1961), while in Nazareth Solotow has used an inverted dome. Beersheba also has a pyramidal synagogue based on a star-shaped plan (1979), the same approach being used in the Afeka district of Tel Aviv (1973, I. Gazith). The Negev seems to generate modernist sculptural responses, an example being the volumes of Dany Karavan's *Monument to the Fighters of the Negev* (1963-68). As David Cassuto points out[5], the tent is a recurring theme: he singles out the synagogues on the kibbutz at Ein-Hamatziv (Auerbach and Baruch) and Ohel Josef, the Yemeni synagogue in Jerusalem. The prize for the most astonishing venture must surely go to J. Toledano and A. Russo for their Hechal Yehuda synagogue in Tel Aviv (1980), built for a community from Salonika. Was it the nearness of the sea that called forth this vividly organic accretion in the shape of a shell?

University campuses have been venues for major experiments. As early as 1957 Heinz Rau and David Reznik, commissioned by the University of Jerusalem, took a highly original approach to their structure on the Givat Ram hill, setting the worship area on pilotis beneath a blind, whitewashed concrete dome resting on its own piers. The building gives the impression of having risen spontaneously out of the ground and, now that the surrounding trees have grown, is almost totally hidden in the wild natural setting of this little-frequented end of the campus. While in some respects reminiscent of the half-dome structure at Miami Beach's Beth Sholom (1953, Goodman), Rau and Reznick's synagogue is more closely related to the organic vernacular approach. Its situation, however, is a paradoxical one. Even before formally becoming a State, Israel had founded its secular university as the spearhead of the new national identity; while the synagogue could hardly be excluded, its location at Givat Ram does not really fit with its function, for even if it is almost always closed, it contributes to the overall symbolism of the campus. The University of Tel Aviv, the largest in the country with 27,000 students, did not even have a large-scale synagogue until 1998! Mario Botta's design there is the perfect expression of a certain duality in Israeli society and culture.

Other campuses have also acquired major synagogues. The modernity of the Technion in Haifa is echoed by Ohel Aharon (1969, A. Kachtan): once again using pilotis, it features a roof detached from the body of the building and supported from the inside by enormous arches, the result being a very distinctive interior lighting. At Mt Scopus, the other campus of the Hebrew University in Jerusalem, the Hecht synagogue (1983, Ram Carmi) is an extremely plain multi-purpose hall, with a Holy Ark at each end of an opening giving onto Temple Mountain. Here there was no choice as to the aspect and the overall impression is that, with the return to Zion now a reality, the synagogue can take second place to the rediscovered Temple. How much more effective and meaningful is this simple use of a point of view than the sheer monumentality of Hechal Shlomo, synagogue of the Grand Rabbinate in Jerusalem (1982): the product of a backward-looking state of mind, its height, massiveness and use of a single symbolic motif—the calotte that tops the structure—succeed only in giving it the look of a public building, as if it were the offices of a Ministry. The façade contains a reminder of the Temple of Solomon, while the interior volume harks back to the monumental synagogues of the West. Fortunately Régine Heim's symbolic stained glass, mingling the tree of life, the tree of the *sefirot*, a rainbow and various inscriptions, is there to inject some colour and life into these chilly expanses of marble.

Working towards a synthesis

What emerges most clearly from all these experiments is the sheer vitality of Israeli architecture, without it being a national priority and without the appearance of any new architectural type as such. Either the old models persist and are enriched in the course of a dialogue with the setting and the various vernacular traditions, or technical innovation takes on a symbolic value of its own, prevails over function and confers on the synagogue an unashamedly modern character. Today's buildings are proof that synagogue architecture can be unfettered and varied, that earlier styles are no longer an issue and that there are no longer any models. The successes can mainly be explained in terms of the synthesis sought since the days of the pioneers, a synthesis of Occident and Orient, modernity and tradition, religion and the secular, the Biblical past and the Israeli present, exile and a return to the roots, Israel and the diaspora. Two synagogues in particular, especially significant because of the internationally famed artists who created or contributed to them, illustrate this ongoing tension in present-day Jewish values: with its Chagall stained glass, the Hadassah synagogue is a veritable Hymn to the homeland regained, a synthesis of the Jewish experience past and present; and set as it is on the Tel Aviv campus, Mario Botta's Cymbalista synagogue both underscores and radically symbolizes the religious-secular duality of contemporary Israeli society.

Known throughout the world and now an obligatory stop for tourists, Joseph Neufeld's synagogue at the Hadassah University Medical Centre was built in 1959 on a hill in Ein Karem, in the Jerusalem suburbs. This is a small, rectangular, detached building at the foot of the

Jerusalem, *Interior view
of Hechal Shlomo, Synagogue
of the Grand Rabbinate of Israel* (1982),
with Régine Heim's stained glass windows.

Jerusalem, *Jechurun Synagogue*
(1935, architects Friedman,
Rubin and Sultzer).

259

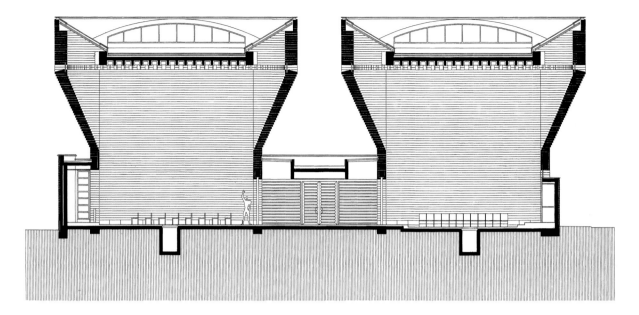

Tel Aviv, *Cymbalista synagogue,*
drawing (1998, architect Mario Botta).

Tel Aviv, *view of Cymbalista synagogue*
(1998, architect Mario Botta).

slabs making up the teaching hospital; once again, then, the setting is an academic one. The building's fame, obviously, derives from the Chagall stained glass.

Founded in 1912 by Henrietta Szold, Hadassah, a Zionist association of American women, opened a hospital on Mt Scopus in 1938. When political unrest forced its closure in 1948, the new hospital at Ein Karem was begun. Stunned by the stained glass they had seen at a Chagall exhibition in Paris, Hadassah leaders and architect Joseph Neufeld commissioned a project from the artist in 1959. Neufeld's idea was for a square-plan synagogue with three large arched windows high up on each side, a layout that led naturally to an art brief based on the twelve tribes of Israel and their disposition around the Tent of Meeting. Although a great admirer of the synagogue of Doura-Europos, Chagall agreed not to represent the human figure, but rather to present the tribes symbolically via their habitual attributes, quotations, the blessings of Jacob and Moses, and the Biblical bestiary, which he revived in ravishing form. To this image of the twelve tribes Chagall added a personal vision of the world, and of the Creation in particular, together with a reconstruction of the early patriarchal society.

Chagall's genius resides here in a use of rich blues, reds and yellows that would not be out of place in

Chartres Cathedral, and in his breathing of new life into Jewish symbols. Forming as it were a jewelled crown whose colours vary in intensity according to the time of day, the windows apply a totally untrammelled artistic language to their evocation of the *shtetl* and the world of the Bible. For the artist himself the creation of this work on the ancestral soil of the newly independent State was a most moving experience, as he was to make clear in the inauguration speech[6] he delivered in Yiddish on 6 February 1962: 'How is it that the air and the soil of Vitebsk, where I was born, and the thousands of years of Exile come to mingle with the air and the soil of Jerusalem?'

'How could I ever have imagined that in my work I would be guided not only by my own hands as they worked with their colours, but also by the poor hands of my parents? And that behind me, too, I would sense a seething, murmuring crowd, its eyes now closed and its lips now silenced, seeking to partake of my life?'

'It seems to me that your tragically heroic resistance movements in the ghettos, and the war you are fighting here in this country, are to be found mingled here with my flowers, my animals, my fiery colours.'

With the backing of the private patron Norbert Cymbalista, the project for a highly symbolic synagogue-

cultural centre on the Tel Aviv campus was entrusted to Mario Botta. Botta's 'vocation for the sacred and the monumental'[7] had attracted considerable commentary and he had already undertaken several Christian projects, among them Every Cathedral (1995) and Monte Tamaro in his native Ticino, Switzerland (1996). Without having formal roots in any specific religious tradition, Botta's overall approach—an aesthetics based on such elementary forms as the sphere, the cube and the cylinder, a capacity for subtle association of high-tech materials and (often polychrome) stone, and above all his handling of light—was eminently suited to contemporary religious sentiment. The same formal approach and religious sense are to be found in his art-related work: the Museum of Modern Art in San Francisco (1995) and the Watari-Um Gallery of Contemporary Art in Tokyo (1990).

Responding to the dualistic implications of the brief, Botta came up with twin forms differing only in terms of their interiors. To the west is the Jewish Heritage Center, a lecture theatre with its dais set in a small apse; to the east—on the Jerusalem side—is the synagogue, with its centrally-located *bimah* and an apse for the Holy Ark. The two flared volumes rise above the base that constitutes the ground floor, the ensemble being clad with stone. Light is brought into the interior of the paired volumes via a circular series of small windows and spread over the walls by a square panel set into each cylinder.

Within this dual-purpose building, intended as the symbolic embodiment of contemporary Israeli culture, the similarity of the volumes and their internal layout points up the equal status of the religious and secular functions. Botta himself wrote of the project in 1996 that 'The use of the same plastic, formal, spatial and lighting characteristics reflects a symbolic choice expressive of the contribution a simultaneously secular and religious space can make to the cultural and spiritual life of students today.' The Cymbalista synagogue thus made its appearance at a crucial stage in Israel's evolution—the fiftieth anniversary of its founding as a State—and succeeded in reconciling not only the secular and religious elements of Israeli society, but its Orthodox and Reformed components as well: while the synagogue follows the traditional plan, the multi-purpose auditorium can also serve as a Reformed synagogue. Once again a university context increases the global symbolism of the synthesis achieved.

Hurva, the Temple's dream

The issue of the synagogue was also to arise in the very heart of Jerusalem: was not an architectural type born of the diaspora rendered totally irrelevant by the Temple? Louis Kahn's project for the city, although it never actually left the drawing board[8], is a supreme illustration of the synagogue's architectural and artistic potential in the Israeli setting; yet the undertaking was haunted by the spectre of the Temple and it is not surprising that it never came to fruition.

Artists have always been fascinated by the idea of a creative return to the land of their ancestors and in this respect Kahn's career was very similar to that of Chagall: both were born in Eastern Europe, succeeded brilliantly in the West and found in Israel the opportunity to create masterworks bearing the stamp of synthesis.

Chagall's stained glass windows were repaired after being damaged during the Yom Kippur war, but this was out of the question for the synagogues in Jerusalem's Old Town, destroyed during the Jordanian occupation in 1948. Especially significant were the losses of the two largest, Hurva (1854-64) and Tiferet Israel (1856-72).

The project for rebuilding Hurva that was set in motion deserves attention, for it symbolizes all the ambiguity of the synagogue's situation in Jerusalem. Unfortunately, however, Kahn was to be no luckier here than in Philadelphia.

Kahn was approached by Yaakov Solomon, the project's instigator, in August 1967, in the wake of Israel's triumph in the Six Day War. Then a pile of rubble, the building had itself been raised on the site of older, destroyed synagogues—in Hebrew *hurva* means 'ruins'. Situated high up to the west of Temple Mountain, it had overlooked the city's Jewish quarter. In an affirmation of Judaism's rightful presence in the city, its dome, drawn against the Jerusalem skyline by an Arab architect[9], maintained a symbolic dialogue with those of the mosques on the Temple esplanade and that of the Holy Sepulchre. With the Israeli recapture of the Old Town, its rebuilding became an immediate priority: Ram Carmi was approached, but reacted with the opinion that a single architect—Louis Kahn—could provide a structure on such a scale. Kahn had first visited the Middle East in 1951 and had been working on the Mikveh Israel project since 1962.

View of Jerusalem. The domes
of the Hurva (1854-1864) and Tiferet
Israel (1856-1872) synagogues
can be seen. Designed by the architect
Assad Bey, come to repair the mosques
on the Esplanade, the former was known
as Hurvat Rabbi Jehuda haHassid,
but sometimes called Beth Yaakov
in honour of Baron James (Jacob)
de Rothschild, who had paid
for its completion.

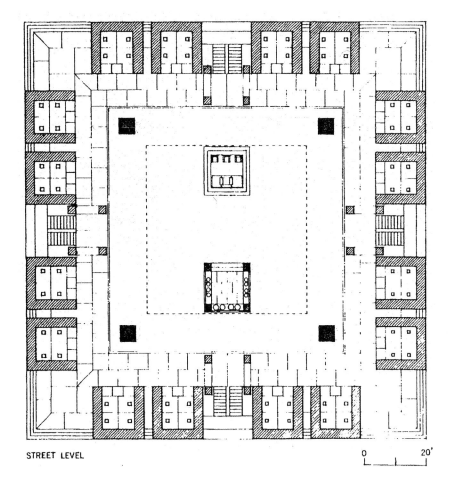

STREET LEVEL

0   20'

Louis Kahn, *Project for the Hurva
synagogue in Jerusalem* (1968).

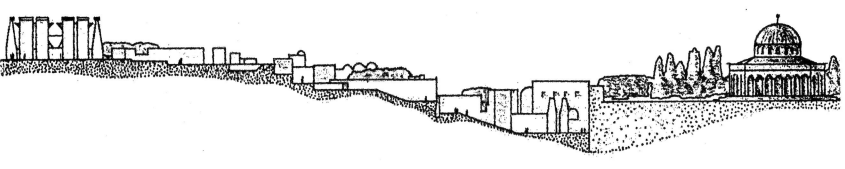

This new project was emphatically a challenge. How, opposite the Dome of the Rock, was he to create something equally splendid and meaningful, something that would match—not only in Israel but all over the world—the expectations of Jews rejoicing in the reconquering of Jerusalem? In other words, how was he to rebuild the Temple—not on the Dome of the Rock site, which was totally unthinkable—but facing both it and the Holy Sepulchre? Doubtless the project's sponsors had less grandiose ambitions, but the brief as Kahn interpreted it rapidly became a major political issue. The sections drawn up in July 1968 are eloquent: Kahn's pylons rise higher than the Dome and a 'Way of the Prophets' was to link the building to the Wailing Wall. In making the synagogue the tallest building in the city, Kahn not only revived the Talmudic prescript, he also proposed what Teddy Kollek, then mayor of Jerusalem, called a 'world synagogue' enjoying the same status as the Dome and the Holy Sepulchre. Kahn continued to work on his impossible project until his death. Between 1969 and 1972 he effected significant internal changes, before returning to what was essentially the initial idea.

And so he too fell prey to the dream of a symbolic re-creation of the Temple of Solomon; not, however, in the spirit of nineteenth-century pastiche, but by approaching earlier reconstructions as a source of certain elements and an Egyptian-style monumentality. At the same time he remained very much aware that he was first and foremost building a synagogue. The square plan decided on, with a centralized layout that could be seen as harking back to his project's predecessor, is surrounded by massively lofty pylons containing prayer cells; the reference here is to the lateral chambers of the Temple as reconstructed by archeologists. Kahn, however, did not settle for a simplistically archeological approach, his concern being a poetical architecture and a use of meaningful form: while he points out that he 'uses the same stone as the western Wall', his pylons also contain 'candle niches', about which he later wrote[10]: 'I sensed the light of a candle plays an important part in Judaism. The pylons belong to the candle service and have niches facing the chamber. I felt this was an extension of the source of religion as well as an extension of the practice of Judaism.' Set in its monumental square pyramid, the central area is surrounded by an ambulatory, a 'serving space' of the kind Kahn frequently used. Roofed with four enormous flared platforms resting on what might be called towers, this is a classical, two-level worship area whose concentric rows of benches face a sanctuary housing the *bimah* and a Holy Ark set between two towers. The interior is a world of shade, the crushing sunlight of the outside being admitted only through the interstices between the roof slabs and the pylons.

The building of the Hurva synagogue would have been a decisive gesture and a source of profound change within the symbolism of the Old Town. But having become politically and aesthetically controversial, the project was halted on its architect's death in 1974. The ruins Kahn wished to preserve as testimony to the past and a link with the future remain as they were. Yet his synagogue, reproduced in a 'fictional', computer-assisted form, continues to generate discussion; for it brilliantly raised the question of the future of the synagogue in Israel and of the Jewish symbol in Jerusalem.

Instead of Jerusalem, it was finally in Sarcelles—emblem of the multicultural new town of the 1960s[11] and a focal point for the new Judaism in France—that Jean-Marc Weill created a surrogate for Kahn's project. His Community Centre features pylons forming a blind wall, overhanging roofs supported by flared towers, interplay between the internal levels, and a ground floor multi-purpose hall with a worship area above it. So maybe there is now a little bit of Jerusalem in Sarcelles…

If ever a synagogue was a political act, it was Hurva, as Jerusalem's mayor had acknowledged. If built, would it have provided the necessary counterweight to the Grand Rabbinate's Hechal Shlomo? The abandoning of the project can be seen to some extent as reflecting a 'heritage' approach to the Old Town and a concomitant rejection of a potent symbol of continuity. True, the ruins are still there, but their style is too indebted to the martyrdom of the past. Until the very end Kahn worked on a garden that would have enveloped the ruins and, in terms of the synagogue, filled this memorial function. Hechal Shlomo, bearing a name so charged with meaning, is above all significant of Judaism's gradual absorption by the State —and, moreover, is situated outside the Old Town.

Nonetheless the future of the Israeli synagogue doubtless lies more with *Beth Hamidrash* (the house of study) than *Beth Hamikdash* (the Temple of Jerusalem). The existence of a Grand Rabbinate—and a dual one at that—can only be justified as part of a diaspora-derived yearning to restore the high priests of the past. There is something Napoleonic about it, as there is about the undisguised monumentality of the building itself. Judaism has no Pope and on Israeli soil should be free to develop more freely; but in any 'normalized' or 'secularized' nation—to use a typically Occidental concept—Church-State relations remain a most delicate business, as the dualist Cymbalista Synagogue illustrates. Trapped between political contradictions, architects have no escape-hatch but their own poetics: yet sometimes, like latter-day prophets—ever on the verge of crying in the wilderness—they succeed in opening up new avenues.

Jean Marc Weill, *Project for the Great
Synagogue at the Sarcelles Community
Centre.* Such was the fame
of Louis Kahn's projects that their
inspiration is felt even here.

Max Beckmann, *The Synagogue*,
1919, oil on canvas.
Frankfurt Stadelsches Kunstinstitut.
A modernist rendering of the Orthodox
synagogue on the Börneplatz
in Frankfurt, opened in 1882.

A Looking-Glass Architecture

Few forms of architecture are as heavily weighed down with notions of representation as that of the synagogue, that mirror of the history and condition of the Jews in the societies in which they have lived. We have seen how the synagogue could conceal itself, move out of the ghetto, raise spires to signal its presence, adapt readily to all imaginable architectural models—but also attempt to be itself, assert its individuality. Its place in the *res publica* is the image of that of the Jew in society, an identification of the Jew with the synagogue that is not without consequences when it crystallizes anti-Semitic hatred. The iconography of the synagogue speaks eloquently of the way Jews have been seen down the centuries: mysterious, foreign, picturesque, fascinating, exaggeratedly Oriental, expressive of the Semitic myth... The image of the synagogue has thus embodied the gamut of the standard literary and pictorial representations by finding equivalents for them on the architectural plane. The canvases of the German Moritz Oppenheim, the Englishman Solomon Hart, the Pole Maurycy Gottlieb and the Frenchman Edouard Moyse lay bare the integrative idealism and confessionalization of the Neoclassical and Neo-Romanesque periods; while the writings of Edmond and Jules de Goncourt project all the fantasies of French society onto a Jewish heroine and a Paris synagogue.

The synagogue's artistic apogees have almost always coincided with periods of profound symbiosis, of syntheses between Judaism and its host civilizations: syntheses with Babylon, the Hellenistic and Arabic worlds, Spain, Germany and so many other nations. And every one of these climaxes has ended in destruction, for civilizations

Berlin, *The Fasanenstrasse synagogue
burning during the Kristallnacht*, 1938.
Built in 1912 by Ehrenfried Hessel,
this enormous building was replaced
by the headquarters of Berlin's Jewish
community. Fragments of the former
synagogue have been incorporated
into the façade of the new structure.

are mortal—especially Jewish civilizations, even more fragile than the others. Yet by a kind of miracle, each time a Jewish culture is extinguished a new point of focus emerges out of exile and dispersion; and the synagogue plays a not inconsiderable role in this capacity for rebirth. Today, moreover, a double destiny is being played out, in the diaspora and in Israel.

It hardly needs to be said, given its endless history of burning and profanation, that the synagogue is also the mirror of Jewish martyrdom. It would take an entire book just to list the destruction so effectively practised by Crusaders, Cossacks, Nazis, caliphs and rabble-rousing preachers. The twentieth century saw more such destruction than any other, with attacks against both of Judaism's major branches: the Nazis and their sympathizers, backed up by the Stalinist regime, almost succeeded in eradicating European Jewry, while certain Arab nations set out to remove the last traces of Sephardic and Oriental Judaism. The events of 1948, ten years after the Kristallnacht, might lack the latter's pretty-sounding name, but the outcome was just as devastating, with 58 synagogues destroyed in Jerusalem alone, not to mention all those that went uncounted elsewhere. Now synagogues disappear in time with the wars in the Middle East: 1948, 1967 and afterwards; and in France, in October 2000, with the burning of the synagogue at Trappes, in the Paris suburbs. Thus the unthinkable, the unnamable can recur amidst near-total indifference. Is it now the case, as Ytzhak Baer observed in 1936, that 'Exile has come back to square one'?

We have a historical duty towards these buildings which, together with the cemeteries, are among the last surviving remains of the Jewish presence. Heritage preservation is only meaningful in terms of the future, but this future is not so much that of Jews themselves as of the nations that have had—or still have—the good fortune to have Jewish communities in their midst. The synagogue's destiny remains the destiny of living Judaism, and fortunately it has always been gifted with the suppleness and adaptability needed to meet changing needs. Its future—certainly tending more to the *Beth Hamidrash* than to the renewed confessional emphasis generating a bunker mentality in certain circles—remains open; the choice is between withdrawal and dialogue. The synagogue continues to exist in a multiplicity of forms and to engage in internal debate as much as it did in past centuries: should it, then, remain an architectural type characterized by a certain monumentality—or sacrality—as an instrument for offering the world an image of Jewish values? Or should it give way to the *shtibl*, where a near-sacredness has become attached to the words of the rabbi rather than to the building itself? Yet it would be a mistake to mistrust the building, be it ancient or modern, for its very walls can speak.

Mauricy Gottlieb, *Jews praying
in the synagogue at Yom Kippur*, 1878,
oil on canvas. Tel Aviv Museum of Art.

Notes

Introduction

1. Mendelsohn, "My approach to building a modern synagogue", *Architectural Forum*, vol. 98, 4/1953, p. 108.
2. "Our prayer spaces have a little of the scarred character of the Temple. They have the right, at least partially, to the application of the precept (Le. 19,30): 'Revere my sanctuary'.", Ernest Weill, *Choul'hâne Aroukh abrégé*, Fondation Sefer, 1980, chap. 39, p. 80.
3. "Le Temple", sermon of Schemini-Atsereth 5633 (1872), *Sermons et allocutions*, 1ère série, Durlacher, 2e ed., 1893, p. 157 and 159.
4. Kafka, "Discours sur la langue yiddish", *Préparatifs de noce à la campagne*, transl. by Marthe Robert, Gallimard-Folio, 1980, p. 479.
5. Jacob Katz, *Exclusion et Tolérance. Chrétiens et juifs du Moyen Age à l'ère des Lumières*, French transl., Lieu Commun, 1987, pp. 7-8.

I. SYMBOLIC ARCHITECTURE

1. Rabbi of the Shearith Israel congregation in New York, inauguration sermon on 20 December 1895.
2. Julien Guadet, *Eléments et théorie de l'architecture*, 1904, tome 3, p. 464.
3. Zadoc Kahn, "Sermon prononcé à l'inauguration de la synagogue de La Ferté-sous-Jouarre, le 21 septembre 1891", *Sermons et allocutions*, 3e série, Paris, Durlacher, 1894, p. 118-121.
4. Ernest Weill, *Choul'hâne Aroukh abrégé*, ed. cit., chap. 39, p. 80.
5. *Etoiles du matin*, French transl. from the Hebrew by G. Deutsch, Albin Michel, 1969, pp. 28-30.
6. In order to finance in part the 'Portuguese' synagogue in Paris, on the Rue Buffault, Daniel Osiris Iffla (from Bordeaux) in the agreement that he made with the community, specified that: "The memories of my family and those of my youth impose the obligation of recalling in the present that in the Synagogue on the Rue Buffault the Sephardic rite—called Portuguese—will be exclusively followed, such as it is presently practiced in Paris at the Temple on the Rue Lamartine, in Bordeaux, in Bayonne, in Amsterdam and in the Ritual of Hazan Mendès." Archives du Consistoire israélite de Paris
7. G. Ben Lévi, "La schoule, la synagogue et le temple", *Archives israélites de France*, November 1846, pp. 663-4. The italics and the spelling are from the original.
8. A temporary synagogue (and with free places) installed during Kippur for the traditionalist Jews of the Marais.
9. According to the analysis of Simon Schwarzfuchs, *Du Juif à l'Israélite. Histoire d'une mutation 1770-1870*, Fayard, 1989.
10. Yaacov Agam, "My Ideal Synagogue", *Reform Judaism*, Autumn 1994.

II. AN ARCHITECTURE OF EXILE

1. 23 January 1903, Rome, *Journal*, extract published from *L'Etat juif*, Stock, 1981, p. 225.
2. Yitzhak F. Baer, *Galout. L'imaginaire de l'exil dans le judaïsme*, French transl., Calmann-Lévy, 2000, p. 63.
3. Masha Itzhaki and Michel Garel, *Jardin d'Eden, Jardins d'Espagne*, Le Seuil/B.N., 1993, p. 109.
4. E. Jabès, *Le Livre des questions*, Gallimard, 1963, p. 113.
5. Franz Kafka, 4e cahier (February 1918), transl. Marthe Robert, *Préparatifs de noce à la campagne*, Gallimard-Folio, 1980, p.130.
6. Yosef H. Yerushalmi, *Zakhor. Histoire juive et mémoire juive*, transl. E. Vigne, 1984, p. 54-56.
7. S. Tigerman, *The Architecture of Exile*, New York, Rizzoli, 1988.
8. J. Roth, *Juifs en errance* (1927), French transl., Le Seuil, 1986, p. 24: "'Temple Jews', that is to say, are clean shaven well-brought up gentlemen with frock-coats and tall hats (...) Organ music can be heard in these temples (...)".

1. The Diaspora in Antiquity

1. *Le monde juif vers le temps de Jésus* (1935), Paris, 1969, p. 93.
2. Lee I. Levine, "The Second Temple Synagogue: the Formative Years", *The Synagogue in late Antiquity*, ed. L.I. Levine, The American School of Oriental Research, Philadelphia, 1987, pp. 7-31.
3. However the Hebrew word used is 'tabernacle', as in the Tent of the desert, *Ohel moed*, and not *knesset*, 'assembly'. The interpretation which proposes to see in the events related here the profanation of the Temple by King Antiochus Epiphane (169 B.C.) allows better to envisage an allusion to synagogues.
4. Aramaic translation of the Bible. After the return from Babylonia, the common language became Aramaic. It was therefore necessary to accompany the reading of the Torah by a translation which was the first commentary.
5. V. Corbo, "Resti della sinagoga del primo secolo a Cafarnao" *Studia Hierosolymita*, 3, 1982.
6. Abraham Galanté, "Les synagogues d'Istanbul", *Hamenora*, July-August 1937.
7. The high density of sites found within the actual borders of Israel can be explained by the fact that excavations are more systematically undertaken there than elsewhere. Listed in: M.J.S. Chiat, *Handbook of Synagogue Architecture*, 1982; L.I. Levine, ed., *Ancient synagogues revealed*, 1981; Dan Urman and Paul V.M. Flesher, *Ancient Synagogues. Historical Analysis and Archaeological Discovery*, 1995; L. I. Levine, *The Ancient Synagogue. The First Thousand Years*, 1999.
8. "On the source of the architectural design of the ancient synagogues in Galilee: a new appraisal", *Ancient Synagogues. Historical Analysis and Archaeological Discovery*, 1995; ed. cited, p. 83.
9. Kohl and Watzinger, *Antike Synagogen in Galilea*, Leipzig, 1916.
10. F. Cumont, *Fouilles de Doura-Europos (1922-1923)*, 1926.
11. See in particular, J. Gutmann, ed., *The Dura-Europos Synagogue: A Re-evaluation (1922-1972)*, 1973; K. Weitzmann and L.H. Kessler, *The Frescoes of the Dura-Europos Synagogue and Christian Art*, 1990. A Franco-Syrian mission resumed excavations in 1986, under the direction of P. Leriche and A. Al Mahmoud: the results are published in *Syria*.
12. A.W. Brunner, "Synagogue Architecture", *The Brickbuilder*, 16, n°3, March 1908, p. 38.
13. He published a work: *Let them make me a Sanctuary. A Contemporary American Synagogue Inspired by the Art of Ancient Israel*, New York, Behrman House, 1978.
14. Famous prayer ritual, the oldest was compiled in Champagne during the 11th century.
15. Agam exposed his mobile star in Paris at the Petit Palais in 1968 before sending it to New Rochelle.
16. Alf Thomas Kraabel, "The Diaspora Synagogue: archaeological and epigraphic evidence since Sukenik", *Ancients Synagogues...*, ed. cited, 1995, pp. 119-120.

2. The Sephardic and Oriental Diasporas

1. This process was not specific to Spanish and Portuguese Jews. In Persia the Shiit persecutions also compelled the Jews to outwardly change their religion and to practise in secret.
2. D. Jarrassé, "*Sefarad* imaginaire. Le style hispano-mauresque dans les synagogues françaises du XIXe siècle", *Mémoires juives d'Espagne et du Portugal* symposium, Publisud, 1996, pp. 261-269.
3. F. Cantera Burgos, *Sinagogas españolas*, Madrid, Instituto Arias Montano, 1955.
4. Id., *Sinagogas de Toledo, Segovia y Córdoba*, Madrid, Instituto A. Montano, 1973.
5. Several sources attribute this synagogue to Joseph ben Shoshan, adviser to Alfonso VIII. His epitaph (he died in 1205) states that it was constructed around this date.
6. Bernard Lewis, *Juifs en terre d'Islam* (1984), French transl. Flammarion, 1989, pp. 146-147.

7. Michaël Molho, *Les Juifs de Salonique à la fin du XVIe siècle. Synagogues et patronymes* (1967), transl. 1991.
8. Elias V. Messinas, *The Synagogues of Salonika and Veroia*, Athens, Gavrielides Ed., 1997.
9. During the reconstruction, completed in 1845, an inscription was found which attests that the synagogue was 460 years old, according to Neumann, *Die heilige Stadt*. 1877, cited by Y. Ben-Arieh, *Jerusalem in the 19th Century, The Old City*, Jerusalem, 1984, p. 299.
10. Gérard Nahon, *Métropoles et périphéries séfarades d'Occident. Kairouan, Amsterdam, Bayonne, Bordeaux, Jérusalem*, Cerf, 1993.
11. *Histoire du peuple juif*, French transl., Stock, 1980, t. 2, p. 77.
12. Theodore Lewis, *History of Touro Synagogue*, Bulletin of the Newport Historical Society, vol. 48, n°158, Summer 1975.
13. "Société civile du Temple Israélite, suivant le Rite Espagnol-Portugais dit Sephardi", statutes registered on the 21 May 1875, Archives of the Consistoire de Paris.
14. Shlomo Deshen, *Les gens du Mellah*, French transl., 1990. This social anthropological work on Jewish life in pre-colonial Morocco gives an important place to the question of synagogue administration.
15. Paul Sebag, *Histoire des Juifs de Tunisie*, 1991.
16. D. Jarrassé, *Une histoire des synagogues françaises. Entre Occident et Orient*, 1997, pp. 302-310.
17. See the works of Jacob Pinkerfeld, "Un témoignage du passé en voie de disparition: les synagogues de la région de Djerba", *Les Cahiers de Byrsa*, Paris, 1957, pp. 127-137; *Bate ha-keneset be-Afrika ha-tsiponit*, Bialik Institute, Jerusalem, 1974
18. *Lettres édifiantes et curieuses de Chine par des missionnaires jésuites*, Garnier-Flammarion, 1979, p. 161.
19. *La Synagogue à travers les âges*, photographs by Neil Folberg, text by Yom Tov Assis, Abbeville Press, 1995.
20. Phyllis Lambert, ed., *Fortifications and the Synagogue. The Fortress of Babylon and the Ben Ezra Synagogue*, Cairo, London, 1994.
21. Laura Rachel Felleman Fattal, "American Sephardi Synagogue Architecture", *Jewish Art*, n°19-20, 1993-1994, pp. 21-43.

3. The Ashkenazic Diaspora

1. J. Roth denotes by this word, the *shtibl*.
2. J. Roth, *Juifs en errance*, French transl., pp. 26-27.
3. Mark Zborowski and Elizabeth Herzog, *Olam. Dans le shtetl d'Europe centrale avant la Shoah* (1952), French transl., Plon, 1992; cit. pp. 42-43.
4. Josef Erlich, *La Flamme du Shabbath. Le Shabbath—moment d'éternité—dans une famille juive polonaise* (1970), transl. from Yiddish, Plon, 1998.
5. " Mutual Influences between Eastern and Western Europe in Synagogue Architecture from the 12th to the 18th Century", *Yivo Annual of Jewish Social Science*, 2/3, 1947-48, pp. 25-68.
6. Certain synagogues of the important Jewish centres in Poland and Lithuania bear the name of the masters who founded or directed them, or even influenced them with their ideas: MaHarShaL refers to Rabbi Salomon Louria; ReMo, Rabbi Moses Isserles; TaZ, Rabbi David ben Samuel by the title of his treatise *Ture Zahab*.
7. A. Grotte, *Deutsche, böhmische und polnische Synagogentypen vom 11. bis Anfang des 19. Jahrhunderts*, Berlin, 1915, p. 39.
8. Maria and Kazimierz Piechotka, *Bóznice Drewniane*, Warsaw, 1957; id., *Bramy Nieba. Bóznice drewniane na ziemeciach dawnej Rzeczypospolitej*, Wydawnictwo Krupski i S-ka, Warsaw, 1996.
9. An article in Yiddish in *Rimon/Milgroim*, n° 3, Berlin, 1923; transl. "Memoirs Concerning the Mohilew Synagogue", in Ruth Apter, ed., *Tradition and Revolution. The Jewish Renaissance in Russian Avant-Garde Art 1912-1928*, The Israel Museum, Jerusalem, 1987, pp. 233-4.

10. Information furnished by Prof. Bernard Keller.
11. Cyril Edel Leonoff, *The Architecture of Jewish Settlements in the Prairies. A Pictorial History*, 1975.
12. Louis Wirth, *Le ghetto* (1925), French transl. Presses universitaires de Grenoble, 1980.
13. *Les Enfants du ghetto* (1892), *Tragédies du Ghetto* (1893), *Les Rêveurs du Ghetto* (1898), *Comédies du Ghetto* (1907), etc. Zangwill taught at one time at a Free Jewish school in Spitalfields.
14. G. and N. Pressburger, *Histoires du Huitième District*, transl. From Italian, Lagrasse, Verdier, 1989, p. 25.
15. H. Hapgood, *The Spirit of the Ghetto. Studies of the Jewish quarter in New York*, New York and London, 1902.
16. Gerard R. Wolfe, *The Synagogues of New York's Lower East Side*, New York, 1978.
17. On this edifice, see III, 2, Nationalization.
18. R. Ertel, *Le Roman juif américain. Une écriture minoritaire*, Payot, 1980, p. 149.
19. E. Fleg, *L'Enfant prophète*, Gallimard, 1926, p. 156.
20. O. Israelowitz, *Synagogues of New York City*, Dover, New York, 1982, p. VIII.
21. Gallimard, 1979, p. 45.
22. "Synagogue Design: Forging an Aesthetic Unbound by Tradition", *Progressive Architecture*, vol. 47/1, March 1966, p. 151.
23. Apropos of Adath Jeshurun, "A Synagogue", *Perspecta*, 1955, n°3, p. 62.

III. AN ARCHITECTURE OF IDENTITY

1. A common expression during the 1840s particularly for Hippolyte Fortoul and Léon Vaudoyer who saw in architecture the most authentic expression of the genius of a people.

1. From the Ghetto to Emancipation

1. Lionel Kochan, "La fin de la Kehila. Forces sociales dans la société juive d'Europe centrale et orientale aux XVIIᵉ et XVIIIᵉ siècles", *La Société juive à travers l'histoire*, t.1, Fayard, 1992, pp. 532-563.
2. A document from the *geniza* of the Ben Ezra synagogue mentions the demolition of a part of a synagogue which was higher than the neighboring mosque, cited in Ph. Lambert, ed., *Fortifications and the Synagogue, The Fortress of Babylon and the Ben Ezra Synagogue*, Cairo, London, 1994, p. 86.
3. Juda ha-Hassid cited by Jacob Katz, *Exclusion et Tolérance. Chrétiens et juifs du Moyen Age à l'ère des Lumières*, French transl., Lieu Commun, 1987, p. 130.
4. It opened after the events of 1848 and lost its walls, but Pie IX, upon his return, remised the principle of enforced residence.
5. Rachel Heuberger and Helga Krohn, *Hinaus aus dem Ghetto... Juden in Frankfurt am Main 1800-1950*, Frankfurt, Fischer, 1988.
6. Alessandria, Asti, Casale Monferrato and Moncalvo (1723), Carmagnola, Chieri and Saluzzo (1724), Vercelli (1727), Cherasco and Mondovì (1730), Acqui Terme (1731), Nizza Monferrato (1732).
7. *Le Jardin des Finzi-Contini* (1962), French transl, Gallimard, 1964, Part I, chapter IV.
8. René Moulinas, *Les Juifs du Pape en France*, Privat, 1981.
9. Dohm, *De la réforme politique des Juifs*, transl. of Bernoulli, reedition, Stock, 1984, p. 34.
10. Herder, *Idées pour la philosophie de l'histoire de l'humanité* (1784-1791), book XVI, chapter 5.
11. A deputy of Paris, who presided over the Assemblée Nationale Constituante, he declared on 23 December 1789, during a debate on the eligibility of non-Catholics: "We must refuse everything to Jews as a nation and grant everything to Jews as individuals." He refered then to the edict of Joseph II.
12. Sendschreiben an seine Hochwürden, Herrn Oberconsistorial Rath und Probst Teller zu Berlin, von einigen Hausvätern jüdischer Religion (1799), cited by Hannah Arendt, "L'Aufklärung et la question juive" (1932) in *La Tradition cachée*, French transl., C. Bourgois, 1987, p. 23.
13. Paragraph 2 of article 12 of the decree of 17 March 1808 (resumed in the *règlement organique* of 25 May 1844) demanded that the *consistoires*, "see that under no cause or religious pretext that there be, without specific authorization, any prayer assemblies".
14. Deliberations of the *Consistoire israélite* of Bordeaux, 23 May 1809: moreover, it referred to the request of the Prefect of Paris to the Jews to meet in "a single location". During the debates, the faithful demanded "a temple", a term henceforth consecrated.
15. Chief Rabbi Andrade, inauguration speech, 14 May 1812.
16. "Discours sur la synagogue de nos jours comparée à celle des temps passés", *La Famille de Jacob*, 17, 1874-75, p. 22.
17. "Le Temple. Schemini-Atsereth 5633", *Sermons et allocations*, 1ʳᵉ série, 1875.

2. Architectural Styles and National Affiliation

1. Isaiah Berlin, The Crooked Timber of Humanity
2. 1772, quoted in Herder, *Von Deustcher Art und Kunst*, 1773.
3. Leon A. Jick, *The Americanization of the Synagogue 1820-1870*, Brandeis University Press, Hanover, New Hampshire, 1976, p. 143.
4. Trad. franç. et présentation Marc B. de Launay, *Pardès*, 5/1987, pp. 13-48.
5. Israel Zangwill, *Comedies of the Ghetto*, London.
6. 'Architecture and Anglicization: London Synagogue Building, 1870-1900', *The Jewish Quarterly*, 34/2 (126), 1987, pp. 16-22.
7. P. Lindsay, *The Synagogues of London*, London, Valentine Mitchell, 1993, pp. 118-19.
8. Ibid, pp. 118-19.
9. *Synagogen in Deutschland. Geschichte einer Baugattung im 19. und 20. Jahrhundert (1780-1933)*, Hamburg, 1981.
10. 'Die neue Synagoge in Kassel', *Allgemeine Bauzeitung*, 1840, p. 205 sqq.
11. *Die Architektonischen Stylarten*, Brunswick, 1857, III, 4, § 402.
12. For details of the debate see D. Jarrassé, *Une histoire des synagogues françaises entre Occident et Orient*, 1997, chapter 8.
13. *Synagogues of Europe. Architecture, History, Meaning*, 1985, p. 311.
14. In a report of February 1864, quoted by H. Hammer-Schenk, 'Edwin Opplers Theorie des Synagogenbaus, Emanzipationversuche durch Architektur', *Hannoversche Geschichtblätter*, 1979, 32/1-2, p. 106 .
15. Wolfram Selig, ed., *Synagogen und jüdische Friedhöfe in München*, Munich, 1988.
16. 'Nouvelles diverses', *L'Univers israélite*, 1864-65, p. 348.
17. J.F. van Agt and E. van Voolen, *Synagogen in Nederland*, Amsterdam, 1988.
18. 'Wie baut man Synagogen?', *Allgemeine Zeitung des Judenthums*, 8 March 1901, pp. 115-17
19. 'Betrachtungen über den modernen Synagogenbau', *Ost und West*, vol. 6, January 1906, col. 35-36.
20. 'Ueber Tempelbau', *Die Neuzeit*, 4 and 18 April 1884, pp. 134-37, 154-56.
21. Charged in 1911-13 with the building of synagogues in Tachov (Bohemia) and Pniewy, near Poznan, he discovered ancient synagogues whose plans he noted and published in his *Deutsche, böhmische und polnische Synagogentypen vom XI. bis Anfang des XIX Jahrhunderts*, Berlin, 1915.
22. It should be remembered that the Kingdom of Hungary then included Transylvania (now in Romania), Slovakia, Voivodina and a part of Serbia and Croatia.
23. Aristide Streja and Lucian Schwarz, *Synagogues of Romania*, Bucharest, 1997, p. 129.
24. Eugen Bárkány and Ludovít Dojc, *Zidovské nábozenske obce na Slovenku*, Bratislava, 1991, pp. 186 and 298.

3. Orientalism: From Temple to Semitism

1. 'L'esprit de l'Orient et le Judaïsme', *Judaïsme*, trad. franç. (1982), Gallimard, 1986, pp. 62-63.
2. As is illustrated by the reconstructions of this period, by Stieglitz (1834), Kopp (1839) and at Canina (1844).
3. Helen Rosenau, *Vision of the Temple*, London, 1979.
4. D. Jarrassé, 'Les mémoires du Temple. Sécularisation du Temple et sacralisation de la synagogue dans la culture juive française du XIXᵉ siècle', *Transmission et passages en monde juif*, Publisud, 1997.
5. 'Über Synagogenbau', *Allgemeine Bauzeitung*, n° XXIV, 1859, pp. 14-16.
6. A. Hirsch, 'Temple consistorial israélite de Lyon', *Revue générale de l'architecture*, 1865, col. 220.
7. P. Hampton Frosell, *Københavns synagoger gennem tre hundrede år*, C.A. Reitzel, Viborg, 1987.
8. Jacob Katz, *Jews and Freemasons in Europe, 1723-1939*, 1970.
9. R. Wischnitzer, 'The Egyptian Revival in Synagogue Architecture', *American Jewish Historical Society*, vol. XLI, n°1, September 1951, pp. 61-75.
10. Robert S. Merrillees, 'Israël en Egypte' aux antipodes: les premières synagogues en Australie', *L'Égyptomanie à l'épreuve de l'archéologie*, R.M.N., 1996, pp. 279-304.
11. Ferguson, *The Temple of the Jews*, London, 1878.
12. Georges Perrot and Charles Chipiez, *Histoire de l'art dans l'antiquité*, vol. IV, Judée, Paris, 1887; Chipiez, *Restitution du Temple de Jérusalem et du palais du Bois-Liban*, 1889
13. Carol Ockman, 'Two large eyebrows à l'orientale': ethnic stereotyping in Ingres's *Baronne de Rothschild*', *Art History*, vol. 14, no. 4, December 1991, pp. 521-538.
14. *Bauwörterbuch*, 1859, vol. 2, p. 276: in H. Hammer-Schenk, *Synagogen in Deutschland*, op. cit., p. 255.
15. Henri Charlet, *Le Gaulois* 11/09/1874.
16. Quoted by Jacob Katz, *Wagner et la question juive*, French translation., Hachette, 1986, pp. 164-5.
17. 'Correspondances…', *Archives israélites*, March 1866, p. 297.
18. Ralf Busch, 'Constantin Uhde als Synagogenarchitekt', *Artibus et historiae*, no. 17, 1988, pp. 39-48.
19. A Jew and a native of Vercelli, Marco Treves worked in Florence and had already rebuilt the Neoclassical synagogue in Pisa. His 1864 proposal for Vercelli had been judged too elaborate.
20. 'Beth Haknesset. Synagogen in België 1865-1914', *Monumenten en Landschappen*, January-February 1993, p. 28.
21. 'The Problem of the Temple and its Solution', *The Architectural Forum*, LII, no. 2, February 1930, p. 168.
22. Ernest Renan, 'Le Judaïsme comme Race et comme Religion', lecture given on 27 January 1883, reprinted in *Discours et conférences, Œuvres complètes*, vol. 1, Calmann-Lévy, 1947.
23. *Israël chez les nations* (1893), new edition, Calmann-Lévy, 1983, pp. 251-52.

IV. A MODERNIST ARCHITECTURE

1. Emil Fackenheim, *What is Judaism: An Interpretation for the Present Day*, New York, Summit Books, 1987.

1. Functionalist Changes

1. 'Betrachtungen über den modernen Synagogenbau', *Ost und West*, vol. 6, no.1, January 1906, p. 30.
2. Perrot et Chipiez, *Histoire de l'art dans l'antiquité*, vol. IV, Judée, 1887, pl. IV, pp. 278-88; Chipiez, *Restitution du Temple...*, 1889.
3. A series of works by students, all featuring a central plan with cupola, was presented between 1886 and 1918, cf. D. Jarrassé, *Une histoire des synagogues françaises...*, 1997, pp. 84-93.
4. This issue dated April-June 1892 (vol. 1, no. 4) gives a clear indication of the concerns of American architects of the time, including as it does, in addition to 'Choice in architectural styles' by Edward A. Freeman, a piece by Aitchison on 'Byzantine architecture' and articles by Jewish architects Dankmar Adler (on the Chicago Auditorium) and Leopold Eidlitz.
5. 'American Synagogue Design: 1729 to 1939', *Architectural Record*, vol. 86, November 1939, pp. 58-59.
6. 'Towards a Modern Synagog Architecture', *The Menorah Journal*, vol. XI, June 1925, pp. 225-240.
7. 'Isaiah Temple, Chicago, Ill.', *The American Architect*, vol. 126, 31/12/1924, pp. 623-626.
8. *Synagogue Architecture in the United States. History and Interpretation*, Philadelphia, 1955, p. 132.
9. In France the symbol of this liberalization was the move from the consistorial system dating from Napoleonic times to the confessional associations born of the legislation separating Church and State.
10. Notably in the Vienna review *Menorah*, where in one article, 'Vom Geist der Synagogue', he compares the Amsterdam-Jacob Obrechtplein synagogue with that of Vienne-Hietzing.
11. 'Synagogue Art and Architecture', *A Century of Anglo-Jewish Life 1870-1970*, Salmond S. Levin, London, 1970, p. 85.
12. 'The Architecture of the Synagogue', *American Jewish Year Book*, vol. 28, 1926-27, pp. 155-192.

2. American and European Experiences

1. 'La Synagogue de l'Unité', *Bulletin de nos Communautés*, no. 6, 21 March 1958, p. 11.
2. Hermann Zvi Guttmann, *Vom Tempel zum Gemeindezentrum. Synagogen im Nachkriegsdeutschland*, Frankfurt, 1989.

3. Already used by the Dutch and especially by Christian architects like Dom Bellot and Dominikus Bohm.

4. In 1900 the Diocese of Paris had begun its 'Œuvre des chapelles de Secours' ('Chapels of Charity') work, which in 1931 became the Oeuvre des nouvelles paroisses' ('New Parish Charities'), better known as the 'Cardinal's building projects', in honour of Cardinal Verdier.

5. 1966, La Courneuve; 1968, Creil; 1971, Créteil; 1975, Choisy-Orly and so on until the total reached 36 in 1982. Then came a new campaign for replacement of prefabricated structures and apartment synagogues.

6. Inauguration speech for the synagogue-community center at Villiers-le-Bel, 17 June 1962, reprinted in A. de Rothschild, *Le Juif dans la cité*, 1984, p. 72.

7. It should be pointed out that in certain synagogues in the Carpentras area, the women assembled on a lower level and only glimpsed the all-male ceremony through a kind of cellar window!

8. Eli Grad, *Congregation Shaarey Zedek 5622-5742, 1861-1981*, Southfield (Michigan), Wayne State University Press, 1982.

9. Ben C. Bloch, 'Notes on Post-War Synagogue Design', *Architectural Record*, September 1944.

10. P. Goodman, 'A Guide for Planning the Synagogue Building', *A.I.A. Journal*, vol. XXXVII, May 1962, pp. 70-74.

11. Published by the Union of American Hebrew Congregations, Peter Blake Editor.

12. Peter Blake (ed.) *A Guide Book to Synagogue Design and Construction*, Union of American Hebrew Congregations, 1954, p. 43. 'Meshugothic' plays on the Yiddish *meshugge*, 'crazy'.

13. 'The Problem of Synagogue Architecture. Creating a Style Expressive of America', *Commentary*, vol. 3, no. 3, March 1947, pp. 233-241.

14. Erich Mendelsohn, 'My Approach to Building a Modern Synagogue', *Architectural Forum*, vol. 98, April 1953, p. 108.

15. An interpretation of I Kings, 6, iv, describing the windows of the Temple, *Vayikra Raba*, 31,6

16. Franz Schulze, *Philip Johnson. Life and work*, New York, A. A. Knopf, 1994, p. 238.

17. See *A Synagogue for today…*, p. 110-111.

18. 'Réflexions' (1965) in Louis I. Kahn, *Silence et lumière. Choix de conférences et d'entretiens 1955-1974*, (French compilation), Ed. du Linteau, 1996, pp. 117-119.

19. 'A Synagogue by Yamasaki', *Architectural Record*, September 1964, p. 192.

20. 'Temple's slanting walls create an upwardly directed symbolic form', *Architectural Record*, vol. 143, March 1968, pp. 133-136.

21. *Choulhâne Aroukh abrégé*, Ernest Weill, chapter 39, Fondation Sefer, 1980, p. 80.

22. 'Site and symbolism dictate design', *Architectural Record*, vol. 107, May 1950, p. 103.

23. Swampscott, Massachusetts (1958), Merion, Pennsylvania (1959), Rochester, New York (1962), Short Hills, New Jersey (1969).

24. 'Creating a Modern Synagogue Style', *Commentary*, June 1947, p. 537-544; 'The Character of the Modern Synagogue', op. cit., pp. 87-97.

25. See in particular Avram Kampf, *Contemporary Synagogue Art: Developments in the United States 1945-1965*, Philadelphia, 1966. A debate on 'Contemporary Art in the Synagogue', featuring Chagall, Lipchitz, Motherwell, Goodman, Gottlieb, Lassaw, rabbis and architects is reprinted in *An American Synagogue for Today and Tomorrow*, pp. 176-197, but is not especially enlightening.

26. 'My Ideal Synagogue', *Reform Judaism*, Autumn 1994.

3. The Synagogue in Israel

1. 'La théologie juive', *Fidélité et Utopie*, compilation in French, Calmann-Lévy, 1978, p. 231.

2. A. Neher, 'Dire: Israël', *Dans tes portes, Jérusalem*, Albin Michel, 1972, p. 127.

3. Theodor Herzl, *Old New Land*, tr. Lotta Levenson, Markus Wiener, 1997

4. First exhibited in 1878, the collection of this noted French conductor was housed in the Cluny Museum before being transferred to today's Musée d'Art et d'Histoire du Judaïsme. It includes an Ark dating from 1472 and said to be from Modena. An Ark from the Benguiat collection is now in the Jewish Museum in New York.

5. 'Il luogo sacro nella modernità. Il caso di Israele', *Architettura e spazio sacro nella modernità*, Milan, 1992, p. 104.

6. Quoted in Sylvie Forestier, *Marc Chagall. L'œuvre monumental. Les Vitraux*, Milan, Jaca Books, 1987, p. 185.

7. Werner Oechslin, 'Mario Botta—Une Vocation pour le sacré et le monumental', in *Mario Botta. Bâtiments publics 1990-1998*, Milan, Skira/Le Seuil, 1998, pp. 26-30.

8. In addition to the bibliography provided on Louis Kahn, see Luis Mariano Akerman, 'The evocative character of Louis Kahn's Hurva synagogue project, 1967-1974", *Jewish Art*, no. 23-24, 1998, pp. 245-253; and especially the computer-assisted reconstruction of the building by Kent Larson, 'A virtual Landmark', *Progressive Architecture*, no. 9, September 1993, pp. 80-87, with an introduction by Vincent Scully.

9. Assad Bey, sent to Jerusalem by the Sultan to restore the mosques on the esplanade, designed the Hurva synagogue in 1854.

10. In the July-August 1972 issue of *Forum*, in which his plans were presented, p. 69.

11. In 1965 French writer Marc Bernard published a book entitled *Sarcellopolis*.

Glossary

Almemor (Yiddish, of Arabic origin): cf. *bimah*.

Altneuschul (Yiddish): name given to the most famous synagogue in Prague. Called the "old—young" because of the existence of an "old" synagogue (Altschul).

Amidah (Hebrew): prayer recited while standing. It forms the essential part of the weekday service and is composed of 19 benedictions. It is first said in a whisper and then aloud.

Ark of the Covenant: the gold covered, wooden chest in which the Tables of the Law were placed. Equipped with handles in order to be transported in the desert, it was also carried into battle. It was surmounted by two cherubim. Placed in the Tent of the Meeting, then in the Holy of Holies, this ark symbolized the covenant between God and Israel. A certain equivalence was established with the Holy Ark of the synagogue: *cf. Aron hakodech*.

Aron hakodesh (Hebrew), "Holy Ark": this word denotes the Ark of the Temple in which the Tables of the Law were kept. Originally, this chest was called the *tebah*. Later the habit began of associating the former Ark of the Covenant with the Ark of the synagogue. For this chest, the Sephardim used the term *hechal*, a word that in the Temple referred to the Holy place, that is to say the ritual space where the sacred objects were kept, and then, during the Talmudic period, to the niche itself. The assimilation of the Holy Ark to the Holy of Holies was reinforced by naming the curtain which covers the chest with the same name (*parohet*) as that which separated the Holies of Holies from the Holy Place. As for the term of Tabernacle, it is sometimes used in reference to the Tent of the Meeting in the wilderness, but it has strong Christian connotations that usually restrict its usage.

Ashkenazic: Denotes the rite and other attributes of the Ashkenazim.

Ashkenazim, plural of Ashkenazi: refers to the Jews whose ancestors originated in Germany. Their language is Yiddish.

Babli Ketuvot (Hebrew): *Babli* denotes the Babylonian version of the Talmud and *Ketoubot*, the name of a book of the Talmud concerning "marriage contracts".

Bene Israel (Hebrew), "sons of Israel": refers to the twelve sons of Jacob, whose name was changed to "Israel" after his struggle with the angel (Genesis, 32,29), and then to all Jews.

Berakhoth (Hebrew), "benedictions": Talmudic treatise concerning the recitation of prayers.

Bessamim (Hebrew), "aromatics": a tower-shaped cassolette is used for the aromatic substances (*bessamim*) employed during benedictions that mark the end of the *Shabbat*. The *bessamim* play upon the five senses.

Beth hakneset (Hebrew), "house of the assembly": this term for the synagogue emphasizes the notion of a gathering of the faithful (as the Greek *sunagoge* and the Latin *ecclesia*). *Cf. beth hamidrash* and *beth hatefila*.

Beth hamidrash (Hebrew), "house of study": this name indicates another essential function of the synagogue.

Beth hamikdash (Hebrew), "house of the sanctuary": the Temple of Jerusalem.

Beth hatefila (Hebrew), "house of prayer": another name for the synagogue.

Bimah (Hebrew), plural *bimot*, "platform": this word is used in the Talmud to denote the platform upon which a table—or a pulpit—is placed. It is from here that the Torah is read. The Sephardim calls this element of furniture the *tebah*. The Ashkenazim add the word *almemor*, a term that is of Arabic origin (*al-minbar*, pulpit), known in old French under the name "*almembre*".

Bimot (Hebrew): plural of *bimah*.

Boaz (Hebrew), "force within him": word inscribed upon a bronze pillar (or detached column) that was cast by Hiram. It stands on the left of the porch of the Temple of Solomon. Associated with *Jachin*, the pillar on the right (I Kings, 7, 21).

Carrière (French), "quarry": name given to the ghettos in Provence and the Comtadin.

Chekhina (Hebrew), "divine presence in the world": this term is even sometimes substituted for the name of God.

Chuppah (Hebrew), "dais": a dais of fabric under which marriage ceremonies are carried out. These had formerly taken place outside, but were now more often held in a synagogue.

Cohanim (Hebrew): plural of *cohen*.

Cohen (Hebrew), plural *cohanim*, "priest": the Levites who participated in the sacrificial ritual of the Temple.

Cohen Gadol (Hebrew), "High Priest": reference to Aaron, then to his descendants who held the position of high priest. The high priest wore a special costume, and certain rites were reserved for him, such as, to enter into the Holy of Holies at Kippur.

Congregation: employed here in the American sense to denote religious associations that in France are more often qualified as communities and, administratively, as Israelite cultural associations.

Consistoire (Consistory): term used in France and Belgium to denote Jewish institutions. *The Consistoire Central des Israélites de France* (Algeria was later added to the name) was founded by Napoleon 1st in 1808, in order to control the regional consistories. Suppressed in 1905, it was reconstituted as the *Union des Communautés Israélites de France* but is often referred to by its former name.

Debir (Hebrew): denotes in the Holy of Holies in the Temple of Jerusalem. This area was reserved for the high priest who entered during *Yom Kippur*.

Dhimma (Arabic), "*ahl al-dhimma*, other people of the covenant": Islamic law according to which Jews and Christians were accepted as subjects in Muslim countries but with an inferior legal status. It entailed specific restrictions and obligations as well as the payment of a special poll tax. It did, however, assure the non-Muslim a legal status as a *dhimmi*.

Dhimmi (Arabic) : indicates a person subject to the *dhimma*.

Edah (Hebrew), "community": denotes the Jewish people or the community.

Eretz Israel (Hebrew), "land of Israel": the land promised by God to Abraham and his descendants. This land is thus holy and plays a key role in Jewish life and religion. Zionism, however, has secularized the value.

Etrog (Hebrew): citron, a citrus fruit used at the feast of *Sukkot*.

Ez haim (Hebrew), "tree of life": symbolic name given to the handles of the Scrolls of the Law.

Ezrat Nashim (Hebrew), "court of women": in the Temple of Solomon this court was reserved for women. It was during the Middle Ages, apparently, that rooms reserved for women were annexed to synagogues. Later, the term was applied to the galleries and tribunes for women.

Gabbai (Hebrew): the administrator or treasurer of the synagogue whose role is mainly to collect donations and subscriptions.

Galut (Hebrew), "exile": this notion appeared as early as the period of Egyptian slavery, but was greatly expanded during the Babylonian Exile. It denotes both the country of exile and an idea that became central to Jewish identity over the ages: it insists on the notion of 'exile' while the more frequently used Greek term *diaspora* rests on the notion of 'dispersal'.

Geniza (Hebrew), "hiding-place": a place for storing books and other objects of a synagogue which have become unusable but which, nevertheless, remain holy and cannot be destroyed. The famous *Geniza* of Cairo, an attic discovered in the attic of the ben Ezra synagogue in 1896, contained very ancient texts.

Gerush (Hebrew): "expelled".

Ghetto (Italian): the district of Venice that gave its name to the segregation of Jews in modern Europe. The process was intentionally discriminatory, but also provided the Jews with protection, and even—sometimes—privileges.

Ghriba (Arabic), "foreigner": the name given to the most famous synagogue of Djerba. It comes from a legend about a young foreign woman who had settled on the island and whose hut was struck by lightning.

Golem (Hebrew), "unformed substance": originally a Biblical term, it later denoted the creation of an artificial being. The most famous account concerning a *golem* is that related by Rabbi Yehoudah Loew of Prague. This legend relates how a servant managed to escape from his master who was then obliged to destroy him.

Grana (Judaeo-Arabic): refers to the Jews from Livorno (Leghorn) who had settled in Tunisia.

Hagbaha: synagogue rite consisting of raising the *Sefer* before (Sephardic rite) or after (Ashkenazic rite) the reading.

Hagada (Hebrew), "narration": this term applies particularly to the "narration of Passover", a work containing texts that concern the escape from Egypt. It is read during the *Seder*.

Hakafot (Hebrew): processions of the Scrolls of the Torah or of the *Lulav* in the interior of the synagogue at *Sukkot* and *Simhat Torah*.

Halakha (Hebrew), "course, procedure": legal part of the Talmud which defines the Jewish religious obligations and practices.

Hanukah (Hebrew): feast of the "inauguration" of the sanctuary. Held on the 25th of *Kislev*, it commemorates the Maccabean victory over Antiochus IV and the miracle of the cruse of sacred oil which burnt for eight days. In remembrance, the eight candles of a candelabra are successively lit over eight days.

Hanukia (Hebrew): an eight-branched candelabra used during the feast of *Hanukkah*. Its form, very different from culture to culture, is sometimes inspired by the *Menorah*.

Hara (Arabic): a Jewish quarter in Tunisia

Hasid (Hebrew), plural *hasidim*, "pious": the word originally denoted a certain religious ardor. It came to mean the charismatic and mystic movement founded by Baal Chem Tov in the 18th century which judged joy and fervor more important than study. This trend was opposed by the *Mitnaggedim*.

Hasidim (Hebrew), plural of *hasid*.

Haskalah (Hebrew): the Jewish Enlightenment movement which developed in the 18th century in Central Europe. Its followers, called *maskilim*, advocated studying secular sciences and an integration into their adopted nations.

Hazan (Hebrew): cantor, officiant.

Hechal (Hebrew): *cf. aron hakodesh.*

Hevra Kadisha (Hebrew), plural *hevrot*: holy brotherhood. These were essentially intended to render funeral duties. However, in the absence of any other community structure, they also sometimes became the base of the community. After the Emancipation, they sometimes grouped traditionalists around an oratory.

Hevrot (Hebrew), plural of *hevra/hevra Kadisha*.

Hidur Mitzvah (Hebrew): the duty to sanctify God through beauty.

Holy (Place, the): refers to the ritual space in the Temple where the sacred objects are found, then during the Talmudic period to the niche itself.

Holy of Holies: *cf. aron hakodech.*

Hulin (Hebrew), "profane things": the book of the Talmud that regulates ritual slaughtering and dietary regulations.

Hukat Hagoy (Hebrew), "imitation of the Gentiles": initially applied to idolatry, this notion tends to condemn all that is borrowed from non-Jewish cultures, particularly concerning religious matters.

Hurva (Hebrew): ruin.

Jachin (Hebrew), "he strengthens": the word inscribed upon a bronze pillar (or detached column) that was cast by Hiram. It stands on the right of the porch of the Temple of Solomon. Associated with *Boaz*. (I Kings, 7, 21).

Judengasse (German), "street of the Jews": in Germanic countries, this was a street inhabited mainly by Jews during Middle Ages or in modern times. Closed, it sometimes became a ghetto. It corresponds to the Spanish *Judería*.

Judenstadt (German), "town of the Jews": this denotes a more or less autonomous Jewish quarter in Germanic countries. It could also become a closed ghetto.

Judería (Spanish), "the Jews": Jewish quarter in Spanish towns.

Kadish (Hebrew): a prayer of praise in Aramaic that is repeated several times during the service. It is also recited for the dead for seven days.

Kashrut (Hebrew), "aptitude": denotes the sum of laws which governs dietary regulations in Judaism.

Kehila (Hebrew), plural *Kehilot*: denotes the community as an institution.

Kehilot (Hebrew): plural of *kehila*.

Keter (Hebrew), "crown": an ornament which crowns the Scrolls of the Torah in order to symbolize dignity.

Kippur (Hebrew), Day of Atonement: Held on the 10th of *Tishri*, this is a day of fasting and prayers which celebrates repentance. It concludes ten days of penitence (*selihot*). It opens with a recitation of the *Kol Nidre*, a prayer of which the melody is famous, and ends with the *Neila* (closure), a service where the *shophar* is blown.

Kislev (Hebrew): ninth month of the Jewish calendar.

Klause (Yiddish): plural klausen "room, cell": a terms used to designate synagogues.

Klausen (Yiddish): plural of *Klause*.

Knesset (Hebrew), "assembly": *cf. beth haknesset.*

Kol Nidre (Aramaic), "all vows": first words of the opening prayer recited on the eve of *Yom Kippur*.

Landmannschaften (Yiddish), "associations of origin": associations formed by immigrant Jews who originated from the same town or region. They were initially social structures of mutual aid, but also often became the base of the religious congregations that founded synagogues.

Lulav (Hebrew), "palm": this term also indicates the bouquet used during *Sukkot*, which associates this palm with myrtle and willow.

Magen David (Hebrew), "shield of David": a six-pointed star. Only recently has it been considered a symbol, often Cabalistic. With its less religious connotations than the more traditional *Menorah*, it was taken by Zionism as the Jewish symbol.

Maharal: acronym of Yehouda Loew, *cf. Index of Names.*

Mahzor Vitry (Hebrew and French), "ritual of Vitry": a famous prayer ritual, the oldest of which was compiled in Champagne during the 11th century.

Mappa (Hebrew), plural *mappot*, "swaddling-cloth": in Ashkenazic communities, the strips of cloth, which are offered after the circumcision ceremony, are used to hold and maintain the Scrolls of the Torah.

Mappot (Hebrew): plural of *mappa*.

Marrano (Spanish), "pork": in the Iberian Peninsula, this contemptuous term was used to indicate Jews that had been converted to Catholicism by force, or New Christians, but who secretly remained faithful to Judaism.

Megillah (Hebrew), "rolls": a name given to scrolls in general, but in particular to the scroll of Esther which is read during the feast of *Purim*. It is also used to designate a Talmudic treatise.

Megorashim (Hebrew), "expelled": applied mainly to the Jews expelled from the Iberian Peninsula.

Mellah (Arabic): a Jewish quarter in Morocco.

Menorah (Hebrew), plural *menorot*: In the Temple, a seven-branched candelabra. In synagogues, there are normally eight branches.

Menorot (Hebrew): plural of *Menorah*.

Middot (Hebrew), "measures": the title of a treatise of the *Mishna*, the Oral Law, describing and interpreting the measurements of the Temple of Jerusalem.

Midrash (Hebrew), plural *midrashim* "study": system of interpreting the Torah which gave rise to a complete set of literary commentaries.

Midrashim (Hebrew): plural of *midrash*.

Mikdash meat (Hebrew), "small sanctuary": a word used by the prophet Ezekiel (11, 16) and interpreted as an allusion to synagogues during the Babylonian Exile.

Mikvaot (Hebrew): plural of *mikve*.

Mikve (Hebrew), plural *mikvaot*, "concentration" of water, pool : a ritual basin fed by natural waters in which people or objects to purify are bathed, in particular women every month.

Minhag sarfati (Hebrew), "French rite": *cf. Minhag.*

Minhag, plural *minhagim*: "custom": comprises all the practices that are not based on biblical or rabbinical injunction and that were established in a given region by tradition. It concerns all aspects of Jewish life and not just religious matters, even if the word has often been used in this sense, in the place of *nossah*.

Minhagim (Hebrew): plural of *minhag*.

Minyan (Hebrew), "number": the quorum of ten adult men required in order to hold a public service. The term also denotes traditionalist oratories.

Mirhab (Arabic): the niche in a mosque that is orientated towards Mecca and where the officiant stands.

Mitnagedim (Hebrew), "opponents": designates the Jewish groups who were opposed to the development of Hasidism and who gave rise to a revival of study.

Mizrah (Hebrew) "orient": direction towards which worshiper turn for certain prayers. Synagogues should have an oriented *aron*. The term also refers to small tableaux that are suspended on the wall to indicate the direction of Jerusalem.

Mitzva (Hebrew), plural *mizvot*, "duty": Judaism has 613 commandments, but many are inapplicable since the destruction of the Temple. This word also denotes the participation in the ritual of which the different acts, being honorary, are sold at auctions.

Mitzvot (Hebrew): plural of *mizva*.

Moriah (Hebrew): the mount to which God sent Abraham to sacrifice Isaac. From the book of Chronicles, this hill is interpreted as one of the hills in Jerusalem where Solomon built the Temple. Two fundamental events are thus superimposed.

Neila (Hebrew), "closure": the name of the closing service during the feast of *Yom Kippur*.

Neologian: the name in Central Europe of the Reform movement. The Neologian (new doctrine) movement arose in 1869 following the Congress of Pest. It established a modern trend in Hungary for integration (emancipation was decreed in 1867). It advocated sermons in Hungarian, and used the organ, but did not go so far as to suppress the separation of men and women (*Kashrut*). The institution of a seminary sanctioned this tendency.

Ner tamid (Hebrew), "eternal light": a lamp usually suspended near the ark.

Nosah (Hebrew), "custom": designates the rite followed by a community.

Parnes (Hebrew): initially meant an administrator of the community in charge of charity, but later its president.

Parohet (Hebrew), "curtain": it separates, in the Temple, the Holy Place from the Holy of Holies. In synagogues, it covers the Holy Ark.

Pesach (Hebrew), Passover: the commemoration of the Exodus from Egypt. It is especially marked by the *Seder*, a banquet served in a specific order and where the lamb is eaten.

Piutim (Hebrew): "liturgical poems" inserted into the ritual over time.

Pletzl (Yiddish), "small place": name given to the Marais quarter of Paris, a traditional district inhabited by immigrant Jews from Eastern Europe.

Proseuche (Greek), "prayer, oratory": the Greek name for the synagogue.

Purim (Hebrew), "lots": the feast commemorating the salvation of the Jews from the Persian empire who had escaped from the destructive intentions of Haman, the prime minister of King Ahasuerus.

Rabbi, *rabbi*, "my master" or "my teacher": the title given to scholars and teachers of the Law of Israel, formerly distinguished by an ordination, the *semikha*. Salaried as of the Middle Ages, rabbis tended to assume the role of the spiritual leader of a community by teaching, preaching, and judging. Institutionalized Judaism established a hierarchy with chief rabbis and rabbis. They do not, however, in any manner have the role of priests. The Aramaic term *rav* is often used in Orthodox circles in order to differentiate the «master» from a «rabbi», the later owing his title more to his institutional role than to his knowledge.

Rav (Aramaic): variant of the word 'rabbi'.

Rimonim (Hebrew), "pomegranates": an ornament in the form of a pomegranate on the handles of the Scroll of the Torah.

Romaniote: refers to the communities of the Byzantine empire, then of the Ottoman empire. It distinguishes the autochthonous Jews from the immigrant Sephardic Jews who arrived after their expulsion from Spain.

Rosh Hashanah (Hebrew), "head of the year" or New Year: this festival opens a series of solemn events during the month of *Tishri*. The *aron* is draped in white and the shophar (ram's horn) is blown.

Sabra (Hebrew), "prickly pear": the name of this fruit, chosen for its quality of being prickly on the outside and tender on the inside, denotes the vernacular culture and the Israelis born in Israel as opposed to immigrant Israelis.

Schule (Yiddish), "synagogue": places the accent on its role of teaching. The equivalent in Mediterranean countries is the *scuola*.

Schulhof (Yiddish), "court of the synagogue": indicates a grouping of the synagogue and the study rooms around a courtyard, most often closed.

Scuola (Italian), "school": another term for synagogues: *cf. Schule*.

Seder (Hebrew), "order": the order in the ceremonial Passover dinner takes place as well as the name of the meal itself.

Sefarim or *sifre* (Hebrew): plural of *sefer*.

Sefer (Hebrew): plural *sefarim* or *sifre*, "book".

Sefer Torah (Hebrew), plural *sefarim* or *sifre*, "scroll of the Law": vellum scrolls on which the Pentateuch is written. It is thus a sacred object *par excellence* in synagogues. It is rolled around two handles (*ez haim*, or tree of life) with *rimonim* (pomegranates), then rolled in a mantle that sometimes bears a *keter* (crown) and decorated with a *tass* (pectoral recalling the high priest). A *yad* (hand), which is suspended there, serves to follow the text without touching it. In some traditions, the scroll is held by *mappot* (strips of cloth offered after a circumcision and which serve as a sort of birth register). The Sephardim place the *sefer* in a casket *(tik)*.

Sefirot (Hebrew): refers to the ten primordial numbers (divine potencies or emanations) and is schematized under the form of a tree through which God is revealed. The Cabalist attempts by his practice, study and prayers to regenerate the human world in order to draw closer to the divine world.

Seliha (Hebrew): plural *selihot* "penitence, pardon".

Selihot (Hebrew): plural of *seliha*: prayer of repentance recited on days of fast and during the ten days that precede the new year.

Semikha (Hebrew), "laying on of hands": ritual of benediction or ordination of rabbis. This ritual is no longer used and has been replaced by a diploma.

Sephardic: Denotes the rite and other attributes of the Sephardim.

Sephardim, plural of Sephardi: denotes the Jews whose ancestors originated in Medieval Spain and Portugal. Their language is Ladino (Judaeo-Spanish). The term is used by extension for all Oriental Jews in general.

Shabbat (Hebrew): The seventh day of the week is consecrated to rest, in remembrance of the seven days of creation. A day of celebration, it is devoted to the reading of the holy texts and to prayer. Numerous actions are forbidden and a special ritual is observed. The sabbath sanctifies time and is a basic tenant of Judaism.

Shabuoth (Hebrew), "weeks": the feast of Pentecost (49 days after *Pesach*) commemorates the gift of the Torah.

Shema Esre (Hebrew): eighteen benedictions. This prayer constitutes the central part of the weekday service. It calls for benedictions on God and formulates requests such as the reestablishment of justice and of Jerusalem. It is inscribed in the *Amidah* (standing prayer).

Shemini-Atzeret (Hebrew), "eighth day of assembly": the feast celebrating the eighth day of *Sukkot*. It is marked by a prayer for rain. Confused with *Simhat Torah* in Israel.

Shophar (Hebrew): a ram's horn which is blown at certain feasts during the month of *Titer* in memory of the ligature of Isaac.

Shtetl (Yiddish), "small town": a town or village inhabited by Central or Eastern European Jews. It later meant the entire area where the Jewish inhabitants had developed a specific lifestyle and culture.

Shtibl (Yiddish) plural *shtiblekh*, "small room": a space devoid of decoration, containing only a few tables and benches, and organized especially with the intent of study. All community activities in the pious circles in Eastern Europe occur here. An Orthodox antithesis to monumental synagogues.

Shtiblekh (Yiddish): plural of shtibl.

Shulha ha-Gadol (Hebrew), "large table": the name given to the synagogue built by the Livornais (Jews from Leghorn) in Tunis.

Shulhan 'Arukh (Hebrew), 'The Well-Laid Table': a work compiled by Josef Qaro in the 16th century. It is an abbreviated summary of the complete codification of the Jewish religion.

Sifre (Hebrew), plural of *sefer*.

Simhat Torah (Hebrew), "joy of the Torah": the feast that follows *Sukkot*. It is marked by processions and festivities linked to the completion of a cycle of readings from the Bible and the commencement of a new cycle.

Sukka (Hebrew), plural *sukkot* "hut": This word also refers to a book of the Talmud concerning the feast of *Sukkot*.

Sukkot (Hebrew), plural of *sukka*: literally "huts", this word refers to the festival in the month of *Tishri* during which a hut is built under which people eat and sleep in remembrance of the march through the desert. The worshipers go to the synagogue with a *lulav* (palm branch) and fulfil certain rites.

Synagogue: from the Greek term which intially translated the Hebrew *edah* ('community') and *knesseth* ('assembly'), before denoting the building itself. During the Alexandrine Diaspora, the term used was *proseuche*. At present, synagogues most often bear the name of the street where they were built. However, in the United States and Canada as well as for Orthodox synagogues, they generally take the name of the congregation which commissioned them

Taanith (Hebrew), "fast": a Talmudic treatise on the laws concerning fasting.

Taleth (Hebrew): the rectangular prayer shawl worn by adult men (over thirteen years old).

Talmud (Hebrew), "learning": denotes the study and the collection of biblical commentaries explaining the Oral Law. It is subdivided into sections concerning legal matters (*halakha*) or narratives (*hagada*).

Talmud-Torah (Hebrew), "study of the Law": refers to religious study and sometimes even to the institution where this takes place. *Cf. Talmud*.

Targum (Aramaic), "translation": the first translations of the Bible from the Hebrew text into Aramaic, the spoken language of the times, they are often paraphrased commentaries.

Tass (Hebrew): an ornament on the Scroll of the Torah that recalls the pectoral of the high priest.

Tebah (Hebrew): the meaning of this term has changed from that of "Holy Ark" in Antiquity to "reading platform" in certain Sephardic contexts.

Teshouva (Hebrew), "return, repentance": refers to the process through which a Jew returns to religious practice.

Tent of the Meeting, in Hebrew *Ohel moed*. This tent was the first sanctuary. It was erected in the desert by Bezalel on divine indication during the time when the Jews were forming as a people. Its plan and its sacred objects prefigured those of the Temple of Jerusalem.

Tik (Hebrew): The Sephardim use this cylindrical casket, which opens in two, to protect the Scrolls of the Torah.

Tishri (Hebrew): a month (September-October) marked by major religious feasts : the 1st and 2nd (*Rosh Hashanah*), the 10th (*Kippur*), and the 15th (*Sukkot*) which lasts eight days and ends on the 23rd with *Simhat Torah*, a day when the annual cycle of the reading of the Torah is completed and a new cycle begins.

Torah (Hebrew), "teaching, Law": this initially referred to the Law that was revealed to Moses, the Pentateuch. The term was then enlarged to all of the Bible (written Law) and to the commentaries (Oral Law).

Tosefta Megillah (Aramaic), "addition": collection of complementary teachings.

Twansa (Judaeo-Arabic): refrs to Jews of Tunisian origin and distinguishes them from the *Grana*.

Veldt (Dutch), "field": refers to the grasslands of South Africa.

Weiberschul (Yiddish): "synagogue of women".

Yad (Hebrew), "hand": a wooden or metal pointer used to read the Torah. The *yad* allows the text to be followed more easily without it being touched by the reader, and thus rendering it impure.

Yerushalmi Megillah (Hebrew): the version in the Jerusalem Talmud of the *Megillah* treatise.

Yeshiva (Hebrew), plural *yeshivot*, "session, to sit": an academy or centre of Talmudic studies.

Yeshivoth (Hebrew): plural of *yeshiva*.

Yiddish: the language used by Ashkenazic Jews. A mixture of Hebrew, German and various other European languages, it is written with the Hebrew alphabet. It has served as a means of expression for a specific sensibility and culture qualified as *Yiddishkeit*.

Yiddishkeit (German and Yiddish): cf. *Yiddish*.

Yiddishland (German and Yiddish): cf. *Yiddish*.

Yishuv (Hebrew), "population": denotes the Jewish population of Palestine before the creation of the State of Israel in 1948.

Yom Kippur, (Hebrew) "Day of Atonement": cf. *Kippur*.

Zohar (Hebrew), "(book of) Splendor": a commentary on the Torah. It is the basis of the Cabala. Attributed by tradition to Simeon ben Yohai, it was later written in Spain during the 13th century.

Glossary
of Architectural Terms

Abacus Flat slab on top of a capital.

Apse Semi-circular end of a nave.

Architrave Main beam resting directly on the capitals of columns.

Attic Upmost storey of a building, concealing the springing of the roof.

Aureole A radiant circle surrounding the head of a saint or sacred person.

Barrel vault Vault comprising a succession of round arches.

Basilica plan Elongated plan inspired by the early basilicas, with a central nave and two side aisles.

Bishop's screen Ceremonial seat reserved for the bishop.

Cella In antiquity, the central room of a temple, housing the statue of the resident deity.

Chancel rail Railing separating the choir from the nave

Chapter house Meeting room for the canons of an abbey, known collectively as the chapter.

Classical orders The Classical styles of architecture—Doric, Ionic and Corinthian—constantly reused in building up until the twentieth century.

Colossal order, giant order An order continuously traversing several storeys of a construction without recourse to the more traditional superposition of columns.

Corbel, corbeling A projection jutting out from a wall to support a structure above it.

Eclecticism Architectural method based on diverse borrowings from earlier styles.

Fabric In eighteenth-century architecture, a small ornamental garden construction, in a Classical, Chinese, Arabic or other vein.

Flying buttress Buttress slanting from a separate column, usually forming an arch with the wall it supports.

Gable The often ornate triangular upper part of a wall, above a window, dormer window or flying buttress.

Greek cross Cross whose four arms are equal in length. This is the basic layout for cruciform plan buildings.

Groin vault Vault formed by the intersection of two diagonal ribs and characterized by the four protruding arches thus produced.

Historicism Architectural method drawing inspiration from earlier stylistic approaches.

Horseshoe arch Arch in the shape of a horseshoe.

Jesuit style A Baroque style whose use of gilt, paint, etc. was calculated to please the faithful.

Knotwork, strapwork Ornamentation consisting of interlaced curves in delicate branching patterns.

Lantern A circular, open-sided structure bringing light downwards into a dome or stairwell.

Latin cross Cross whose vertical arm is longer (in its lower part) than the horizontal. This arrangement is used for structures with a nave and transept.

Lombard bands A series of small, round, blind arches set against a wall and separated by vertical strips in relief.

Merlon Term used mainly in military architecture: the solid part of a battlement between the crenellations.

Mudejar Term used to describe Spanish Christian art (12th-14th century) showing a Muslim influence.

Narthex (or **Antechurch**) Porch or antechamber, usually surrounded by columns, at the western entry to a church.

Nave Elongated volume beneath the highest part of a church.

Oculus (or **Roundel**) Small circular opening.

Palladianism Building style based on the work of the Italian Andrea Palladio (1508-80), designer of houses inspired by the architecture of antiquity.

Pendant Sculpted ornament suspended from the apex of a vault.

Peristyle A space surrounded by columns.

Pilaster An imitation pillar protruding slightly from a wall.

Pinnacle A small, pointed, decorative turret serving to ensure the stability of a small building.

Pyramidion The pyramidal portion forming the apex of an obelisk, often cut from a single block of stone.

Quatrefoil Symmetrical decorative element resembling a flower or a four-leafed clover.

Rustication Smooth or sculpted stone whose surface protrudes from the basic masonry.

Serliana "Venetian window": triple opening defined by four columns. The taller, central opening is arched, the other two having horizontal lintels.

Shingle Rectangular wooden tile used for covering walls and roofs.

Side aisles Lateral naves as high as or lower than than the main nave and running parallel to it.

Stall Compartment for one person, usually aligned in rows on each side of the choir.

Stereotomy The art of cutting stone.

Stucco A malleable mix of lime and powdered marble, used for creating various forms of ornamentation.

Tempietto 'Little temple' in Italian. Circular private chapel surrounded by columns, drawing its inspiration from the Roman style.

Three-pointed arch A pointed arch based around an equilateral triangle.

Tracery Ornamental stone open-work around stained glass windows.

Transept crossing Point of intersection of the nave and the transept. A secondary nave at right angles to the principal nave.

Triclinium In Roman times, a dining room with couches along three sides.

Truss Triangular element of a roof frame.

Bibliography

GENERALITIES

Architettura e spazio sacro nella modernità, Biennial of Venice, Milan, Abitare Segesta, 1992.

De Breffny (Brian), *The Synagogue*, Macmillan, New York, 1978.

Folberg (Neil*), "Et je demeurerai parmi eux". La Synagogue à travers les âges*, with a text from Yom To Assis, Abbeville Press, New York, Paris, London, 1995.

Grotte (A.), *Deutsche, böhmische und polnische Synagogentypen vom 11. bis Anfang des 19. Jahrhunderts*, Berlin, 1915.

Gutman (Joseph), *The Synagogue: Studies in Origins, Archaeology and Architecture*, New York, Ktav Pub. House, 1975.

Kaploun (Uri), *The Synagogue*, Keter Press, Jerusalem, 1973.

Krautheimer (Richard), *Mittelalterliche Synagogen*, Berlin, 1927.

Krinsky (Carol H.), *Synagogues of Europe, Architecture, History, Meaning*, The Architectural History Foundation, MIT Press, Cambridge, Massachusetts, 1985.

Künzl (Hannelore), *Islamische Stilelemente im Synagogue des 19. und frühen 20. Jahrhunderts*, Frankfurt am Main, 1984.

Künzl (Hannelore), *Jüdische Kunst. Von der biblischen Zeit bis in die Gegenwart*, Verlag C.H. Beck, Munich, 1992.

Lamm (Hans), "Synagogenbauten gestern und heute", *Der Baumeister*, 63, 1966, t.1, p.53-59.

Loukomski (Georges), *Jewish Art in European Synagogues*, London, 1947.

Meek (Harold A.), *La Synagogue*, Phaidon, London, 1995.

The Real and Ideal Jerusalem in Jewish, Christian and Islamic Art, ed. Bianca Kühnel, *Jewish Art*, vol. 23-24, 1998.

Rosenau (Helen), *Vision of the Temple. The Image of the Temple of Jerusalem in Judaism and Christianity*, London, Oresko, 1979.

Schwarz (Hans-Peter), ed., *Die Architektur der Synagoge*, catalogue of the expostion, Architectural Museum of Germany, Frankfurt, 1988.

Sed-Rajna (Gabrielle), Jarrassé (Dominique), Amishai-Maisels (Ziva) et al., *L'Art juif*, Paris, Citadelles-Mazenod, 1995.

Tigerman (Stanley), *The Architecture of Exile*, New York, Rizzoli, 1988

Wigoder (Geoffrey), *The Story of the Synagogue. A Diaspora Museum Book*, Domino Press, Jerusalem, 1986.

Wischnitzer (Rachel), *The Architecture of the European Synagogue*, The Jewish Publication Society of America, Philadelphia, 1964.

Wischnitzer (Rachel), "The Egyptian Revival in Synagogue Architecture", *Publications of the Jewish Historical Society*, 51, 1951, pp.61-75.

Wischnitzer (Rachel), "The Problem of Synagogue Architecture", *Commentary*, 1946, pp.233-241.

ANTIQUITY

Chiat (Marilyn J.S.), *Handbook of Synagogue Architecture*, Brown Judaic Studies, 1982.

Cumont (F.), *Fouilles de Doura-Europos (1922-1923)*, 1926.

Gutman (Joseph), ed., *The Dura-Europos Synagogue: A Re-evaluation (1922-1972)*, 1973.

Kohl (Heinrich) and Watzinger (Carl), *Antike Synagogen in Galilea*, Leipzig, 1916.

Levine (Lee I.), ed., *Ancient synagogues revealed*, Jerusalem, 1981.

Levine (Lee I.), *The Ancient Synagogue. The First Thousand Years*, Yale University Press, New Haven-London, 1999.

Levine (Lee I.), ed., *The Synagogue in late Antiquity*, The American School of Oriental Research, Philadelphia, 1987.

Urman (Dan) and Flesher (Paul V.M.), *Ancients Synagogues. Historical Analysis and Archaelogical Discovery*, Leiden, New York, Köln, 1995.

Weitzmann (K.) and Kessler (L.H.), *The Frescoes of the Dura-Europos Synagogue and Christian Art*, 1990.

NORTH AFRICA

Fargeon (Maurice), *Les Juifs d'Egypte*, Cairo, Imp. Barbey, 1938.

Lambert (Phyllis), ed., *Fortifications and the Synagogue. The Fortress of Babylon and the Ben Ezra Synagogue*, Cairo, London, 1994.

Pinkerfeld (Jacob), *Bate-knesset veAfrika hatsiponit*, Bialik Institute, Jerusalem, 1974.

Id., "Un témoignage du passé en voie de disparition: les synagogues de la région de Djerba", *Les Cahiers de Byrsa*, Paris, 1957, pp. 127-137 et 14 pl.

Zack (Joel), *The Synagogues of Morocco: an Architectural and Preservation Survey*, photographs by Isaiah Wyner, The Jewish Heritage Council, World Monuments Fund, New York, 1993.

NORTH AMERICA

Batkin (Stanley I.),*Let them make me a Sanctuary. A Contemporary American Synagogue Inspired by the Art of Ancient Israel*, New York, Behrman House, 1978.

Brunner (Arnold W.), "Synagogue Architecture", *The Brickbuilder*, 1907, XVI, 2, pp. 20-25; 3, pp. 37-44.

Clarke (Peter), ed., *A American Synagogue for Today and Tomorrow. A Guide Book to Synagogue Design and Construction*, The Union of American Hebrew Congregations, New York, 1954.

Felleman Fattal (Laura Rachel), "American Sephardi Synagogue Architecture", *Jewish Art*, n°19-20, 1993-94, pp. 21-43.

Greenberg (Evelyn L.), "The Tabernacle in the Wilderness: the *Mishkan* Theme in Percival Goodman's Modern American Synagogues", *Jewish Art*, vol. 19-20, 1993-94, pp. 44-55.

"L'Héritage juif au Québec", *Continuité. Le Patrimoine en perspective*, n° 45, Autumn 1989, pp.31-57.

Israelowitz (Oscar), *Synagogues of New York City*, New York, Dover, 1982.

Israelowitz (Oscar), *Synagogues of the United States. A Photographic and Architectural Survey*, Israelowitz Publishing, New York, 1992.

Jick (Leon A.), *The Americanization of the Synagogue 1820-1870*, Brandeis University Press, Hanover, New Hampshire, 1976

Kampf (Avram), *Contemporary Synagogue Art. Developments in the United States 1945-1965*, Philadelphia, Jewish Publication Society of America, 1966.

Korros (Alexandra S.) and Sarna (Jonathan D.), *American Synagogue History: A Bibliography and State-of-the Field Survey*, Markus Wiener Publishing, New York, 1988.

Levitt (Sheldon), Milstone (Lynn) and Tenenbaum (Sidney T.) *Treasures of a people: the synagogues of Canada*, Toronto, Lester & Orpen Dennys, 1985.

Mumford (Lewis), "Towards a Modern Synagog Architecture", *The Menorah Journal*, vol. XI, June 1925, pp. 225-240.

Recent American Synagogue Architecture, catalogue, The Jewish Museum, New York, 1963.

Torrey (Charles C.), *Touro Synagogue of Congregaton Jeshuat Israel. Founded 1658, dedicated 1763, designated as a national historic site, 1946*, Newport (R.I.), 1948.

Two Hundred Years of American Synagogue Architecture, catalogue, American Jewish Historical Society, Waltham, Mass., 1976.

Wertheimer (Jack), *The American Synagogue: a sanctuary transformed*, Cambridge University, New York, 1988.

Wischnitzer (Rachel), *Synagogue Architecture in the United States*, Jewish Publication Society, Philadelphia, 1955.

Wolfe (Gerard R.), *The Synagogues of New York's Lower East Side*, photographes by J. R. Fine, texts by G.R. Wolfe, Washington Mews Books, New York University Press, New York, 1978.

CENTRAL AMERICA

Oldest synagogue in the New World. Pictures, facts, figures. Three centuries of Jewish life in Curaçao, 2nd ed. Revised and augmented, by Rabbi Js. Jessurun Cardozo, Curaçao, 1955.

ASIA

ISRAEL

Ben-Arieh (Yehoshua), *Jerusalem in the 19th Century, The Old City*, Jerusalem, Institut Itzhak Ben Zvi, 1984.

TURKEY

Galanté (Abraham), "Les synagogues d'Istanbul", *Hamenora*, July-August 1937

Halperin (Don A.), *The old synagogues of Turkey: a pictorial narrative*, Wyndham Hall Press, Bristol (Ind), 1986.

AUSTRALIA

Merrillees (Robert S.), "'Israël en Egypte' aux antipodes: les premières synagogues en Australie", *L'Egyptomanie à l'épreuve de l'archéologie*, colloque du Louvre, Paris, R.M.N., 1996, pp. 279-304.

EUROPE

GERMANY

Altaras (Thea), *Synagogen in Hessen: was geschah seit 1945? Eine Dokumention und Analyse aus allen 221 hessischen Orten, deren Synagogenbauten die Progromnacht 1938 und des 2. Weltkrieg überstanden: 223 architektonische Beschreibungen und Bauhistorien*, Königstein im Taunus, K. Langewiesche, 1988.

Davidovitch (David), *Wandmalereien in alten Synagogen. Das Wirken des Malers Elieser Sussmann in Deutschland*, Hameln-Hanover, 1969.

Graefraeth (Robert), "Die Neue Synagoge in Berlin. Ergänzung eines fragmentarisch erhaltenen Repräsentationsbaus des 19. Jahrhunderts", *Deutsche Kunst und Denkmalpflege*, Munich-Berlin, 1992, n°1, pp.22-32.

Hermann Zvi Guttmann. Vom Tempel zum Gemeindezentrum. Synagogen im Nachkriegsdeutschland, ed. Sophie Remmlinger and Klaus Hofman, Frankfurt am Main, Athenäum, 1989.

Hahn (Joachim), *Synagogen in Baden-Wurtemberg*, Stuttgart, 1987.

Hammer-Schenk (Harold), *Synagogen in Deutschland. Geschichte einer Baugattung im 19. und 20. Jahrhundert*, Christians Verlag, Hamburg, 1981.
Rieger (Paul), *Jüdische Gotteshäuser und Friedhöfe in Württemberg*, herausgegeben vom Oberrat der Israelitischen Religionsgemeinschaft Württembergs, Stuttgart, 1932.
Rosenau (Helen), "German Synagogues in the the Early Period of Emancipation", *Yearbook Leo Baeck Institute*, 8, 1963.
Selig (Wolfram), ed. *Synagogen und jüdische Friedhöfe in Munchen*, Aries Verlag, Munich, 1988.
Die Synagogen des Oldenburger Landes, ed. Erno Meyer, Oldenburg, Holzberg, 1988.
Synagogen in Berlin. Zur Geschichte einer zerstörten Architektur, Willmuth Arenhövel and Berlin Museum, Berlin, 1983.
Wischnitzer (Rachel), "Mutual Influences between Eastern and Western Europe in Synagogue Architecture from the Twelfth to the Eighteenth Century", *YIVO Annual of Jewish Social Studies*, 2/3, 1947-8, pp. 25-68.

AUSTRIA
Genée (Pierre) and Lindner (Walter), *Wiener synagogen 1825-1938*, Löcker, Vienna, 1987.

BELGIUM
Braeken (Jo), "Beth Haknesset. Synagogen in België, 1865-1914", *Monumenten en Landschappen*, 12/1, January-February. 1993. p. x-45.
Dratwa (Daniel), "De Synagoge in België: Geschiedenis en cultuur", *Monumenten en Landschappen*, 12/1, January-February. 1993. p. 8-x.

BOSNIA
Gotovac (Vedrana), *Sinagoge u Bosni i Hercegovini*, Muzej Grada Sarajeva, Sarajevo, 1987.

CZECH REBUBLIC
Adler (Norbert), *Die Jüdischen Denkmäler in der Tschecoslowakei*, Prague, 1932.
Fidler (Jirí), *Jewish Sights of Bohemia and Moravia*, Prague, Sefer, 1991.
Parík (Arno), *Die Prager Synagogen in Bildern, Stichen und alter Photographien*, Stadliche Jüdische Museum, Prague, 1986.
Volavkova (Hana), *The Pinkas Synagogue. A memorial of the Past and of our days*, Prague, 1955.

DENMARK
Frosell (Preben Hampton), *Københavns synagoger gennem tre hundrede år*, Copenhagen, C.A. Reitzel, 1987.

FRANCE
Jarrassé (Dominique), *L'Age d'or des synagogues*, Herscher, Paris, 1991.
Jarrassé (Dominique), ed., *Le Patrimoine juif français, Monuments Historiques*, n° 191, February 1994.
Jarrassé (Dominique), *Une histoire des synagogues françaises entre Occident et Orient*, Actes Sud, Arles, 1997.
Meyer (Pierre-André), "Synagogues anciennes de Moselle", *Archives Juives*, 17ᵉ année, 1981, n° 2, p.19-33.
Rothé (Michel) and Warschawski (Max), *Les Synagogues d'Alsace et leur histoire*, Chalom Bisamme, Jerusalem, 1992.

GREAT BRITAIN
Barnett (Arthur), *The Western Synagogue through two centuries (1761-1961)*, with a foreword by C. Roth, London, 1961.
Glasman (Judy), "Architecture and anglicization : London synagogue building, 1870-1900", *The Jewish Quarterly*, 34/2 (126), 1987, pp. 16-22.
Kadish (Sharman), *Building Jerusalem. Jewish Architecture in Britain*, Vallentine Mitchell, London,Portland, Or., 1996.
Levin (Salmond L.), ed., *A Century of Anglo-Jewish Life 1870-1970*, London, 1970
Levy (Matthias), *The Western Synagogue: some materials for its history*, London, 1897.
Lindsay (Paul), *The synagogues of London*, London , Portland (Or.), Vallentine Mitchell, 1993.
Roth (Cecil), *The Great Synagogue, London, 1690-1940*, London, 1950.

GREECE
Messinas (Elias V), *The Synagogues of Salonika and Veroia*, Athens, Gavrielides, 1997
Molho (Michaël), *Les Juifs de Salonique à la fin du XVIᵉ siècle. Synagogues et patronymes* (1967), French transl. 1991.
Stavroulakis (Nicholas), *The Jews of Greece*, Talos Press, Athens, 1990.

GERMANY
Altaras (Thea), *Synagogen in Hessen: was geschah seit 1945? Eine Dokumention und Analyse aus allen 221 hessischen Orten, deren Synagogenbauten die Progromnacht 1938 und des 2. Weltkrieg überstanden: 223 architektonische Beschreibungen und Bauhistorien*, Königstein im Taunus, K. Langewiesche, 1988.
Davidovitch (David), *Wandmalereien in alten Synagogen. Das Wirken des Malers Elieser Sussmann in Deutschland*, Hameln-Hanover, 1969.
Graefraeth (Robert), "Die Neue Synagoge in Berlin. Ergänzung eines fragmentarisch erhaltenen Repräsentationsbaus des 19. Jahrhunderts", *Deutsche Kunst und Denkmalpflege*, Munich-Berlin, 1992, n°1, pp.22-32.
Hermann Zvi Guttmann. Vom Tempel zum Gemeindezentrum. Synagogen im Nachkriegsdeutschland, ed. Sophie Remmlinger and Klaus Hofman, Francfort a/Main, Athenäum, 1989.

Hahn (Joachim), *Synagogen in Baden-Wurtemberg*, Stuttgart, 1987.
Hammer-Schenk (Harold), *Synagogen in Deutschland. Geschichte einer Baugattung im 19. und 20. Jahrhundert*, Christians Verlag, Hamburg, 1981.
Rieger (Paul), *Jüdische Gotteshäuser und Friedhöfe in Württemberg*, herausgegeben vom Oberrat der Israelitischen Religionsgemeinschaft Württembergs, Stuttgart, 1932.
Rosenau (Helen), "German Synagogues in the the Early Period of Emancipation", *Yearbook Leo Baeck Institute*, 8, 1963.
Selig (Wolfram), ed. *Synagogen und jüdische Friedhöfe in Munchen*, Aries Verlag, Munich, 1988.
Die Synagogen des Oldenburger Landes, ed. Erno Meyer, Oldenburg, Holzberg, 1988.
Synagogen in Berlin. Zur Geschichte einer zerstörten Architektur, Willmuth Arenhövel and Berlin Museum, Berlin, 1983.
Wischnitzer (Rachel), "Mutual Influences between Eastern and Western Europe in Synagogue Architecture from the Twelfth to the Eighteenth Century", *YIVO Annual of Jewish Social Studies*, 2/3, 1947-8, pp. 25-68.

HUNGARY
Gerö (Lázló), *Magyarországí zsínagógák*, Müszaki Könyvkiadó, Budapest, 1989.
Heller (Imre) and Vajda (Zsigmond), *The Synagogues of Hungary. An Album. A magyarországí zsínagógák albuma*, World Federation of Hungarian Jews, New York, 1968.
Somogyi (György) and Gerle (Janos), *Baumhorn Lipot zsinagogai*, MIOK évkönyv, Budapest, 1979.

ITALY
Cassuto (David), *Ricerche sulle cinque sinagoghe (Scuole) di Venezia*, Jerusalem Publishing House, 1978.
Cassuto (David), "The Scuola Grande Tedesca in the Venice Ghetto", *Journal of Jewish Art*, 1977.
Curiel (Roberta) and Coopermann (Bernard Dov), *Le Ghetto de Venise*, Herscher, 1990.
Il Centenario del Templio Israelitico di Firenze, Atti del Convegno, Giuntina, Florence, 1982.
Pinkerfeld (Jacob), *The Synagogues of Italy*, Jerusalem, 1954.
Sacerdoti (Annie) and Fiorentino (Luca), *Guida all'Italia ebraïca*, Marietti, Casale Monferrato, 1986.

NETHERLANDS
Agt (J.F. van), *Synagogen in Amsterdam*, 's-Gravenhage, 1974.
Agt (J.F. van) and Voolen (E. van), *Nederlandse Synagogen*, Weesp, 1984.
Agt (J.F. van) and Voolen (E. van), *Synagogen in Nederland*, Amsterdam, Joods Historich Museum, Hilversum, Gooi & Sticht, 2ⁿᵈ ed., 1988.

POLAND
Balaban (Majer), *Die Judenstadt von Lublin. Mit Zeichnungen von K.R. Henker*, Berlin, 1919.
Gruber (Samuel) and Myers (Phyllis), *Survey of Historic Jewish Monuments in Poland. A Report to the United States Commission for the Preservation of America's Heritage Abroad*, Jewish heritage Council, World Monuments Fund, New York, 1994.
Piechotka (Maria and Kasimirez), *Wooden Synagogues*, Warsaw, 1959.
Piechotka (Maria and Kasimirez), *Bramy Nieba. Bóznice drewniane na ziemeciach dawnej Rzeczypospolitej*, Wydawnictwo Krupski i S-ka, Warsaw, 1996.
Wisniewski (Tomasz), *Boznice Bialostocczyzny/Heartland of the Jewish life: synagogues and Jewish communities in Bialystok region*, Bialystok, Wyd, 1992.

ROMANIA
Streja (Aristide) and Schwarz (Lucian), *Synagogues of Romania*, Editure Sefer, Bucharest, 1997.

RUSSIA-UKRAINE
Yargina (Z.), *Wooden Synagogues*, Masterpieces of Jewish Art, n°5. A Pictorial Series of Treasures in the Commonwealth of Independant States, Image Publishing House, s.l., (1993).

SLOVAKIA
Bárkány (Eugen) and Dojc (Ludovít), *Zidovské nábozenske obce na Slovenku*, Bratislava, 1991.

SPAIN
Cantera Burgos (Francisco), *Sinagogas de Toledo, Segovia y Córdoba*, Instituto Arias Montano, Madrid, 1973.
Cantera Burgos (Francisco), *Sinagogas Españolas con especial estudio de la de Córdoba y la toledana de El Tránsito*, Instituto Arias Montano, Madrid, 1955.
Sepharad, Jewish Art, n° 18, 1992.

Index

NAMES OF INSTITUTIONS, OF PEOPLE AND OF PLACES

Abbreviations used: a.: architect;
cong.: congregation; j.: Jewish.
The mention of belonging to Judaism,
relevant in the case of synagogue
architecture, is only specified
for assured cases. It is used in the same
spirit as the appendix of *Synagogues
of Europe* (1985), by Carol H. Krinsky.